Praise for *Paradoxical Leadership*

"Ivo Brughmans's book discusses how leadership that embraces a paradoxical perspective is so much needed for our modern civic and organizational lives to transcend a sense of paralysis and to assume better kinds of responsibility. May future leaders think, act, and morally grow towards working within this possibility!"

KLEIO AKRIVOU, **Professor of Business Ethics and Sustainability and Director of the Centre for Business Ethics and Sustainability, Henley Business School, University of Reading**

"In this deeply divided and fragmented time, recognizing paradoxes and embracing ambiguity is of existential importance. This requires a holistic perspective and the ability to connect polarities, to transform 'either/or' into 'both/and.' This book fulfils both, making it a very valuable and useful tool for the future."

CHRISTINE BOLAND, **Trend analyst, brand purpose specialist, and keynote speaker**

"In my practice I see that the ability to effectively deal with tensions and paradoxes has become a key differentiator for excellence in leadership. With this book Ivo Brughmans provides a unique guide to how to bring this into daily practice. *Paradoxical Leadership* invites you to reflect on yourself and your own fundamental assumptions, while providing a wealth of practical methods, tools, and skills to support you on your leadership journey."

KARSTEN DE CLERCK, **Senior Partner at Egon Zehnder and Chairman of the Board at Vrije Universiteit Brussel**

"*Paradoxical Leadership* offers an inspirational and thought-provoking reading for leaders, and leadership/MBA students. This book contains both fresh perspectives and practical guidance on handling the paradoxical nature of our complex world, be it in a profit or non-profit context, or a leader or professional role. Ivo Brughmans's book adds great value for everyone who wants to learn how to come to grips with conflicting goals and opposing views."

DR. UWE NAPIERSKY, **Associate Professor for Business Psychology, Aston Business School, Aston University, Birmingham**

PARADOXICAL
LEADERSHIP

HOW TO MAKE COMPLEXITY AN ADVANTAGE

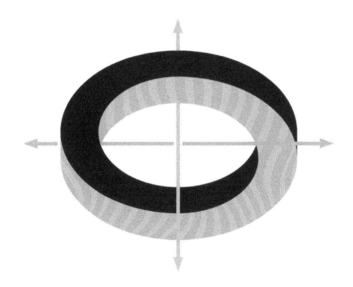

IVO BRUGHMANS

UNIVERSITY OF TORONTO PRESS
TORONTO BUFFALO LONDON

Rotman-UTP Publishing
An imprint of University of Toronto Press
Toronto Buffalo London
utorontopress.com
© University of Toronto Press 2023

ISBN 978-1-4875-0763-3 (cloth)
ISBN 978-1-4875-3664-0 (EPUB)
ISBN 978-1-4875-3663-3 (PDF)

Previously published as
Paradoxaal leiderschap: Soepel schakelen tussen tegenpolen © Boom, 2016

Library and Archives Canada Cataloguing in Publication

Title: Paradoxical leadership : how to make complexity
an advantage / Ivo Brughmans.
Names: Brughmans, Ivo, author.
Description: Includes bibliographical references and index.
Identifiers: Canadiana (print) 20220480222 | Canadiana (ebook) 20220480354 |
ISBN 9781487507633 (cloth) | ISBN 9781487536633 (PDF) |
ISBN 9781487536640 (EPUB)
Subjects: LCSH: Leadership. | LCSH: Paradox. | LCSH: Management. |
LCSH: Organization.
Classification: LCC HD57.7 .B78 2023 | DDC 658.4/092 – dc23

We wish to acknowledge the land on which the University of Toronto Press
operates. This land is the traditional territory of the Wendat, the Anishnaabeg, the
Haudenosaunee, the Métis, and the Mississaugas of the Credit First Nation.

University of Toronto Press acknowledges the financial support of the Government
of Canada and the Ontario Arts Council, an agency of the Government of Ontario,
for its publishing activities.

When trying to outline their identity, people often make a grocery list of common traits. That's a mistake. They would fare much better if they made a list of common conflicts and dilemmas.

Yuval Noah Harari, *21 Lessons for the 21st Century*

Contents

Part 2: At Work

INTRODUCTION

As I was putting the finishing touches on the first edition of this book in 2016, I saw the perfect example of a paradox on the news: the glorious comeback of vinyl records. Just when we could get all the music we want through virtual means, and we were no longer restricted by material limitations, vinyl LPs became extremely fashionable again. Record stores could hardly handle the demand. And it wasn't just older listeners looking for LPs out of nostalgia but mostly enthusiastic young people, many of whom had never even seen a record player before. They were now on the lookout for cool stuff in vintage stores, but also in the rapidly growing range of brand-new vinyl releases. Having something awesome and tangible in one's hands, the color, the scent, and the amazing artwork on the cover, the slow and careful ritual of placing the LP on the record player, the authentic soundscape with its soft crackle, soothing hiss, and familiar pops … This is difficult to grasp using plain logic; there is no rational explanation for this. Records need storage space, they are sensitive to scratches, and we need to get up and turn them around if we want to continue listening to the B-side. Instead of simply opting for digital music which we can get anytime and anywhere with just one tap, we're suddenly making our lives less convenient again.

From a paradoxical perspective, however, this is pure logic. Every movement in one direction creates a countermovement in the opposite direction. The more we turn toward the virtual world, the stronger our desire to hold something tangible in our hands. The faster we live, the more we want to slow down and be mindful. The easier it is to buy everything ready-made, the more we want to craft things ourselves. When abundance reigns, limitation beckons.

I wrote this book because the dominant paradigm of either/or thinking is grossly inadequate. We cannot solve today's problems in business and society if we continue to look at them as simple and clear-cut either/or choices: either we control or we empower; either we are cosmopolitans or we foster our own identity; either we empathize or we are strict; either we focus on personal responsibility or on group solidarity; either we innovate according to our own vision or based on client demand; either we change incrementally or we come up with a master plan.

We always need both sides of the coin. If we stick to rigid either/or choices, we will not only limit our own opportunities and potential but also create a structural imbalance in organizations and in society as a whole. Systems that are chronically out of balance will sooner or later correct themselves, usually in a quite brutal and disruptive way. The challenge lies in consciously learning how to balance and connect opposing poles, making full use of the tensions and complementary aspects of opposing forces instead of choosing one side of the coin or merely being satisfied with a gray compromise.

In 2013, I published my first book on this subject, *The Art of Paradoxical Life*,[1] which focused on polarities in society and our daily lives. I was disappointed with its lukewarm reception but still strongly believed in its message. My core business for over twenty years had been in management consulting, and I decided to write a new book on the theme of paradoxes, this time focusing on leadership,

---

1   Ivo Brughmans, *De kunst van het paradoxale leven: Gebruik je tegenpolen als kracht* (Tielt: Lannoo, 2013).

organization, and business. It was published in Dutch in 2016, and it also forms the foundation of this book.

To my great satisfaction, this second book flew off the shelves. Times had changed. In the past ten years we have only seen the level of volatility, unpredictability, complexity, and ambiguity sharply increase, a growing challenge to which this book attempts to provide a practical answer.

The demand for lectures, workshops, and training sessions on paradoxical leadership grew so strong that I had to leave my job at an international consultancy firm to dedicate myself completely to this work. Interest in this theme is growing in a diverse range of companies and organizations: government agencies, family businesses, private equity firms, educational and cultural institutions, health care providers, professional service providers, city councils, financial service firms, manufacturing companies … In short, wherever today's challenges are felt most. This is not surprising because companies and public organizations that operate close to markets and citizens, respectively, have to deal with dilemmas on a daily basis and have to be able to adapt ever faster to changes in the environment.

The urgent need for a both/and perspective arises from several broader societal developments.

Rapid Change

We live in a turbulent world of rapid change that requires us to adapt and shift gears quickly and smoothly. Ideally, we should do this efficiently, without wasting huge amounts of capital and value by replacing everything old with something new, only to change everything back again just a few years later. How can we stay agile and easily cope with sudden external turbulence without creating an organization that is constantly in a state of unrest, stress, and confusion? Wouldn't it be wonderful if we could be like a Japanese

swordsman who can move into action at lightning speed from a
state of deep tranquility?

Unproductive Polarization

We live in a world in which we waste too much energy on positioning ourselves: on "us" versus "them," on polarization, and on
fighting each other, both in society and in organizations. In society
and politics we see steady movement toward the extremes, driven
by seemingly irreconcilable values, views, needs, and concerns, and
nearly every topic can quickly become loaded with strong emotions,
causing deep divides. But this also happens in organizations: "We
(in sales) know that flexibility and creative solutions are the key to
survival in this competitive market, but they (the back office) rigidly
stick to their bureaucratic standards and procedures. They simply
don't understand what this business is all about!" Energy is spent
on separating and dividing, instead of on joining forces, causing dialogue to falter or slide into mere finger pointing. The solution is not
to try to eliminate contradictions, but to use the inevitable tension
between opposing forces in a productive way.

Complexity

Simple, straightforward recipes no longer work long term in our
complex society. Systems (economic, political, business, health)
are interconnected, and an imbalance in one part of the world can
have immediate repercussions for the balance of the whole. Organizations have to think more about the wider context in which they
operate and about a broad group of potential stakeholders with
divergent interests. In our globalized world, dealing with different
cultures is essential, and solutions that work well in one part of the
world don't always work well elsewhere. In this world of diverse
and articulate people, it is no longer possible to quickly identify and
impose "the only right way of thinking and acting."

The clue is a strategy that is less angular, one-sided, rigid, and wasteful when dealing with opposites. This strategy gives us a broader range of options than the familiar playing field of extreme positions or halfhearted compromises. How can we adopt a new way of thinking and working, focused on finding the right combination of opposite approaches in any situation?

This book offers both a conceptual framework and concrete models and tools for putting the both/and perspective into personal and organizational practice. It doesn't dwell on spelling out the problems, but rather on formulating solutions.

In preparing this new edition, I came across a whole international research community on organizational paradox. This book was written based on my own practice and reflections, but I was very happy (and lucky) to find that the principles and conclusions I came to were corroborated by scientific research. And I'm happy not to be alone! In this new edition, I have included references to key publications in this new, booming field of academic research.

The book is divided into two parts. Part 1 (In the Lab) takes you through the basic principles of dealing with opposites. You will become thoroughly acquainted with the both/and perspective and gain tools for its practical use in your personal and professional lives. Part 2 (At Work) shows you how to apply these principles to a number of well-known management and business challenges, including strategy, governance, performance management, innovation, change, corporate identity, diversity, and talent management.

A Book for Everyone

This book's title, Paradoxical Leadership, may suggest that learning how to deal with polarities is only for people in leadership roles and management positions. But nothing could be further from the truth. Polarities and the ways we deal with them are relevant to everyone, although this may be in a slightly different way for each:

- **Board members, executives, and senior managers** must keep
  the organization on the right track, navigating a fickle sea and
  juggling conflicting demands and interests. They determine the
  options on different strategic dimensions (such as cost-cutting –
  investing, focusing – diversifying. centralizing – decentraliz-
  ing, etc.) and are confronted at the organizational level by the
  negative impact of any unilateral choices. They do not have the
  luxury of moving within a clearly defined and sheltered playing
  field with straightforward objectives. Their challenge is to pave
  the way in the chaos of opposing forces and to create structure
  and direction. For senior managers, it's all about dealing with
  ambiguity and looking for the right balance for each complex
  challenge.
- **Managers** (of an organizational unit) have to strike a balance
  between the opposite demands that arise within a more defined
  playing field (for example, between standardized procedures
  and customized solutions, between quality and speed, or between ensuring compliance and offering room for personal interpretation and initiative). They are also often caught between the
  wider objectives of the organization and the concrete challenges
  on the shop floor, and between the specific views, needs, and interests of team members and customers.
- **Professionals** have to constantly weigh their options. "Should I
  go after this overdue payment with legal action, or should I take
  the client's situation into account and give them more time?"
  "Should I make an unprofitably low first offer to potentially gain
  an important new client, or pitch at a premium price to ensure
  profitability and risk not getting the deal?" On top of their own
  professional considerations, professionals often have to compromise between the guidelines of the organization and the wishes
  of the client: "My manager says that I can spend a maximum
  of seven minutes on each patient, but most patients need much
  more attention and time."

At all these levels, it is necessary to strike the right balance between conflicting demands, values, and needs. The tools provided in this book are useful for all of these groups.

A Personal Note

This book contains not only detached observations and analyses but also a personal quest. I have three different perspectives on the challenges of paradoxes: my concern for today's global challenges (macro), my role as a management consultant in organizational change (meso), and my own personal life (micro). On all three levels, the theme of bringing together opposing views and values appeals to me deeply.

From the Perspective of Society and the Way We Live

I have been interested in paradoxes my whole life, but the search for a more sustainable way of life really triggered my need for a deeper exploration. A truly sustainable way must take into account the natural limitations of our planet but still offer opportunities for personal and economic growth. When I started thinking about this, I was quickly confronted by two extremes: the world of abundance and the world of limitations.

On the one hand, there is the model of unlimited economic and personal growth and ever-increasing material wealth. This model still lies at the heart of nearly every national and international policy, as it is the driving principle of economic development, job creation, and raising the standard of living. At an individual level, this model is reflected in the adage "the sky is the limit," whether in pursuing personal growth, material wealth, or breathtaking experiences. At present, the benefits of this model are mainly reserved for a select group of developed and developing countries, but they are clearly at the expense of the climate, biodiversity, and working and living conditions elsewhere. Under this model, can every human being on this planet attain a similar level of prosperity? Aren't such aspirations more than fair? We are already on the brink of ecological disaster. Can our planet sustain any further growth?

The other extreme is that of austerity: distancing ourselves from material wealth and living modestly. Individuals can stop traveling by airplane or car, become vegetarian and eat only local and seasonal products, swap second-hand items instead of buying new, and use as little energy and water as possible to keep our ecological footprint small. This may be an alternative for a few, but for most it would remain unappealing. It is human nature to want to grow and fully enjoy the abundance and fullness of life.

This was one of the first examples of an apparent contradiction, in which I fully realized that neither of these opposite approaches is optimal and that the only long-term solution is a both/and approach. How can we achieve both abundance and limitation at the same time? Or even better: How can we find "abundance in limitation"? This immediately became the working title of my first book. But going further, I realized that it was even more relevant to focus on the method – this new way of thinking in terms of "both/and" – rather than on only this specific dilemma. It became clear to me that all major social, economic, cultural, and political challenges of today – such as migration, national sovereignty/identity, gender, diversity, climate, digitalization, handling a pandemic, etc. – need a fresh look from a both/and perspective.

The same is true on an individual and day-to-day level. I am always moved when I see total acceptance of people who are "different" and who are appreciated for who they are, without having to conform to the mainstream. Lisbeth Salander comes to mind: in Stieg Larsson's *Millennium* novels, she is both "our best data analyst" and an all-out nonconformist cyber punk. Or the totally shy and introverted waiter at a restaurant I frequent who, together with his two very extroverted colleagues, has been doing his job for years and is notably appreciated and accepted as one of the team, not as a kind of mascot but as an indispensable link in the chain. The authenticity, warmth, and tenderness that emanate from the attitude of this team characterize the atmosphere of the whole restaurant, making it extremely popular – and thus also a thriving business. It is always motivating to see how opposite poles can coexist and even reinforce each other when we do not try to iron out the differences and level everything to a universal standard.

From a Consultant's Perspective

As a consultant, I have all too often been confronted with (one-sided) management trends that replace each other in relatively quick succession. Process Redesign is old school and Lean Management and Agile are the subsequent fashions, until one starts to realize that all those incremental changes aren't the solution either; next a revamped and updated Process Redesign 2.0 will come into vogue. Organizations that were involved in the first wave of outsourcing and offshoring were working hard to bring these outsourced tasks back home only a few years later. Almost every large organization has already made the transition from centralized support functions to "organizing the support processes as close as possible to the business" and then back again to shared service centers. What will be the next step?

If you were to look at this cynically, you could say that this is the inexhaustible livelihood for a consultant because there is a lot of work to be done every time the organization needs to change. Consultants are often the first to hype new trends in management, and many consultants will not turn down the opportunity to exchange an old trend for a promising new one. An ironic example would be a consultant who first helps to structure and professionalize a fast-growing start-up company by introducing formal operating procedures, only to discover later that the entrepreneurial culture of yesterday has started to fade, and who now pushes for a program of cultural change for staff to take more ownership and initiative.

Shouldn't the role of a good consultant be to advise the client to take a critical look at all these trends, to make them aware of the unstable swings within the organization – which often cost vast amounts of money and resources – and to stimulate the client to search for sustainable both/and solutions?

From a Personal Perspective

My fascination for polarities and paradoxes goes much further than a critical analysis of society and my own profession. It has to do with who I am and how I feel about life. My motto is "Nothing in moderation, everything in excess." According to one personality test, I am a complete extrovert; according to another, a complete introvert. I can be extremely businesslike but also very empathetic. I can enjoy doing nothing at all and relish emptiness and space, but at the same time I make sure that I am fully booked from morning until evening. My main personal challenge is to find the happy medium among these extremes.

When I was a teenager, this was all very confusing because I was searching for a clear and well-defined identity, and that is not easy when you feel like a dandy one day, a punk the next, and a hippie the day after that, with all the clothes to match! But as I got older, I learned that I can also use these opposing aspects of my personality to my advantage. It allows me to switch from a broad and abstract perspective to practical details and back, or to balance between empathy and professional distance. It certainly came in handy in my work as a consultant. At some organizations, my role was mainly to create urgency and spur the company to meet the goals they had laid out in elaborate and uninspiring documents. At other organizations, I had to slow down the roaring stream of improvement programs and initiatives and encourage the company to critically reflect on their core purpose.

This is not just about shifting from one extreme to the other. What really fascinates me about this subject is the interweaving of different worlds. How can we link a fundamental philosophical lens to our pragmatic ideas on how to run a profitable business? How can we bring the business side and people side together? How can we adapt ourselves to our clients or the people around us and still stay close to ourselves? The thing that affects me most on a personal level is the magical moment when two opposite forces come together to form one new whole, for example: a timid-looking girl turns out to be a fierce drummer in a heavy metal band, a seemingly shapeless and rotting plant suddenly sprouts new shoots, or a melancholic song sounds cheerful at the same time.

I invite you to join me in my search for new ways to combine and mix colors.

PART 1

IN THE LAB

This part of the book introduces you to both/and thinking. It starts by creating a conceptual framework that describes what paradoxes and polarities are and how they work. It then addresses the shortcomings of traditional either/or thinking. You will learn what thinking in terms of both/and thinking actually entails and why it is required to enable us to effectively tackle the issues and challenges of our time. Finally, I will give you practical steps and tools for applying this way of thinking as a person and as a leader or professional.

A both/and lens, where opposing visions, ideas, values, strategies, and interests can coexist and even be reconciled, can sometimes feel awkward and counterintuitive. Familiarizing yourself with this way of thinking and really coming to grips with it requires time and energy. This part of the book will show you how polarities work and how to experiment with them, just like in a lab. You will then be fully equipped to enter the workplace in part 2 ("At Work"), and to look at various business challenges in a new light.

POLARITIES AND PARADOXES: WHAT ARE THEY AND HOW DO THEY WORK?

This chapter introduces you to the key concepts of paradoxical leadership and to the paradoxical lens through which we examine the world, organizations, and ourselves. First, let's see some concrete examples of polarities in organizations.

A social housing association has a dual purpose: it has to build and maintain good quality and cost-efficient housing infrastructure, and it strives to provide its residents with a pleasant and affordable living environment. Both objectives are of course closely interlinked, but each is allocated to a different department within the organization. One focuses on infrastructure maintenance ("the bricks"), and another focuses on the living conditions and experiences of residents ("the people"). There are inherent tensions between these objectives and accordingly between the departments. For example, residents might have specific needs that cannot be met due to building code and maintenance standards, and some habits and behaviors of residents might have a negative impact on the condition of the infrastructure.

Sometimes these conflicting priorities fall on one person. In this example housing association, there is a general rule that climbing plants on the walls are not allowed as they damage the bricks. However, during an inspection, the property manager notices a recently planted ivy bush growing up a wall. Before removing it, he approaches the residents to remind them of the rules. The culprit turns out to be to be a young girl of eleven who planted the ivy bush with her family as a symbol of new hope after her operation to remove a brain tumor. What should the property manager do: show his big heart or stick to the rules? What would his colleagues do? Some of his people-oriented colleagues would probably allow it, while others would say that they are very sorry, but it needs to be removed. It all depends on whom you have in front of you. And if you allow this exception, what should you do when other residents, based on this precedent, start asking for exceptions? How are you going to explain to others that this bush of ivy is allowed but their requests are not? People may feel unfairly treated and may accuse the manager of having double standards.

This tension gives rise to some key challenges on an organizational level too. How do you strike the right balance between compliance to general rules and standards on the one hand and personalized and human solutions on the other? How can an organization make sure that its staff finds the right balance in every situation, knowing that you cannot cover all possible cases with clear if-this-then-that rules? How do you create consistency and avoid arbitrariness in your team while empowering people to work out tailored solutions for exceptional situations?

A family-owned dredging company has grown into a leading global player, delivering projects in the most challenging environments all over the world. One of its successful lines of business is to lay the foundations for oil and gas rigs on the ocean floor. With their family business background, the company has a very flexible, informal, "hands on" and "can do" culture and is adept at improvising and finding solutions to all kinds of difficult and unexpected challenges. However, over the course of a few months, they experience two identical critical equipment failures on two different ships. At first, these incidents are seen as unconnected technical issues, but the client, a major oil company, is not satisfied with this explanation and demands an audit. The audit reveals that the issue was not technical but arose from the company's culture: corners were cut, standard operating procedures and contingency plans were lacking, and safety measures were insufficient. This is the downside of their operational flexibility and their talent for improvisation. The oil company issues an ultimatum: either the dredging company installs solid procedures and immediately complies with rigorous standards, or the contract will be terminated.

The challenge for the company is finding a way to comply with procedures and work in a more structured and transparent way while keeping its crucial strength of rapid deployment and flexibility. How should it become more professional and accountable without creating a cumbersome bureaucracy and losing its informal and flexible culture?

A municipality of a major city wants to be more innovative in finding breakthrough solutions for the city's many challenges. Therefore, it wants to start conducting small-scale experiments with short learning loops. This also means taking risks, as the outcomes are never known in advance. Some experiments may be successful, but these might only be a fraction of all the experiments run. So, community funds are invested in projects with uncertain outcomes. The municipality has a strong culture of accountability, justifying that every cent of taxpayer money has been well spent. In the past, the municipality has always funded programs with clear budgets, elaborate business cases, and precise delivery dates that were closely monitored so that expectations could be managed and expenditures justified. However, those programs always took more time than expected and the solutions were often already outdated before they were fully implemented. This new experimental way of working means loosening control and allowing for mistakes and failures in order to learn from them. This is quite scary because eventually someone will be held accountable by the city council, the press, or the tax payer for all activities and spending.

The executive board faces a complex challenge: How can we make room for experiments and justify uncertain outcomes but at the same time also remain in control and on budget? How does the municipality avoid saying one thing ("Experimenting and making mistakes is fine!") and doing another (tightening control mechanisms and assigning blame when things go wrong)?

1.1 Polarities Are the Lifeblood of Adaptive Systems

Every complex system – whether it is an ecosystem, the human body, a person, a couple, a team, an organization, an economy, a national state, or the international community – consists of opposing forces that self-regulate and adapt to changes in the environment. These opposing forces allow a system to move in different directions and to be flexible in dealing with changing requirements. A bike that can only be steered in one direction is not very useful. We call these pairs of opposing forces "polarities." We can define polarities as "interdependent pairs that need each other over time"[1] or as "contradictory or oppositional elements that are interrelated and persistent over time."[2] I deliberately don't call them "paradoxes" or "dilemmas," as those have, in my view, another meaning. I will clarify these conceptual differences in the next section.

Our bodies provide many examples of polarities. Pairs of hormones often act antagonistically. For example, insulin lowers blood sugar levels by making the sugar available to our cells, whereas glucagon raises the blood sugar level if it falls below the normal

---

1 Barry Johnson, *And: Making a Difference by Leveraging Polarity, Paradox or Dilemma* (Amherst, MA: HRD, 2020).
2 Jonathan Schad, Marianne W. Lewis, Sebastian Raisch, and Wendy K. Smith, "Paradox Research in Management Science: Looking Back to Move Forward," *The Academy of Management Annals* 10, no. 1 (2016).

level. We inhale fresh air to feed our cells and exhale the waste products of cellular processes.

There are also examples in human relationships. In her book *Mating in Captivity*,[3] psychotherapist and relationship expert Esther Perel explores the secret to happy, long-term relationships between couples. She refers to the polarity of safety, familiarity, closeness, honesty, and equality on the one hand and danger, distance, inequality, manipulation, and power games on the other. Where you might think that long-term couples should primarily focus on the first set of qualities, it's the second set that appears to be just as important for a lasting relationship. Relationships that are only built on the first set lose their strength and radiance after a while. Partners may become so familiar with each other that the seductive tension between them disappears. When couples are asked when they find their partner most attractive, oddly enough the answer is often "when my partner goes away for a while" or "when I see my partner in a totally different context than the one I am used to."

Organizations are no different. An organization must be outward-facing to serve its clients, respond to the market, identify developments and innovations, and enter into collaborative partnerships. But it must also be inward-facing to set out its own vision, develop unique solutions, create cohesion by forming a common identity, and have well-functioning processes in place. Similarly, there must also be a balance between corporate guidance and local initiative, between people and results, between change and stability, between taking and avoiding risks, between making a profit and making a social contribution, and between creative ideas and bottom-line financial results. Organizations need both poles to function, and they must be flexible in shifting the balance between the two poles in order to adapt to constantly changing circumstances.

---

3 Esther Perel, *Mating in Captivity: Unlocking Erotic Intelligence* (London: Yellow Kite, 2007).

Both poles of a given polarity are interdependent. This means that they are inextricably linked and trigger each other through a feedback loop. If there is too much of one pole, a feedback mechanism activates the opposite pole, like how our bodies produce insulin when the blood sugar level is too high. This way, a complex system regulates itself and keeps its balance. After intense activity, our body will signal us to rest by feeling tired. After a period of very focused and concentrated work, we will feel the need to relax and free our minds. In organizations there are vertical feedback loops (between bottom and top) and horizontal ones (between different organizational functions), such as formal and informal communication channels, reporting lines, escalation procedures, and IT systems.

A system's self-regulation can be smooth or slightly bumpy. Let's consider, for example, a well-adjusted thermostat: we don't notice any small fluctuations in temperature. With a poorly adjusted thermostat, on the other hand, the temperature first has to drop considerably before the thermostat kicks in, and then lots of energy has to be used to reheat the room. It is always either too cold or too hot. Similarly, an organization that is sensitive to signals and which reflects critically on itself can quickly adjust its course and adapt to changing circumstances. Other organizations first have to face a problem a number of times or go through a major crisis before they start learning.

As a consequence of this interdependence, polarities cannot be "solved" by eliminating one of the poles: the system will lose its ability to self-regulate and adapt and will eventually collapse. Without self-regulation, your body will collapse due to exhaustion; an organization that is too opportunistic will lose its focus and identity. The interaction between the two opposite poles ensures a dynamic balance. Each time a system receives a new input, its balance will shift from right to left or vice versa to find a new equilibrium, depending on environmental factors (e.g., how big is the pressure to finish your work despite fatigue, or how much market pressure is there to deliver) and the energy and resources available to continue in one direction or the other.

Every movement creates its own countermovement. If there is someone in a group who firmly believes that one first has to talk to clients before developing a new product, there will always be someone else who will say it is better to first develop one's own vision and then check with the clients. For every plea for radical change, there is a contradictory plea to strengthen and build on what already exists. Every idea evokes the opposite idea because both are necessary for balance. People unconsciously sense this and provide the necessary counterbalance. The extraordinary thing is that the balance-seeking system strongly determines the individual views. You may believe that solidarity, on the whole, is extremely important. However, if solidarity is the mainstream belief within a system, you might start to find yourself emphasizing the importance of personal responsibility, especially if you are a bit of a rebel. Just like when you – perhaps unconsciously – feel the urge to tone down someone else's extreme opinion or, inversely, when you start to challenge someone who doesn't want to speak up. Because providing counterbalance is often an unconscious process, it might lead to irritation and to polarization. How much more effective would it be to consciously organize this confrontation between different views, with the goal of more balanced conclusions?

1.2 Polarities in Our Minds

We need to differentiate between polarities in the physical world (like ecosystems, bodies, organs, and weather systems) and polarities in our inner mental world. Polarities of the first type are tangible physical forces, and we will not further elaborate on these in this book, except now and then as metaphors. We are primarily interested in the polarities that work through the human mind. They are opposing values, needs, emotions, intentions, and aspirations that drive our behavior. Their outcomes may be tangible and observable, but they all start in our heads. On a larger scale, they determine the functioning of all our social systems, such as families, organizations, economies, political systems, and societies. Some poles seem to be radically opposed to each other, such as slowing down and speeding up. Others are more complementary, such as an output-oriented and a process-oriented approach.

We are full of contradictory needs and drives. We want to be adventurous but also feel safe; loyal to the group but also to ourselves; connected but also autonomous. In contrast with physical systems, whose polarities are factors outside us, we feel these mental polarities as tensions in our inner world. We're not always aware of all these polarities within ourselves, even though they determine our behavior. Sometimes we just don't see that we are trapped in a recurring dynamic between force and counterforce. We might oscillate between being too agreeable and being too assertive, between shame and anger, or between micromanagement and laissez-faire. When we are in the city, we long for the peace and tranquility of the countryside, but when we are finally in the silence of nature, we yearn for the excited buzz of the city. We may be too focused on what we experience at that moment (the longing for the city), so that the other side (the longing for the countryside) drops off our radar for a while, and we don't see the pattern.

We may become aware of certain polarities when the level of tension between them increases. This usually happens in the following circumstances:

- You are confronted with a dilemma: two contradictory motives at the same time. You actually want both, but in this situation you can't have your cake and eat it too. For example, this evening you could go out with your friends and have some fun (need to unwind) or you could finish this client proposal (need to fulfill your duties and commitments). You feel pressured to make a choice.

- You have gone too far toward one pole, and you have been neglecting the other pole so much that it starts to dominate your mind. For example, you have been working so hard lately, that you desperately crave relaxation and fun.
- You are confronted with a part of yourself you don't like or want to see. You feel ashamed or guilty about it, and you move as far away as possible toward the other pole. For example, you dislike your need to spend time alone, without any responsibility for others, so you deny yourself the alone time you need.
- You are confronted with someone adhering to values you dislike or defending a point of view that you find abhorrent, leading to a situation of mutual tension, polarization, or conflict. The emotional charge may be so high because it mirrors a part of yourself that you don't want to allow. For example, as a disciplined worker you might get irritated when confronted with someone who does not put in any extra effort, because you deny or do not recognize your own need to be lazy sometimes.

The examples above are about polarities at an individual level, but the same mechanisms work when people become aware of polarities on a collective level.

In these situations, it may be apparent a polarity is at work, but that doesn't mean that it is immediately clear which polarity that is. Take the example of the dilemma between going out and finishing work. The polarities that make up this dilemma can be very different:

- Need to relax vs. need to achieve
- Self-care vs. self-discipline
- Personal development vs. professional development
- Extroversion vs. introversion
- Setting my own priorities vs. living up to expectations of others

- Freedom to make my own choices vs. conforming to "the system"
- Feeling vs. reason

We can go on and on with this list. You cannot say by just looking analytically and objectively at the statement of the dilemma what the underlying polarities are that make this a dilemma for yourself or for someone else. You can dig deeper with exploratory questions or introspection, but the only way to know that you have identified the right polarity is through inner experience and feeling. "What tension do I feel the most in this dilemma?" "In how I experience this situation, which parts of myself are clashing?" "What is this conflict really about?" When you know a polarity is at work, you must always look below the surface to find the source, so self-reflection, introspection, and self-knowledge are important skills (see section 9.2 about paradoxical skills).

One polarity can manifest itself in multiple recurring dilemmas. For example, the tension between "pursuing personal gratification" and "contributing to a better world" can manifest in many dilemmas. "Am I going to join this fancy corporate law firm or am I going to give legal support to refugees?" "Do I take my car or my bike?" "Do I eat an apple or a mango?" Every trivial incident you encounter can be used by your mind – consciously or unconsciously – as a focal point for an internal polarity, loading small dilemmas with meaning and emotion.

For you, the choice between an apple or a mango may simply be a matter of taste and not of conflicting values, and therefore it does not create any inner tension whatsoever. It's only when similar dilemmas manifest themselves over and over again that we should look for the underlying polarity. Nor does a polarized conflict need to be rooted in a deeper polarity. Many ideological conflicts today may give the impression that they are about conflicting values, but in fact they are often about such basic needs as "recognize me, listen to me, see me and respect me." Joining the discussion about the content of the "different values" will only serve to make tensions rise because it completely misses the point of giving recognition to the other party. Therefore, when confronted with specific manifestations of tensions, it is critical to first explore what is driving them and what – if any – polarities play a key role.

1.3 How to Engage with Polarities

That polarities are the lifeblood of complex adaptive systems is one thing; how we view and manage them is another. Polarities are a given, but the way we engage with them directly impacts the level of tension generated between the poles and how productive or destructive their interaction will be.

Many polarities balance themselves without any intervention. If the feedback mechanisms work well, the balance will be automatically and continuously restored. For example, if everything works well, insulin and glucagon ensure the right level of blood sugar. When feedback mechanisms are disturbed, outside interventions must bring the system back into balance. The same applies to polarities in our inner world. If we're emotionally and mentally balanced, we don't have to think about maintaining balance. If there are imbalances – due to factors such as cultural or social pressure, stress, trauma, or biochemical disruptions – we have to consciously correct and take action to restore the balance.

However, we have a tendency to not just accept what is, but to optimize systems for maximum value and yield. We weaken or eliminate some feedback mechanisms to shift the balance point to our advantage. We can do this up to a certain point, but if we go too far, systems become unstable and collapse. In fact, they may brutally rebalance themselves, creating collateral damage. For example, if you can only spend what you have already earned, then there is a closed feedback loop that prevents you from spending more than you have. However, to grow the economy, people need to have the opportunity to take on debt. So long as loans and credit levels are still based on real income, there is a feedback mechanism to prevent overspending and serious debt problems. Without these requirements, the system will get out of balance and correct itself with a credit crisis. A similar bubble arises when there is a disconnect between the virtual and speculative world of financial markets and the real economy.

Another example: in our economy the consumption stream (shiny products in shiny shopping windows) and the waste stream are strictly separated and disconnected. Since the waste is out of sight for the consumer (waste exported to faraway countries, plastic soup somewhere in the ocean, invisible CO_2 in the atmosphere), there is no feedback mechanism since consumers are not confronted directly with the consequences of their behavior. After a given time, however, we will all be brutally confronted with the effects of global pollution and climate crises, with wildfires, floods, and hurricanes as tangible manifestations.

Polarities themselves cannot be resolved; the poles are intrinsically connected and inseparable. We can favor one of the poles for a while, but not indefinitely. If we always choose option A and never choose B, the system will tip out of balance. In the long term, our choices need to reflect a sustainable balance between A and B. It is crucial to give each opposing side enough slack so the system can counterbalance. We can of course stretch and shift the balance, but it becomes unhealthy if tension is allowed to build up like a volcano about to erupt.

The "right balance" does not necessarily mean 50/50. In every situation, the right balance is different (for example, some people need less sleep than others, and some organizations are more aggressive or consensus seeking than others). The right balance can be 70/30, 80/20, or maybe even 95/5, but never 100/0.

Therefore, how we engage with polarities is paramount. We can do that in different ways:

1 Deny the interdependence between the poles and foster one pole above the other or make fundamental choices between them (either/or thinking).
2 Respect the interdependent nature of polarities but see them as opposing forces that need to be kept separate so that they do not contradict each other or cancel each other out.
3 Seek a compromise, where some noncontradictory elements of both sides are combined, although the strengths of both sides are not fully used and the end result may be a somewhat diluted version of both.
4 Create a "paradoxical" solution by bringing contradictory forces together in a new, integrated form; both sides are fully present and enhance each other through generative tension.

The last three approaches are all based on both/and thinking, acknowledging the interdependence and value of both sides. This book will not focus exclusively on the paradoxical approach (option 4), as options 2 and 3 can also be helpful. Even either/or thinking may be beneficial. Sometimes you have to make black-and-white decisions, but these can only be temporary stopgaps, and in the long term the balance should be restored. More about this when we talk about the Polarity Wheel in section 3.3.

This brings us to the difference between a polarity and paradox. A polarity is a pair of interdependent forces – either physical or in our minds. Paradoxes, compromises, and separated solutions are different *ways to handle* polarities. Creating a paradoxical solution brings together both poles in their purest undiluted form and optimally exploits their synergies. In a paradox both seemingly contradictory forces are present at the same time without obstructing each other.

Paradoxical solutions will mainly be applied to the polarities in our minds. Radically opposing physical forces are difficult to bring together. The moment they arise in the same place and at the same time, they collide, stand in each other's way, build up destructively high tension, or destroy each other. Think of what would happen if you pressed on the brake pedal and the accelerator of your car at the same time. On the other hand, if you consider human intentions, they can actually coexist without destroying each other. For example, in your change plan, you can aim for speed when building the new technical infrastructure while slowing down when it comes to getting everyone on board with the new process.

Bringing together conflicting demands by formulating them as a paradoxical challenge can be a powerful source for innovation. For example, how can we create unity in a team and at the same time allow for diversity? How can we build close partner relationships but also increase our own autonomy? The seemingly contradictory demands force us to look beyond the obvious. Instead of thinking in limiting choices, we are stimulated to break our assumptions in search of new possibilities.

A paradoxical solution may be something to strive for, but it is not always feasible or even desirable to do so. Paradoxical solutions require a lot of energy and creativity to hold both poles together. For this reason, compromises and separated solutions may be useful alternatives.

DEFINITIONS

Let's wrap up this section by recapping the key definitions and illustrating them with an example.

At the level of manifestation:

- **Dilemma**: You are confronted with a choice between two mutually exclusive options. "Am I going to the movies tonight, or am I going to do my paperwork?" It is difficult to do both at the same time, so you need to make choice. A dilemma may be a manifestation of an underlying polarity.

- **Opposition and conflict**: Two parties have opposing interests or views: "I want to finish my paperwork, but my partner wants to go to the movies tonight." This will give rise to tensions between the parties (having fun vs. doing my duties), but also within each party (doing it my way vs. compromising).

At the underlying level:

- **Polarity**: "My sense of duty and responsibility is at odds with my need to relax and have fun."

At the level of engagement:

- **Either/or solution**: "Duty comes first" or "carpe diem."
- **Separated solution**: "Today I will work late to finish all my paperwork so that I can go out tomorrow." Both poles (sense of duty and need to have fun) are valued, but you experience them separately (in time and/or in place).
- **Compromise**: "I try to do my paperwork as quickly as possible so that I'm just in time for the late evening picture." However, by rushing, you might be jeopardizing both the quality of the work and the full cinema experience.
- **Paradoxical solution**: "How can I do my boring duties in a fun and relaxing way?" In order to find a paradoxical solution, we need to leave the level of concrete manifestations ("going to the movies" and "doing my paperwork") and connect with the underlying polarities in order to come to a new form where both needs can come together (for example, by doing this boring paperwork together or introducing some elements of play or competition).

In the coming chapters we will elaborate further on the strengths, limitations, and modalities of either/or and both/and thinking.

1.4 How Polarities Work in Organizations and Social Systems

The same basic principles about polarities apply to organizations and broader social systems. However, these are different in that they are built up from different subsystems (functions, divisions, teams, professional groups, factions, tribes, individuals), each with their own particular polarities, on top of the polarities that they all share.

Shared polarities are often linked to the core business, such as the polarities between speed and quality, long-term innovation and short-term operations, internal and external focus, or risk and stability. These themes will determine the overall culture of an organization. Then, each part of the organization could also have its own specific polarity. For example, the IT department balances user-friendliness with security, or enterprise architecture with local solutions. Some polarities will also create tensions between different groups or functions within the organization, where each party has identified itself with one pole or another. The tension between sales and production or between financial control and innovation are well known. These horizontal tensions are especially felt at the next hierarchical level, which needs to take care that these groups or functions work together productively. Often there is also a vertical tension between the corporate center and the business units.

The fact that polarities are nested and intertwined makes it much more complex to know which polarities to focus on. As with personal polarities, the key indicator is excessive tension: where exactly it is felt and what it is about. Some polarities will recur often because

they are about the core business of the organization and its changing relations with the outside environment (the market, sharehold-
ers, or regulators, for example). Tensions arise in these polarities as
there is always a delay between changes in the environment and the
adaptive response of an organization.

It's interesting to look through the various, seemingly unrelated
polarities of an organization and check if they are variants of one
deeper polarity. For example, healthcare workers in a care facility
may struggle with the following:

- "aligning with colleagues" and "developing own initiatives"
- "following the protocol" and "starting from the specific needs of
  the clients"
- "tradition" and "innovation"
- "together" and "alone"
- "rigid" and "flexible"

Looking at all of these from a little distance, a pattern appears. Are
they not all about the tension between "structure and compliance"
and "freedom and autonomy"? Finding the right balance for this
underlying key polarity will also have an impact on all the polarities
that are linked to it.

Other polarities in organizations are triggered by unique events,
such as a pandemic. These can become dominant themes at one
point in time, but after a while may completely disappear into the
background like the discussion of whether an organization can force
its staff to be vaccinated.

Some organizational polarities are well balanced. Keeping the
right balance for these polarities is a kind of second nature. Therefore, they are nonissues and go largely unnoticed. For example, the
tension between private life and work life may be something that

sorts itself out and isn't an issue in the least within an organiza-tion. However, it can be made into an issue, for example by specific external causes, such as a new project that demands a lot of extra effort and energy. It's also possible for our perception of what the right balance should be to gradually shift over time. New hires or members of younger generations may hold a completely different view on this balance, for instance. It can even become the sub-ject of a fierce polarization when some people are very vocal and militant about it and turn it into a zero-sum game. Latent polari-ties can effectively be made salient by these changes in perception and may become overwhelmingly dominant, not unlike how black holes trap anything that crosses their event horizon. Every previ-ously insignificant fact or incident can be used as a focal point for a polarizing movement. Here, too, the key is to look beneath the surface and address the underlying polarities that drive and fuel this tension.

Another specific feature of organizations is that they are not self-regulating but need to be managed in one way or another. This sets high expectations on the quality of leadership. How competent is the leadership team in balancing organizational polarities?

In order to work with polarities in organizations, it is important to be aware of the following basic mechanisms.

1. Engage with Those Polarities That Are within Your Circle of Influence

If you take any random situation and list all the polarities that are involved, they may be overwhelming. Suppose that every Saturday you're standing at the soccer field where your child plays. Every week, you are annoyed by a few other parents who smoke while cheering for their kids. If you take a closer look at this situation, there are many polarities involved at different levels:

- "healthy" – "unhealthy"
- "health" – "personal freedom"

- "personal needs" – "general interest"
- "taking responsibility as a role model" – "pursuing your own comfort"
- "sports performance (of the children)" – "moments of fun (for everyone)"
- "introducing rules" – "everyone must take their own responsibility"
- "asking kindly (sociable)" – "banning (strict)"
- "sticking to principles" – "looking for a workable compromise"
- "confrontational" – "seeking harmony"
- "loyalty to my parents (if they complain about my teammates' smoking parents)" – "loyalty to my teammates"

It can seem extremely confusing to analyze this situation in terms of polarities. But it becomes a lot clearer when you realize that for each of the parties involved (smoking parents, nonsmoking parents, children, sports coaches, club management, government policy makers) there are different polarities at play.

- At the general policy level (**macro level**) it is about "health" and "personal freedom" or about "personal needs" and "general interest." This may be the level of policy makers at the Ministry of Health.
- At the level of the management of the soccer club (**meso level**), they will especially feel the tensions between "sports performance (of the children)" and "moments of fun (for everyone)"; between "imposing rules" and "leaving it to personal responsibility" or between "kindly asking" and "banning."
- At the level of the parents and their children (**micro level**) it is about other things:
  - The smoking parent might struggle between "positioning myself as a role model" and "fulfilling my own smoking needs" or between "adapting myself to the group" and "going my own way."

- ○ The nonsmoking parents, on the other hand, feel the tension between "sticking to my principles" and "looking for a workable compromise" and between "seeking confrontation" and "seeking harmony."
- For the child it's about "loyalty to my parents" and "loyalty to my teammates."

In an organization it is never about the polarities "in general" but always about the polarities as experienced by a specific actor. The key question is always: "What tension do *you* feel in this situation?" This can be a very different tension than that felt by other parties in the same situation and may be completely unrelated to the specific content (in this case "healthy" and "unhealthy").

I term the person who feels a certain polarity the "polarity owner," similar to "the problem owner." Your first focus should be on balancing those polarities of which you are the "polarity owner" and that are within your circle of influence. You can of course report polarities that are outside your own circle of influence to the proper polarity owners – in case they have not noticed them themselves or don't see them as a priority – as they will be in the best position to take further action.

2. A Stable System Contains Both Opposite Poles
to Maintain Internal Balance

A system that contains both opposite poles is more stable than a system that relies on an external pole to keep itself in balance. For example, if you completely lean against someone else to keep your balance and that person takes a step to the side, you will fall over; you need the other person to help you stand up. But if you activate your internal balance while leaning against someone and that person suddenly steps to the side, you can quickly find your balance again.

This is how many dictators manage to stay in power for so long: by creating a common enemy. To avoid internal polarization, polarization is externalized. The in-group can then fully lean on the out-group. The activism of citizens is suppressed and curtailed by directing this energy at resisting an external enemy and not at their own political system. This is useful because this requires much less repression and fewer secret police and prisons to get the population to stay in line. If this external enemy suddenly disappears, then this curtailed energy is directed inwards again, and the dictator must use draconian means to keep the whole thing together. The system then wobbles or collapses.

The same principle applies to organizations. What is more stable: a strong HR department that is sufficiently people-oriented to counterbalance the highly content- and task-driven line managers … or line managers who are just as interested in the development and well-being of their staff members as in achieving results? A strong finance and control department keeping a close eye on the IT department so that budgets are not exceeded, or an IT department that thinks and acts while bearing costs in mind? A commercial bank can invest heavily in a large risk and compliance department to "control" the traders who are mainly supposed to hunt for lucrative and thus risky deals, sometimes pushing the boundaries of what is permitted. But wouldn't the balance be better if the trade department regulated itself as much as possible so that the compliance department would only have to perform a quick check?

3. The Lower the Level at Which Opposite Forces Can Interact and Be Counterbalanced, the More Stable the System Is

A system in which opposite forces can correct each other through feedback loops at the lowest level adapts more gradually and smoothly than a system where these corrective mechanisms only occur at a later stage. For example, it is more effective for the human body to continuously produce antibodies to fight germs than for someone to get sick first and then have to take antibiotics. If the feedback mechanisms are disrupted or removed at the lowest level, drastic and costly measures are required at a higher level.

The same applies to organizations: if the sales department and production department do not communicate with each other on a daily basis, then problems can easily escalate. These problems often don't reach the ears of senior management until they are about to get out of hand or already have. And then it takes a tremendous amount of time and effort to get them back under control.

You could also turn things around and stimulate self-regulation at the lowest level. Instead of destroying aphids by using pesticides – which is drastic, costly, and unhealthy – you could also get rid of them by allowing ladybugs to flourish, which would save time, money, and energy. This is also the idea behind the Agile software development method: by getting the user and developer to engage with each other from the start and give each other feedback, no one wastes time and energy on developing applications that do not meet user requirements.

1.5 Are Polarities Inherent or Socially Constructed?

There is a debate in academic literature about the fundamental nature of polarities in organizations. The question is: "Are paradoxes something inherent and 'out there' in organizations, prior to their recognition by the organizational actors, or merely socially constructed by the organizational actors? Or are they both?"[4] In this academic debate "paradoxes" are defined as "contradictory yet interdependent demands that appear simultaneously and persist over time." This definition is very similar to the one I use for "polarities," except for the aspect of "appearing simultaneously," as I argued that both poles can also appear sequentially or separated from each other.

---

4 This question is raised in a number of articles; see Wendy K. Smith and Marianne W. Lewis, "Toward a Theory of Paradox: A Dynamic Equilibrium Model of Organizing," *Academy of Management Review* 36, no. 2 (2011): 381–403, and Tobias Hahn and Eric Knight, "The Ontology of Organizational Paradox: A Quantum Approach," *Academy of Management Review* 46, no. 2 (2019): 362–84.

The issue has already been partly resolved by differentiating between "polarities" (opposite forces that drive dynamic systems) and "paradoxes" (one of the different ways to handle these polarities, by bringing both poles together). From this perspective, polarities are innate in organizational systems and "out there," and paradoxes are social constructs as they require that people deliberately balance the polarities. But there is more to say on this topic.

Some scholars defend the view that "paradoxes" (using the academic definition above) are both inherent and social constructs.[5] Although I am using different terms and definitions, I believe the same, mainly by looking at organizational practice.

On the one hand there are some polarities embedded in the architecture of an organization that can be felt by everyone, regardless of personal perceptions. For example, in a municipal organization everyone will feel the tension between experimenting with new methods and ensuring continuity, and between what is good for the city in the long term and what is expedient for the elected politicians to make their mark in their four-year terms. This tension is real and will influence the behaviors of everyone in the organization. For example, no matter who holds the title of CEO, they will all face the same key challenges of balancing between innovation and continuity and between the short and the long term. The system itself dictates what it needs. Personal perception will only influence how you handle the polarity (either/or or both/and), not the fact that it exists. An organization and its conflicting goals are by definition social constructs, but once the system is created it follows its own logic. Of course, you can try to change the setup or the goals of the organization, and as a consequence change its polarities. But this is not easy as it is seldom a merely internal tension but rather a tension between the organization and its wider ecosystem. Ultimately, this

---

5 Smith and Lewis, "Toward a Theory of Paradox"; Hahn and Knight, "The Ontology of Organizational Paradox."

would only result in exchanging one set of polarities for another. Polarities cannot be entirely eliminated or evaded.

On the other hand, people inside and outside the organization seek a sense of purpose and identity. They will use the polarities of the organization as a focal point for their own search for purpose, meaning, and identification. Or they may try to introduce their own polarities as a theme within the organization. As a result, the inherent tensions of the organization can be inflated or reduced, depending on how people cope with these organizational polarities. Polarities that were nonissues in the past and went unnoticed can suddenly become big issues. For example, taking a strong stance that "the generation of old fossils within the municipality systematically blocks all innovation" will inevitably trigger counterreactions and probably spark a conflict. Every difference can be used as focal point for a polarizing confrontation. We see this trend in society, where there is polarization on nearly all issues, all going back to the same root: people feel that their values and lifestyle are threatened. However, we can also try to reduce the tension by looking for a paradoxical solution. So, it's clear that the way people deal with these inherent polarities is a social construct.

KEY POINTS
- Every complex system consists of opposing forces to self-regulate and adapt to changes in its environment. We call these "polarities."
- Polarities consist of two interrelated poles and are persistent over time. Polarities can therefore never be "solved."
- Both poles trigger each other with complex feedback mechanisms to keep the balance.
- We can try to shift the balance of a system to our advantage by weakening or eliminating some of the feedback

mechanisms, but there is clearly a limit. Eventually the system always will self-correct.

- Polarities in our inner world drive our behaviors, and we feel them as internal tension.
- Our inner polarities manifest themselves in different ways. We don't know what the polarities are, just by looking at their external manifestations. We need to go beneath the surface to discover which polarities are really driving behaviors.
- The only method to pinpoint the key polarities is to find where you experience the highest level of tension.
- There are different ways to engage with polarity: (1) either/or choices, (2) separating interrelated poles in time and/or space, (3) seeking a compromise, or (4) paradoxical solutions. The last three may all provide sustainable solutions.
- Paradoxical solutions bring together both poles, creating a productive tension that makes optimal use of the power of both sides. However, this may not always be possible.
- In organizations polarities are nested and there may be different polarities on different organizational levels. You should focus on the polarities that are within your own circle of influence.
- A stable system contains both opposing poles, where they can interact freely with each other.
- Polarities in organizations are both inherent realities and social constructs.

THE LIMITATIONS OF EITHER/OR THINKING

The basic mechanisms in the previous chapter seem logical but are not easy to fully accept or apply in practice. It can feel awkward and confusing to adopt contradictory values, to focus on two different directions, or to bring opposite forces together. We have a strong urge to pull them apart and make unilateral choices by associating ourselves with one and distancing ourselves from the other or even rejecting it. Why? Because this approach provides us with direction; it keeps things clear, unambiguous, and simple. And then we know how to act.

2.1 Various Forms of Either/Or Thinking

Thinking and acting in terms of either/or solutions can take on various forms:

- **Absolute unilateral**: Only one of the two poles is considered correct, and the opposite pole is totally rejected: "Things can only be changed top-down. Bottom-up initiatives are doomed to fail." Or: "Abolish corporate headquarters and let us organize our own affairs. We know best what the local market needs and how to get things done." These beliefs make life simple and clear.
- **Relative unilateral**: There is a ranking between the two poles, and one pole is clearly ranked higher than the other. In this case, we do not reject the other pole, but we do considerate it inferior.

For example: "A change process should always be initiated top-down. We're open to bottom-up initiatives, but these should be carefully considered and should always fit into the overall strategy." Or: "It is the business units that determine the success of the company. Corporate headquarters should listen to us and support us. After all, we are the ones bringing in the money." There is clear difference with temporarily shifting more to one side or the other, due to the specific context, situation, or external pressure. By contrast, relative unilateral choices are a matter of principle and made for an indefinite period.

- **Externalization**: This happens when we have completely externalized one of the two poles and projected it onto another party. We actively distance ourselves from the party that represents the opposite pole for us, and by doing so we reinforce our own identity. For example: "That internal shared service center with its standard services, air-tight agreements, and bureaucratic rules is not client-friendly at all. They don't take into account what we need as a business. If we worked like that for *our* clients, we would have been out of business ages ago. Let's just go get the services we need outside the company." Or, as seen from the other side: "Every business unit thinks it's so special and unique and uses this as an excuse to go its own way. As a shared service center, we are not going to accept any more exceptions but adhere strictly to each service agreement and make sure everyone uses *our* services."

2.2 Why Is Either/Or Thinking So Attractive?

Why do we feel the urge to associate ourselves with only one of the two poles? There are several reasons for this:

- **Logic**: We have learned to use our logic which clearly tells us that A and the opposite of A cannot exist at the same time. It is difficult and confusing to accept two opposite facts at the same time without feeling that you are directly contradicting yourself, so you have to make a choice.

- **Ease**: Looking at things from all sides may allow us to better grasp the complexity and nuances of a given situation, but unilateralism is easier to handle. It takes less effort. Choosing one side is easier because you do not have to divide your attention.
- **Certainty**: One-sidedness gives us a sense of certainty and control. Ambivalence takes away familiar points of reference. We need a good dose of self-confidence in order to cope with ambivalence as it does not offer any clear direction or practical steps when we want to make a decision or take action. We risk running in circles, wondering what to do and being thrown back and forth between the two extreme positions. Ambivalence makes us vulnerable to doubts and misgivings.
- **Purity of principles**: We have learned to think in binary ethical and judgmental categories, such as in "good" and "bad" or "right" and "wrong." Our values, principles, and beliefs form a clear moral beacon. We want to stick to our principles, come across as being pure and consistent in our convictions, and not be seen as an opportunist without a backbone.
- **Identity**: We like to associate ourselves with a clear set of values. This allows us to build our own identity and distinguish ourselves from others. We do this by associating ourselves with one view and distancing ourselves from the opposite. For example, you may be rallying for innovation and fighting against those who are opposed to change, or you may be in favor of traditional values and against those who want to break with these traditions.
- **Group bonding**: We define our identity by our connection to others. We look for familiarities and tend to associate ourselves with people who resemble us. The things we have in common are hereby intensified as are the things that distinguish us from other groups. This fundamental mechanism is always at work, whether we're talking about a group of human rights activists, financial controllers, or football fans.

- **Communication**: Finally, an either/or decision is easy to communicate to others: there's a clear direction, clear principles, clear choice, and clear profile. An unambiguous message can often be transmitted more easily and is also easier to remember. If you show that you value both sides of the coin, you run the risk of being labeled as someone who is unclear, noncommittal, opportunistic, spineless, or indecisive.

In short: either/or thinking holds all the cards when it boils down to pure logic, certainty, decisiveness, adherence to principles, a sharp profile, group bonding, and clear communication. These are the qualities that are commonly highly valued in the context of leadership and management and are viewed as the essence of well-functioning and stable organizations. But is this high valuation justified?

2.3 Why Doesn't the Either/Or Approach Work?

Systematically choosing one pole and disregarding the other will lead to problems that can shake the foundations of an organization: a wobbly course, unconnected links in the value chain, paralyzing dilemmas, polarization, and uninspired solutions.

2.3.1 A Wobbly Course

Many organizations are thrown back and forth between extreme positions, without even being aware of it. Just think of the classic example of the perpetual pendulum swing back and forth between centralization and decentralization, which is something that every large organization deals with. Let's start with a centrally managed organization that is doing well. The CEO and management team are strongly convinced of this course because of its success in the past, and they fully identify themselves with this direction.

As the organization grows and transforms, and the environment becomes more complex, this model becomes increasingly difficult to maintain. Even the smallest decisions have to be made at the top; the decision-making process takes on the shape of a funnel. Moreover, those at the top are too alienated from the day-to-day operations to be able to make sound judgments. They need lots of time to gather advice and often end up making the wrong decisions. The organization is no longer capable of reacting quickly and adequately, and this is also reflected in its performance. Eventually, a miscalculation has a serious negative impact on the business. The highest governing body sends the CEO and management team home and installs a new management team to make the company more flexible and capable of operating closer to the market. "Decentralization and de-regulation" becomes the new motto.

Business units are then given more power and autonomy to make strategic decisions, and each business unit is free to organize itself as it wants. Also a new way of working with self-organizing teams is introduced in many parts of the business. Initially, this is very liberating. The business sheds the straitjacket of the past and comes back to life. Because of its success, the new course is fully embraced and followed even more closely. The management team totally identifies itself with this course, and the answer to many problems is further decentralization and empowerment, until this also goes too far: each business unit is reinventing the wheel, there is no cohesion or synergy, there is no talent sharing, and in some areas, the business units are competing and even fighting with each other. The self-organizing teams mainly do their own thing, without a clear direction or any coordination. Eventually, dysfunction starts to outweigh the benefits. The management team sees this too late or is unable to change course. The highest governing body has to step in again, the management team is replaced and … history repeats itself: all focus is on tightening control and reporting, centralizing authority over budgets, standardization, shared systems, and "One Company."

Figure 2.1. How an organization oscillates between the two poles of a core polarity

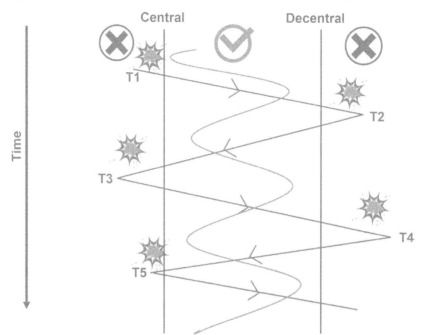

In figure 2.1, the pendulum motion is the zigzagging line with its abrupt, sharp turns. In this figure, two vertical lines represent the boundaries between which the course of direction is still functional (the benefits outweigh the limitations) and outside of which it becomes dysfunctional (the limitations outweigh the benefits).

The pattern illustrated by this specific example of centralization and decentralization is of course applicable to any core polarity in an organization. Organizations may, for example, zigzag between "diversify" and "back to the core business," "entrepreneurship" and "procedures," or a "visionary" and an "opportunistic" market strategy, etc. Also, in culture and society we see similar patterns, oscillating between "opening up to the world" and "strengthening regional or national identity," "social cohesion" and "individual freedom," "integration" and "autonomy," or "liberal" and "conservative."

This pendulum motion occurs when a one-sided focus is maintained for too long. This one-sided focus works well in the beginning as it compensates for the flaws of the previous one-sided focus. But when the new course in turn becomes dysfunctional, it is often difficult to correct it. One reason for this is that some natural feedback mechanisms are blocked. As organizations grow, they become complex with different hierarchical layers and organizational structures, so information can't flow as freely as it used to. When the top becomes aware of important issues that were long known and even reported by people on the shop floor, it's often already too late. Another reason is cognitive dissonance at the top. Management has invested so heavily in this direction and linked their entire identity and reputation to it, so they just cannot accept any dissenting messages.

After the organization has gone too far in one particular direction, it will become clear that a change of course is unavoidable. As the problem has by then grown out of proportion, drastic measures are needed to get the organization back on track. Everything that is "old" is thrown overboard because it is part of the problem and not the solution, and the organization is then radically steered in the opposite direction. Organizations often are not aware of this because their collective memory is short. Management teams often only survive one stroke of the pendulum, and new management teams often start anew as if there were no past. It might not be such a bad idea to systematically keep track of the history of an organization and learn from the past.

The result of the swinging pendulum is that value and capital are destroyed, a lot of energy is lost, and unrest and turmoil are created by the turbulent changes. Wouldn't it be possible to start steering in the other direction at an earlier stage so that balance could be sought in a more controlled, gradual, and less disruptive way, without having to resort to extreme measures? Or maybe a solution could be found whereby two poles are combined and integrated so that the pendulum would swing more gently ... ? Both scenarios are represented in figure 2.1 by the more meandering line within the boundaries of what is considered functional.

2.3.2 Unconnected Links in the Value Chain

An organization is made up of a wide range of opposing and complementary functions that it needs to be able to operate and survive, like the examples of innovation vs. continuity or internal efficiency vs. individual customer needs that we have already seen. In an organization operating smoothly, all of these crucial functions are in balance with each other, and their interaction ensures a healthy, dynamic environment.

These opposing and complementary functions are often separated from each other in different departments. There is nothing inherently wrong with this tactic except that these departments tend to focus primarily on their own targets and less on the functioning of the organization as a whole. This is understandable because they are often only held accountable for their own targets. Friction arises from these conflicting interests. In a best-case scenario, this friction is openly discussed and resolved in a constructive dialogue. In a worst-case scenario though, the departments become internally focused, go their own way, defend their ground, and do not hesitate to blame the other if something goes wrong. They may even go to battle with each other. The organization ends up with a poorly connected chain of departments that work apart from each other or even compete against each other.

When the opposing and complementary functions are not integrated within the organizational units, integration has to take place at a higher level. For example, there may be regular meetings between all parties involved, new horizontal "value chain management" roles, or other structural solutions to coordinate activities between the different silos. However, these integrative solutions at a higher level are often inadequate, as the diverging power of the individual departments is very strong.

When the links in the value chain are not properly connected, the performance of the whole organization is directly impaired. Moreover, a lot of energy is spent on fighting battles and on polarization. The larger and more complex the organization is, the more this problem arises. The higher the hierarchical level at which these opposing interests come together, the greater the chance of escalating conflict. The question is whether it is possible to achieve a balance of opposing and complementary forces at a lower level in the organization – within every position, every team, and even every individual – so that this process can take place in a smoother and less agonizing way.

2.3.3 Paralyzing Dilemmas and Polarization

Organizations and management teams often spend hours discussing the best way to move forward. For example, should we work on reshaping the structure of the organization to bring about a change in corporate culture, or does the key lie in radically changing the old culture so that a new structure will automatically follow? There never seems to be one good answer. Sometimes these discussions have surprising outcomes: new insights arise from the juxtaposition of opposing views, and the strong elements of each suboptimal solution are combined. But in many cases, these discussions turn into arguments between the believers and the nonbelievers. After all, they boil down to fundamental convictions and values, of which there is small chance of convincing the other party. And then these discussions can go on forever, leading nowhere.

Both parties can become so stuck on their points of view, feeling more convinced of themselves by proving the other wrong, that polarization occurs. These types of discussions are often settled by power. There are those who are "for" and those who are "against," and both sides defend their views with great passion. Depending on the situation, sometimes one side has the upper hand and then the other. In short, any proposed solution is suboptimal, and energy is lost in fighting battles. Is it possible to have these exchanges of complementary visions in a more constructive and productive way?

2.3.4 Solutions That Lack Inspiration

When we want to reconcile opposite poles, we usually start looking for a compromise to connect two opposing interests or values. A well-thought-out compromise can be very effective. However, we often end up clinging too tightly to a specific solution at the surface level, losing sight of the essence of the matter. For example: to defend the interests of employees, we might fight to keep a thirty-eight-hour workweek or previously acquired pension rights. However, these are only specific elaborations of what employees' interests might be, the relevance of which greatly depends on time and context. These solutions may even have turned into symbolic values that have little to do with the underlying essence of long-term employee well-being. If we hold on to a specific solution too strongly, it is difficult to take a broader view on what really matters for both parties and to come up with a creative solution. Such compromises end up little more than acts of sharing losses evenly between both sides. All we end up doing is making compromises that lack vision, which meet the underlying needs of neither party.

The question is whether we can't find more creative ways to connect opposite poles, ways that do not lead to dilution (1+1=1.5) but to mutual reinforcement (1+1>2), ways in which we explore the essence of both poles at a deeper level to enable reconciliation at a higher level. Maybe we can find a completely new solution where both parties are able to fully realize their underlying goals. For example: instead of cutting fewer costs so that the quality of the customer services can be more or less preserved, we could make targeted investments to improve specific services, which would lead to a significant reduction of costs.

2.4 The Challenge

Now that we have explored the challenges of the either/or lens, we can conclude that this way of thinking and acting often leads to suboptimal solutions, wasted energy, time, and money, and even to an irresponsible destruction of value. We need both sides of the coin.

We can indeed deal with polarities in a different, more inclusive way. In the following chapters, I am going to elaborate on paradoxical leadership and on both/and thinking as a comprehensive alternative, as well as exploring how we can apply this in practice. Up to now, we have been looking at the question from a negative angle, namely: how can we avoid a lot of grief with both/and thinking? Formulated positively, the ultimate goal of both/and thinking is to achieve sustainable success. In order to sustain a positive result, we do always need to include both opposite poles in every strategy, approach, or solution. We need to be able to adapt in our ever-changing environment, and this requires us, as individuals and as organizations, to be more flexible than ever. Switching smoothly between opposite poles is essential for the agility of our organizations and businesses.

In short, and in positive terms, the main question of this book is thus: "How can we turn opposite forces into positive energy and get the most out of them for ourselves and for our businesses?"

KEY POINTS
- Either/or thinking involves separating two opposite poles and associating ourselves with only one of them.
- Either/or thinking is appealing because it offers pure logic, a sharp profile, group bonding, clear communication, certainty, and decisiveness.

- Either/or thinking nevertheless leads to destruction of value, polarization, paralyzing dilemmas, and uninspired solutions.
- Focusing exclusively on one pole calls for a self-corrective pendulum swing to the other side, trading one extreme for another and causing organizational disruption. The challenge is to navigate more fluently between both sides, avoiding the dysfunctional extremities.

THINKING FROM A BOTH/AND PERSPECTIVE

A new way of thinking is required; a way of thinking where it is not necessary to choose between opposing sets of approaches and values, but where two opposite poles can exist side by side or even be interwoven to form something new. In this chapter, we will focus on what both/and thinking actually looks like and the different forms it can take.

We would already be undermining the basic principle of both/and thinking if we were to push aside either/or thinking and replace it entirely. In some situations, it may of course be advisable or even necessary to make unilateral moves, or to even go for one of the two extremes, but through the lens of both/and thinking, these can only be temporary shifts. Either/or thinking can keep its place as one of the possible courses of action. Both/and thinking is all about creating a wider range of options.

3.1 Why Is a Paradigm Shift Necessary and Inevitable?

Given the problems described in the previous chapter, shouldn't we all be adopting a both/and approach? Can we actually even avoid doing so? The current way of living, working, and doing business is forcing us more and more to think and act in both/and terms.

This section describes seven trends that make both/and thinking inevitable, at least in the long term. However, it is interesting to note that this is a paradoxical development in itself: both/and thinking is already in full swing in some ways, but there is simultaneously a strong polarizing movement in the opposite direction, toward more "either/or."

3.1.1 Fading Boundaries

We used to be able to clearly distinguish between complementary and opposing forces and place them in separate "boxes," but the boundaries are starting to fade. This development is noticeable in our daily lives, at work, in business, and in our society.

Let's look at the division between work life and personal life. In some professions, people can still go home from the office or factory at the end of the day and leave work behind, but these professions are becoming few and far between. With today's technology, we can be reached at all times of day and wherever we are. For many professionals and managers, the idea of having strict working hours belongs to the past. How many of us have not spent an evening or weekend working on a presentation that requires some serious thinking, or had a brilliant idea about an innovation while taking our morning shower, or called our project team while on vacation to help solve some unexpected hiccups? During the COVID-19 pandemic, working from home was even mandatory for many jobs, with the challenge of combining professional and private life.

On the other hand, this fading boundary also offers people more opportunities to complete their own tasks during working hours, such as going to the dentist, picking up the kids from school, doing some shopping for dinner while working from home, or creating a spreadsheet while sitting on a sunny terrace. Sometimes it's annoying when our work and personal lives overlap, and it feels like work is taking over, but it is a reality that every professional and organization must learn to deal with. Now that the clear boundaries of the past have faded, the trick is to be able to switch back and forth between these two worlds and to find a right balance. This balance will be different for each of us and at every moment in time. It requires us to self-regulate with a both/and frame of mind.

Another example of fading boundaries: Health, vitality, a sense of well-being, and happiness all used to be aspects of our personal lives, but now organizations are paying more and more attention to these and their significant impacts on productivity. We now realize that we have to see a person as a whole and cannot superficially divide someone into a professional entity and a personal entity.

This blurring of boundaries is also visible in the way organizations operate. In a network economy, the clear boundaries between an organization and its clients, suppliers, professional institutions, and colleagues/competitors are disappearing. Individual companies will increasingly work in dynamic ecosystems. You may have colleagues within your industry with whom you work very closely in some areas but compete against in other areas. Nowadays, we collaborate more equitably in cocreation partnerships, such as when developing new products and services together with our clients and suppliers. The traditional approaches based on the belief that "I am the client and you are the supplier, so you have to listen" are vanishing and being replaced by new business models based on equality and fading boundaries between internal and external services. The delineation between organizational divisions themselves is also under pressure, and it is becoming increasingly necessary to form an integrated value chain.

This trend toward intermingled opposites is also in full swing in other areas of society: organic vegetable gardens on the rooftops of skyscrapers; elder care facilities joined to kindergartens, allowing the old and young to connect with and stimulate each other; cradle-to-cradle production methods in which waste is fully recycled into new raw material.

These all require a different way of thinking, beyond strictly separated boxes. The key question is this: How can we creatively connect things that at first sight appear to be totally different or even contradictory?

3.1.2 Ambiguity Is the Norm

The world is overflowing with information that is sometimes vague, incomplete, or contradictory. In retrospect, it may be easy to put all the pieces of the puzzle together, but it is much more difficult to see the connection between all the contradictory information at the outset.

Everything depends on how we interpret the data and from which perspective. Taking the same information, we can conclude contradictory "truths," depending on the angle we take. For example, is the rise of jihadism a sign of an aggressive religious and cultural expansion or a reaction to socioeconomic deprivation? In the post-truth era "facts" have lost much of their importance as it has become common practice to selectively use or even fabricate them to support a preconceived idea.

Moreover, the whole world has become increasingly unpredictable, with the COVID-19 pandemic as a striking example. Long-term planning is hardly possible anymore. We can only take a number of possible scenarios into account, and these can very quickly turn into entirely different scenarios, perhaps even one that nobody could have predicted. For example, who would have thought that after twenty years of nation building and military action in Afghanistan, the Taliban would take over again in mere months? Or that with the Russian invasion of Ukraine old school and brutal territorial war would make its comeback in Europe?

This means that we have to be able to accept that not everything is straightforward, clear, and "under control," that we sometimes make the wrong decisions and, above all, that we always need to be able to adjust our sense of what is true when faced with new information. Public image and ego can get in the way because we are often viewed as weak when we change our point of view. Although determination is still an important leadership quality, it is nevertheless extremely dangerous to stick stubbornly to a single interpretation of the truth. Leaders have to be able to change course quickly and perhaps even head in the opposite direction. They have to take contradictory scenarios into account and correct quickly when things unexpectedly turn the other way. The "ability to deal with ambiguity" is an increasingly important competency in the recruitment and selection of executives.

3.1.3 The Need for Speed and Flexibility

The days when we could set up a company and continue on the same course for a number of years are over for many businesses. The increasing speed at which technology and markets are developing requires us to be able to shift gears quickly and smoothly, as in switching from a traditional manufacturing company to a digital service provider, from products to solutions, from growth in Europe to growth in Asia, from working with distributors to using direct sales channels, from insourcing to outsourcing. And perhaps everything will soon have to go in the opposite direction again. Companies also have to be strategically and organizationally agile to move quickly from one end of the spectrum to the other. So how do we ensure continuity and maintain our identity in a world where our business can look very different from one day to the next? Different markets, different products, different clients, different people ... How can we keep on reinventing ourselves without losing our core purpose and values?

3.1.4 Diversity

We need to work with people across different geographies, disciplines, and organizations. To do this, we must leave our own comfortable world, its familiar values, views, culture, and jargon and connect with others who might interpret us and express themselves quite differently. How can we build bridges and open up to new perspectives without losing our own sense of identity and retreating back into our bubble?

3.1.5 Increasing Complexity and Soaring Expectations

As customers we are used to getting everything we want, any time, any place, and anywhere, and especially right here and now: demands are going through the roof. It has become common practice to expect both/and: both top quality and low prices, both customized and best practice solutions, both highly innovative experiments and predictable and stable outcomes, both excellent customer service and maximum cost efficiency.

Many companies can no longer excel in only one area; they have to excel in various areas to make a difference in a highly competitive market, and they have to be creative in coming up with uniquely combined solutions. How can we exceed our climate targets and at the same time expand our production facilities? How can we leverage our strength as a discounter and still provide a range of high-end products?

We need multidimensional organizations that can arrange themselves along different axes at the same time: market segment, service channel, region, product, and customer type. We need multipurpose and at the same time versatile organizations, without the pitfall of creating complicated structures with sluggish communication and reporting lines. We must think multidimensionally and search for smart ways to bring together contradictory goals and interests.

3.1.6 Seeking Balance in a World Where Everything Is Interconnected

Globalization has turned the world into one big interdependent system. When the dot-com bubble burst in 2001, this led to an unprecedented global economic crisis. The US housing market crisis led to a global credit crisis. The coronavirus outbreak, starting in one Chinese city, ended up disrupting the whole world in a matter of weeks. These are all examples of the butterfly effect: the flapping of a butterfly's wings in one part of the world can cause a hurricane in another part. This is why it is essential for these interconnected systems to be in balance with each other and not be based on one-sided principles, creating bubbles which then have to be corrected by draconic measures in the opposite direction. If the global economy is primarily focused on boosting economic growth, then it shouldn't come as a surprise when companies start to do strange and questionable things to meet these soaring expectations. When disappointing results come to light, the inflated bubble bursts and entire interconnected system is at the brink of collapse. These systems can only be sustainable if counterbalancing forces and feedback mechanisms are built into them.

3.1.7 Digital Transformation as a Catalyst

All the above trends are compounded by digital transformation. In his article about digital leadership, industry expert Wim van Hennekeler[1] shows that digital transformation is different from more traditional transformation. It necessitates that silos be broken down, both within the organization and within the wider ecosystem, that organizations be competent in coping with opposite demands, and that they combine different viewpoints to boost innovation and look for hybrid solutions. For example, how to combine customer centricity with operational excellence, entrepreneurship with compliance to strict privacy and security regulations, or remote working

---

1 Wim van Hennekeler, "Digital Leadership: Ten Reasons Why Leading Digital Transformation Is Different," *Wim van Hennekeler* (blog), 2020, https://wimvanhennekeler.com/en/digital-leadership-6.

with face-to-face encounters? Technology itself can bring a brief competitive advantage, but it quickly turns into a commodity that anyone can buy. What really differentiates digital leaders from their competitors is the way they cope with these paradoxical challenges.

3.1.8 Countermovements

These trends show us that both/and thinking is not only "nice to have," but is, for many organizations, a "must have" in order to survive in the twenty-first century. So we are compelled to go in this direction, but are we really following its principles?

If we look at the world today, we also see just the opposite happening: more polarization, more black-and-white thinking, more political and religious extremism, the rise of ultra-nationalism, authoritarian leaders, and outright dictators, with authoritarian rule increasingly presented as an alternative to slow and indecisive democracies.

However, these are two sides of the same coin and both answers to the same question: how to cope with a world that has become increasingly VUCA (Volatile, Unpredictable, Complex, and Ambiguous). One way of dealing with VUCA is to try to return to the "old" world where things used to be more simple, clear, and less confusing, with a solid identity and straightforward values, following single-minded and infallible leaders who give us the illusion of being safe and protected against all these external threats. However, appealing these simple and one-sided solutions may sound in the short term, in the long term they can never match the increasing complexity of our world.

The other way is much more challenging because it entails embracing complexity and ambiguity, allowing tensions and discomfort, and going beyond the safety of simple one-liners, dogmatic prescriptions, and straightforward solutions. This both/and method is more demanding because it requires that we take full responsibility

for the consequences of our actions and learn how to balance. This
book explores this second way, by not only providing inspiration
and food for thought, but also practical models and tools.

3.2 The Rise of Paradoxical Leadership and Both/And Thinking

The idea that creation, evolution, and history are driven by encounters between opposing forces has been around for millennia. You
will come across this view in the works of many great philosophers,
across cultures and time. As early as the sixth century BC, Laozi
taught that the fundamental forces of nature – yin and yang – are
antagonistic but inseparable. They are complementary generative
forces that drive an eternal flow of transformation. We should follow this flow and not go against it. Around the same time, the Greek
philosopher Heraclitus saw the continuous flux of nature as a dialectical clash between opposite forces: "War is the father of all and
king of all." In Hinduism, the cosmic functions of creation, maintenance, and destruction are personified as a balanced triad of deities:
Brahma (the creator), Vishnu (the preserver), and Shiva (the de-
stroyer). Throughout the course of Western history and in very different contexts, various thinkers have put this concept at the heart
of their work, including Nicholas of Cusa ("Coincidentia opposito-
rum") Hegel (dialectical stages of development: thesis, antithesis,
and synthesis), Marx (history as class struggle), Jung (the feminine
and masculine archetypes), and Nietzsche (artistic creation as the
tension between the Apollonian and the Dionysian principles).

However, this paradoxical paradigm has always been overshadowed by the mainstream belief in dualism, in which opposites are
strictly separated from each other or placed in a hierarchical order.
Influential proponents of this school of thought include Plato, whose
allegory of the cave depicts the real world of ideas and the unreal
shadow world of physical manifestation; the Abrahamic religions,

which set the divine and immortal soul apart from the perishable and sinful life on earth; Descartes, who theorized the separation of body and mind and the noncontradiction principle of classical logic, in which A and not-A are mutually exclusive. These are all examples of either/or thinking.

Since either/or and both/and thinking have existed for millennia, it is inevitable that both persist in modern theories of business and leadership as well. Compared to the mainstream either/or model, the both/and movement in management theory and practice has been rather small-scale. Either/or thinking is extremely appealing: It is clear, simple, and straightforward, it appeals to our instinct for logical thought and action, and it allows us to plan and follow a clear direction. However, it is also a way of thinking that relies on a relatively simple and predictable world: that is not our world today.

In management literature the interest in the power of opposites and paradoxical leadership is relatively recent. In their trend-setting article "Toward A Theory of Paradox,"[2] Wendy K. Smith and Marianne W. Lewis put the rise of paradoxical thinking in management research into a broader historical context:

> Early researchers responded to tensions by seeking "one best way to organize ... In the reaction to this perspective, contingency theory emerged in the 1960s calling for researchers to consider the conditions under which alternative elements of tensions were most effective. According to this lens success depends on alignment within the internal system and with the external environment. The role of management is to recognize and then resolve tensions ... In contrast to contingency theory, a paradox perspective assumes that tensions persist within

---

2 Wendy K. Smith and Marianne W. Lewis, "Toward a Theory of Paradox: A Dynamic Equilibrium Model of Organizing," *Academy of Management Review* 36, no. 2 (2011): 381–403.

complex systems. These underlying tensions are not only normal but, if harnessed, can be beneficial and powerful.

The authors clearly point out the differences in perspective: "Early organizational theories asked, 'Is A or B more effective?' Contingency theory asks 'Under what conditions is A or B more effective?' A paradox perspective, in contrast, asks, 'How can organizations and their managers effectively engage A and B simultaneously?'"

In the last quarter of the twentieth century, leading management thinkers and early pioneers such as Paul Hersey and Ken Blanchard (Situational Leadership[3]), Robert Quinn and Kim Cameron (Competing Values Framework[4]), and Charles Hampden-Turner and Fons Trompenaars (Dilemma Theory and its application to cultural differences[5] and leadership[6]) have demonstrated that effective leadership is characterized by both/and thinking and the flexibility of applying different management styles depending on the situation.

In the 1980s and 1990s, pioneers such as Barry Johnson,[7] Fons Trompenaars, and Charles Hampden-Turner developed groundbreaking, research-based practical models, tools, and applications. Johnson developed the Polarity Map® to map and explore polarities in real business challenges and situations. It provides an attractive visual format to identify the strengths and limitations of each

---

3   The original theory was first published in Paul Hersey and Ken Blanchard, "Life Cycle Theory of Leadership," *Training and Development Journal* 23, no. 5 (1969): 26–34.

4   Robert E. Quinn and Kim S. Cameron, *Paradox and Transformation: Toward a Theory of Change in Organization and Management* (Cambridge, MA: Ballinger, 1988). Kim S. Cameron and Robert E. Quinn, *Diagnosing and Changing Organizational Culture: Based on the Competing Values Framework* (Reading, MA: Addison-Wesley, 1999).

5   Fons Trompenaars and Charles Hampden-Turner, *Riding the Waves of Culture: Understanding Cultural Diversity in Business* (London: Nicholas Brealey, 1997).

6   Fons Trompenaars and Charles Hampden-Turner, *21 Leaders for the 21st Century: How Innovative Leaders Manage in the Digital Age* (New York: McGraw-Hill, 2002).

7   Barry Johnson, *Polarity Management: Identifying and Managing Unsolvable Problems* (Amherst, MA: HRD, 1992); Barry Johnson, *And: Making a Difference by Leveraging Polarity, Paradox or Dilemma* (Amherst, MA: HRD, 2020).

pole and to leverage the power of both.[8] Trompenaars and Hamp-den-Turner developed a dilemma reconciliation process to transform leadership dilemmas and cultural differences into both/and solutions.

In the last decade a whole new academic research field and a global research community on organizational paradox has emerged, with Marianne W. Lewis and Wendy K. Smith as important theoretical founders, protagonists, and inspirational drivers. This field covers both theory building and empirical studies on a wide range of organizational topics from a paradoxical perspective.[9]

I'd like to highlight one article here: "Paradoxical Leadership to Enable Strategic Agility"[10] by Marianne W. Lewis, Constantine Andriopoulos, and Wendy K. Smith. The authors explicitly link agility and continuous innovation to thinking in terms of paradoxes. They cite practical examples from companies such as Unilever, Lego, and IBM Global Services. Their article starts with a quote from Paul Polman, former CEO of Unilever: "The difference between average and outstanding firms is an 'AND Mentality.'" From this perspective, paradoxes are seen as the driving force behind creativity. Polman is quoted again: "We actively look for points of tension, many of which come naturally with size and complexity – Do I take the lead or do I rely on others? Do we aim for short-term profitability or long-term sustainability? Do we seek social responsibility or minimise costs? …

---

8 Brian Emerson and Kelly Lewis build further on the thinking and models of Barry Johnson with their Polarity Navigator. Brian Emerson and Kelly Lewis, *Navigating Polarities* (Washington, DC: Paradoxical Press, 2019).

9 You can find more about the publications and activities of this vibrant and productive research community at https://leveragingtensions.com. For a comprehensive overview of academic literature on organizational paradox, I refer you to the bibliography by Wendy K. Smith and Simone Carmine: "Organizational Paradox," in *Oxford Bibliographies in Management*, ed. Ricky Griffin (New York: Oxford University Press, 2021).

10 Marianne W. Lewis, Constantine Andriopoulos, and Wendy K. Smith. "Paradoxical Leadership to Enable Strategic Agility," *California Management Review* 56, no. 3 (2014): 58–77.

My goal is to create an environment of positive energy that values these friction points."

In their 2022 book *Both/And Thinking*,[11] Wendy K. Smith and Marianne W. Lewis build on their years of academic research to develop a practical framework with four sets of tools to effectively work with paradoxical tensions: (1) shifting to both/and assumptions by adopting a paradox mindset, (2) creating boundaries to contain tensions and structures to stabilize uncertainty, (3) finding comfort in discomfort, and (4) enabling dynamics that unleash tensions to avoid getting stuck in a rut. These four levers are in themselves paradoxical, comprising opposing yet interwoven elements.

Closely linked to the academic work on organizational paradox is the research done on organizational ambidexterity.[12] The specific focus here is on the tension between "exploitation" and "exploration." "Exploitation" refers to running the current business in an efficient and controlled manner. It is a predictable process with straightforward lines between input and output. Managing it properly is essential if an organization wants to be and stay competitive. "Exploration" is about structural innovation and is a much more unpredictable process in which flexibility, autonomy, and the freedom to experiment are important. Exploration is essential for the long-term survival of a business. Exploitation and exploration often involve contradictory goals, and organizations need the ambidexterity of two nimble hands to excel in both areas. Data analysis shows a positive correlation between the application of the principles of ambidexterity and growth in sales figures, the capacity for innovation, and market valuation.

---

11 Wendy K. Smith and Marianne W. Lewis, *Both/And Thinking: Embracing Creative Tensions to Solve Your Toughest Problems* (Boston, MA: Harvard Business Review Press, 2022).
12 An article presenting an overview of ambidexterity by Charles A. O'Reilly III and Michael L. Tushman, "Organizational Ambidexterity: Past, Present and Future," *Academy of Management Perspectives* 27, no. 4 (November 2013): 324–38.

The literature makes a distinction between sequential and simultaneous ambidexterity. With sequential ambidexterity, a company shifts its focus from one aspect to another for longer periods of time throughout its life cycle. With simultaneous ambidexterity, an organization focuses on both aspects at the same time. The most obvious way to do this is by creating a dual structure, for example, having one business unit focused on exploitation and another one focused on innovation. This is called "structural ambidexterity." It gets even more interesting with the concept of "contextual ambidexterity" or "the behavioral capacity to simultaneously demonstrate alignment and adaptability across an entire business unit."[13] I will come back to the pros and cons of these different strategies in the next section when we discuss the Polarity Wheel. Academic research on contextual ambidexterity also focuses on the key question of how to make it work, revealing that leadership is the crucial factor here.[14]

In the article "Leadership and the Art of Plate Spinning,"[15] Colin Price, based on his research for McKinsey & Company, shows the importance of embracing paradoxes to achieve corporate success. In contrast to a traditional consultancy-like plea for "boosting innovation," "accelerating change," or "increasing shareholder value," the article indicates that such unilateral actions often have the opposite effect. Good leadership is all about finding the right balance between opposites. In this article Price addresses three paradoxes in management:

- Leaders need to create a sense of stability in order for change to take place.

---

13 Cristina B. Gibson and Julian Birkinshaw, "The Antecedents, Consequences, and Mediating Role of Organizational Ambidexterity," *Academy of Management Journal* 44, no. 2 (2004): 209–26.

14 Kathrin Rosing, Michael Frese, and Andreas Bausch, "Explaining the Heterogeneity of the Leadership-Innovation Relationship: Ambidextrous Leadership," *The Leadership Quarterly* 22, no. 5 (2011): 956–74.

15 Colin Price, "Leadership and the Art of Plate Spinning," *McKinsey Quarterly* (November 2012).

- Organizations are more likely to succeed if they simultaneously control and empower their employees.
- As a company, we have to encourage consistency and standardization as well as innovation and experimentation.

Price states that embracing paradoxes feels awkward at first because it is to a certain degree counterintuitive and contrary to our straightforward, logical way of thinking. He concludes thus: "Far more centered and high performing, in my experience, are those leaders who welcome the inconvenient contradictions of organizational life."

In short, both/and thinking involves an important change in traditional management thinking. It means, among other things, that "values" that were previously frowned upon are gaining recognition again. For example: the focus used to be on maintaining standards and on ensuring consistency, with deviations and variations usually being considered as sources of error and a waste of time. It is now widely recognized that it is better to create some space to experiment and "mess around" so that creativity and initiative can again start to flourish.

3.3 The Fundamentals of Both/And Thinking

Now that we have covered why both/and thinking is important, we will turn to the "what" and the "how": What does both/and thinking actually look like, and how does it work? I will first lay out the three basic principles of both/and thinking, as they provide the lens through which we will look at people and organizations. I will then highlight some principles of practice.

In the next chapter we will go further into the details of the "how" and in part 2, we will apply the both/and lens to specific organizational challenges and functional business areas.

The three fundamentals of both/and thinking are:

1 Valuing the power of both sides
2 Reframing the question: from limiting choices to unexpected possibilities
3 Balancing opposite poles in different ways

These principles can help us cope with polarities both in ourselves and in our relationships with others. We can struggle to bring together different sides of ourselves and to bridge the gap when others represent the opposite pole from our position. I strongly believe that we can only embrace the diversity of others if we are able and willing to embrace the diversity within ourselves. Therefore, I will focus most of the examples on coping with our internal polarities.

3.3.1 Valuing the Power of Both Sides

Both/and thinking basically involves considering the two seemingly contradictory poles as being fundamentally equivalent. It's about recognizing the power of both. For example, the power of centralization lies in creating unity, synergies, and economies of scale; the power of decentralization in being close to the client and being able to adapt quickly to day-to-day challenges.

This does not mean that they need to have the same value in every context or that they even have to be present at the same time, let alone balance each other in a nice fifty-fifty ratio. What a both/and approach does mean, however, is that neither pole is excluded in advance and that sooner or later the other pole will also be needed for balance.

It is always possible to find a context in which even the less attractive of two opposite values can "shine." This is easy to see when both poles have a positive meaning and when it is obvious that they are both needed, such as with "convergence and divergence" and "overview and details." But what happens when one pole in a polarity carries a distinct negative charge? Can concepts like "disintegration," "uncertainty," "loss," "cowardice," "selfish-ness," "sense of superiority," and even "dictatorship" be positive and worthwhile in a specific context? For the sake of consistency, we should all be shouting "yes!" Yet they are not values that we typically come across in an organization's mission statement or list of core values. These are attributes that we prefer to stay as far away from as possible, and yet they also contain positive elements despite their negative appearance and play a vital role in keeping balance.

To be able to see that positive element, we have to distance our-selves from the often extreme form in which these "values" (or rather "un-values") appear and the negative connotation they conjure up in our minds. When we hear the word "coward," we immediately think of a wimp without a backbone who would sell his soul to save his own skin. But beneath this negative behavior, there are also positive intentions, like having legitimate doubts and being cautious about taking personal risks. And in some circumstances, a little bit more cowardice at the senior management level could help to avoid expos-ing the organization to excessive risks and to save it from collapsing.

When we think of "disintegration" or "decay," we think of some-thing that was once beautiful and strong falling apart. But disinte-gration also gives rise to new growth and development. Sometimes it is better to let something disintegrate and to even speed up the process rather than to artificially try to slow it down, since rapid de-cay will create a sense of urgency for renewal. The influential econ-omist, Joseph Schumpeter, saw breakdown as a motor for renewal, and he introduced the term "creative destruction": a never-ending process of rise and fall in which old companies are destroyed and replaced by new ones.

In the material world, something "old and disintegrated" can also be something beautiful and commercially exploitable: the ruins of lost civilizations, picturesque medieval villages that we love visiting as tourists, the mystique of old factory buildings and warehouses, an antique cupboard with that deep patina (or a new cupboard in shabby chic style), an old cemetery with moss covered stones ... In all of these contexts, disintegration is highly valued, as in descriptors like "authentic," "weathered," "containing soul," or "back to basics." Many culinary delicacies also derive their unique taste from fermentation and processes of decomposition and decay, such as that runny ripened cheese, that exquisite sweet wine that gets its special taste from noble rot, or that special top-fermented beer.

Despite the repression, excessive violence, and fear that dictatorships entail, people may turn to them for order, security, and stability. In some circumstances autocratic rule may be the preferable option to avoid civil war, anarchy, terror, or the chaos of a failed state where extreme factions are in charge.

These negative values are thus not only necessary for balance but are explicitly desirable in certain contexts. They are also part of each and every one of us. We all carry around these "shadow sides" to a greater or lesser extent in order to remain adaptable, even if we don't want to admit this to ourselves and project them mainly onto others. It is better to acknowledge and work with our shadow sides in a conscious and constructive way than to pretend they do not exist, and to then unconsciously let them determine our behavior, or – at an unguarded moment when the pressure gets too high – to shift out of balance to our darkest side. In part 2, section 7.1 ("The Power of What Is Hidden in the Shadows") we will explain how we can deal with these shadow sides and use them to our advantage.

3.3.2 Reframing the Question: From Limiting Choices to Unexpected Possibilities

Confronted with a dilemma or a polarized situation, the two poles seem to be unreconcilable, and our options seem to be narrowed down to only these two. But is that really so? If we stay at the surface with the options as they manifest themselves, then it certainly does. If we leave the level of manifestation and go to the underlying values and needs, a wider space of new possibilities will arise. The key is to reframe the question from "Do I choose A or B?" to "How can I use and combine the underlying power of both A and B?"

These four steps, which build on the groundwork of the mutual gains approach to negotiation,[16] can be very helpful to reframe the question in any dilemma:

1 **Recognizing a dilemma or a polarized situation** that seems to be insurmountable. Consider, for example, the dilemma between "Am I going to travel the world?" or "Should I stay at home to minimize my ecological footprint and my impact on climate change?" At this superficial level of concrete options (either traveling or not), one may feel the need to make a clear choice (or feel paralyzed with indecision). The best thing that can happen at this level is some kind of in-between solution or compromise, such as flying less often or less far, eating less meat, or driving an electric car as a form of compensation.

2 **Examining the essence of each pole.** In order to create more space for finding a solution that values both sides of the coin, one needs to get to the underlying needs, concerns, values, and principles. You might ask: What does each side of this dilemma stand for? What does each option mean to me? What deeper purpose does each side serve?

For example: "Travel and see the world" may contribute to my deeper needs for (1) excitement, magic, fun, and fulfillment, (2) my personal growth and broadening of my horizons, and (3) recognition by my peer group. "Minimize the ecological footprint," on the other hand, could be driven by my needs and values, such as (1) taking responsibility for the planet, (2) promoting another way of living and being an example to others, and (3) being seen and valued by others as someone who is morally correct.

---

16 Roger Fisher, William L. Ury, and Bruce Patton, *Getting to Yes: Negotiating Agreement without Giving In* (New York: Penguin Books, 1983).

3 **Defining a paradoxical challenge**. Looking beyond these contradictory manifestations, how could we realize the underlying values of both poles? What are the specifications for a new both/and solution?

An example of a paradoxical challenge could be: How can I grow personally and broaden my horizons while at the same time minimizing my ecological footprint and being seen and recognized for my efforts?

4 **Achieving a new combined form**. What would be a new concrete form or solution in which these specifications could be realized? This search can be best started with clearly defining the requirements for a good both/and solution. These criteria are even more important than the solution itself, as they are less transient over time.

Searching for a new both/and solution requires some creativity and imagination. It means leaving behind all well-known formulas and traditional assumptions of what a solution should look like and looking at it in a completely fresh way. By doing so, we escape from the narrow path of choosing one solution or another and allow for a multitude of possible solutions. Such a fresh perspective could be a strong driver for breakthrough innovation.

For example: Maybe I could grow and develop myself in my vast inner world and in my unlimited imagination. I could read beautiful books about faraway countries, without actually going there, or become more aware and mindful of the hidden magic and beauty of my "ordinary" day-to-day environment, becoming a tourist in my own city, neighborhood, street, or house. Like the French novelist Marcel Proust said: "Mystery is not about traveling to new places but about looking with new eyes."

Or if this doesn't work for me, there's also the virtual world that could enable me to explore and experience new realms: meeting people around the world online, exploring new universes in virtual reality, etc.

These four steps can be visualized in figure 3.1.

Figure 3.1. From dilemma to paradox

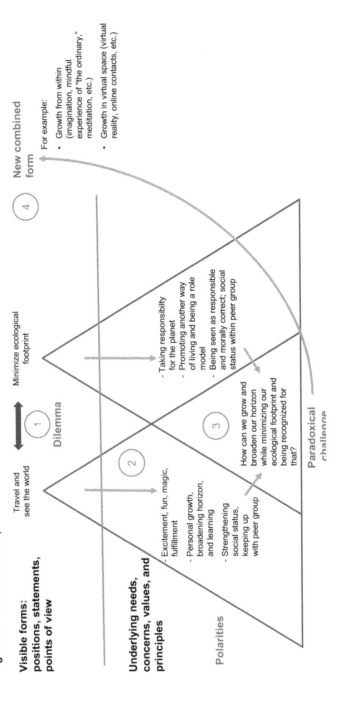

Visible forms: positions, statements, points of view

Travel and see the world — Minimize ecological footprint

① Dilemma

Underlying needs, concerns, values, and principles

- Excitement, fun, magic, fulfillment
- Personal growth, broadening horizon, and learning
- Strengthening social status, keeping up with peer group

②

- Taking responsibility for the planet
- Promoting another way of living and being a role model
- Being seen as responsible and morally correct; social status within peer group

③ How can we grow and broaden our horizon while minimizing our ecological footprint and being recognized for that?

Polarities

Paradoxical challenge

④ New combined form

For example:
- Growth from within (imagination, mindful experience of "the ordinary," meditation, etc.)
- Growth in virtual space (virtual reality, online contacts, etc.)

In conclusion, we have to make two movements: We first need to go from the very concrete level down to the more abstract level of underlying values in order to go back up again to a new concrete and workable form. The crucial point of transformation in this process is the definition of the paradoxical challenge: How can we realize both the underlying value of X and the underlying value of Y?

The challenge lies in pinpointing what is really causing tension. Sometimes you might focus too much on the content of the matter and therefore lose sight of the real issue. In the traveling example: It could very well be that the essence is not about traveling and the magic of new experiences, nor about saving the planet. It could be that the two poles are primarily about the identity and public image that you want to cultivate, and the social recognition that you long for. In that case, the paradoxical challenge (the answer to step 3) is completely different. It might be something like: "How can I be seen and accepted as both a responsible and cosmopolitan person?" Consequently, the new synthesis could also be quite different. Therefore, it is crucial to get to the core polarity before formulating the paradoxical challenge. And this involves listening very well – both to yourself and to others – often reading between the lines and particularly focusing on what is not being *said* but is being *felt*.

3.3.3 Balancing Opposite Poles in Different Ways

From the example above you might think that you must always look for a paradoxical solution on a deeper level where both poles are completely integrated, or an ultimate synthesis where 1+1=3. As I pointed out in chapter 1, this is not always possible or even desirable. There are other both/and solutions, acknowledging and seizing the value of both sides, that work just as well. In chapter 1 we already showed two alternatives: tuning in to both poles separately, or seeking a compromise. If we drill down, we can distinguish

Figure 3.2. The Polarity Wheel

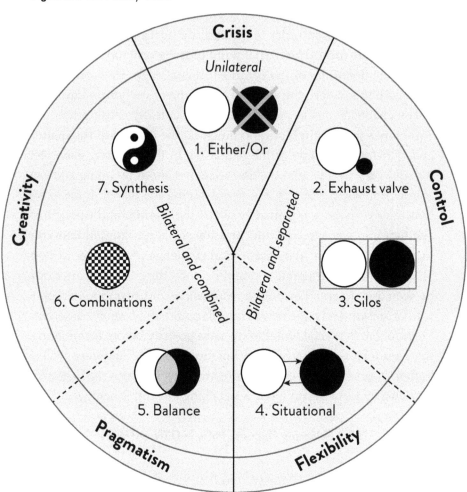

seven strategies of integrating opposites. They can be presented in the Polarity Wheel.

Strategy 1 in the Polarity Wheel represents the either/or perspective in its purest form, where there is only room for one of the two poles (unilateral). In strategies 2 to 4, there is room for both poles (dualistic), but they are still strictly separated from each other, either in space (Strategies 2 and 3) or in time (Strategy 4). In Strategies 5 through 7, the two opposite poles are brought together to create combined solutions; in Strategies 5 and 6, the two opposing elements can still be distinguished from each other; in Strategy 7, they are merged to form something completely new.

The numbering of these strategies may give the impression of an ascending order, as in the more integration between the opposites, the better it is. However, that is not necessarily the case. The most useful strategy depends entirely on the situation. That is why the model is not depicted as a hierarchical ladder or a maturity or growth model but as a wheel from which you can choose a level depending on the context. The keywords in the outer circle of the wheel give the context in which each of these different strategies might prove to be useful.

Making a conscious choice is therefore more important than the level of integration that you choose. Every strategy has its strengths and its limitations. It is important to carefully weigh the pros and cons for every case or situation and to take full responsibility for the consequences. Nevertheless, the strategies with the highest levels of integration are quite attractive as they hold the most potential for innovative and sustainable solutions; but they can also take a lot of creative effort to create and maintain them and not every situation needs a solution of this level. Sometimes a basic compromise or simply placing the poles side by side separately is more than enough.

Finally, these strategies should never be thought of as permanent solutions, but only as temporary forms in which both underlying poles can come together. The Polarity Wheel represents the different steps in the eternal dance between separating and connecting opposing poles.[17] Separation provides focus and clarity while connection provides integration and synergy. All these different strategies need

---

17   Wendy K. Smith and Marianne W. Lewis also describe the dynamic between separa-
     tion (pull apart) and connection (bring together) as a key tool to effectively navigate
     paradoxes as it allows us to structure the boundaries around paradox. Wendy K.
     Smith and Marianne W. Lewis, *Both/And Thinking. Embracing Creative Tensions to Solve
     Your Toughest Problems* (Boston, MA: Harvard Business Review Press, 2022), 139.

to be regularly reviewed to check if they are still fit for purpose and reflect the relationship we want to have with both underlying poles.

The seven strategies of the Polarity Wheel are generic and applicable to all levels of polarity ownership: individual, team, organization, or society. In the following explanation I will take an organizational polarity as an example: the well-known tension between innovation and running daily operations.

Strategy 1: Pure Either/Or Thinking

All the efforts and resources are concentrated on keeping the current operation running, and there is no room for innovation. Or the reverse: a creative start-up focuses entirely on developing innovative solutions, without bothering about clients or business. This is actually level zero with respect to integration. Nevertheless, at a certain phase and for a limited period of time, it can be a conscious and beneficial choice to do so. It can bring focus and in a period of crisis or struggle to survive, it is sometimes unavoidable to make black-and-white choices. "We are going through a very rough period, so we will cancel all new initiatives and refocus on the core tasks." This level cannot be maintained for long because without renewal the organization cannot survive, just as a start-up cannot keep experimenting in the garage. That is why sooner or later the organization must shift away from strategy.

Strategy 2: Exhaust Valve or Sanctuary

Strategy 2 is the first small step toward both/and thinking. One of the two opposite poles is clearly dominant, but a small niche is created for the other pole. This secluded spot can serve as an "exhaust valve" through which any built-up tension can be released in a more or less controlled manner or as a cosmetic measure to appear balanced to the outside world. For example, a busy, heavily polluted city might offer here and there some tiny little parks as sanctuaries of peace and quiet. In Strategy 2, both poles are clearly separated from each other in space or time. It is often a strategy to maintain the dominant pole and to keep control by creating a contained solution which offers just enough release to vent negative tensions and keep the system from bursting and subsequently collapsing. However, it can also be a positive attempt to create a kind of sanctuary for something that we consider precious and want to protect from being absorbed or pushed aside by the dominant pole.

In an innovation/operation example, an organization might keep a free space to experiment in an otherwise highly structured environment: "We are actually a rather traditional, business-as-usual organization, but we ought to do something to innovate." A small innovation cell would be able to come up with out-of-the-box ideas without being engulfed by daily operations and without being restricted by the traditional way of thinking and acting. However, without connection or substantial impact, a cell like this is sometimes nothing more than a management team toy or a PR-showcase. Nonetheless, this "sanctuary" can have a positive role as a protected testing ground where experiments can be carried out and where not everything has to run according to strict processes and well-defined procedures. It can be a feasible and controlled first step to making the entire organization more innovative.

Strategy 3: Equivalent Silos

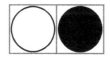

An organization can extend Strategy 2 to achieve an equal balance between the two opposite poles by strictly separating them.

In Strategy 3 both sides have comparable resources and impact but work independently from each other and follow their own logic.

For example, a traditional and an innovative organization coexist in separation, managed as two carefully delineated organizational entities, such as an internet bank alongside a traditional bank, or a standardized production organization and an innovative project organization. This can work well because every organizational component has its own focus and can develop specific work processes and methods. But in many cases, cooperation is unavoidable; for example, the prototypes that are developed in the innovative project organization have to land in the standardized production organization. In that case, organizational walls can constitute a major obstacle and may lead to conflict and competition.

Strategy 4: Situational Switching

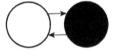

This is a more dynamic way of using the power of both sides. The choice to bring one pole forward and move the other back depends on the requirements of a specific situation. The ability of an organization to switch according to the situation makes it adaptable to changing circumstances. The two opposite poles are thus separated in time and do not occur simultaneously. Situational switching, however, is not just about switching between pitch black and bright white. The organization can switch more subtly between various shades of gray by changing the ratio of the combined poles (100/0, 50/50, 5/95, etc.). Situational switching can also cover longer phases of organizational development.

For example, in successive periods the organization shifts its focus from innovation to stabilization and back to innovation in a cyclical movement. For each phase the organization exchanges old ways of working for new ways and develops or buys new competencies. Once a new product or service offer has been developed and finalized, it is put into production, and it is then all about volume and operational excellence. A biotech start-up might invest years in the development and patenting of a revolutionary drug and then market and produce it on a large scale.

Ideally, to safeguard the continuity of income, the development of new products and services should begin while the existing ones are still going strong. In those overlapping periods, both daily operations have to be run and new products and services have to be developed, which puts significant pressure on the organization. In order to absorb this pressure, the organization can work with a separate development and production organization, like with Strategy 3. The disadvantage of serial switching is that it costs a lot of energy and money, especially during the changeover periods. The advantage is that the smoother an organization can switch between exploration and exploitation – for example through a good mix of widely deployable employees or a large flexible resource pool – the more agile it is and the faster it can respond to changes in the environment.

Strategy 5: Balance

In all previous strategies the complementary functions were separated, either in space or in time. From Strategy 5 onwards they are interwoven.

Seeking balance may take the form of a compromise, with both poles having to yield a bit. It could also result in an equally balanced win-win situation. Strategy 5 types of solutions are often chosen because they are pragmatic and feasible, with each party gaining something and usually giving something up. An interesting variation of this is a "trade-off," as in the example of a coalition government where the left-wing parties are given some explicit left-wing policies and the right-wing parties some clear right-wing points to score, to prevent them from losing the votes of their respective supporters. The advantage of this variant is that it avoids a gray compromise, which makes no one happy, and preserves the full potential of each pole. This exchange could be a stepping stone to Strategies 6 and 7.

Back to the innovation/operation example: innovation is no longer a separate process but belongs to the integral responsibility and objectives of the operation. Since the organization's attention must be divided, it must find a feasible and pragmatic mix. The advantage is that innovation is permanently on everyone's agenda and the innovations probably fit well with the needs of the operation. The disadvantage may be that innovation gets diluted or buried under day-to-day operational work, and as attention is divided, there's a real risk of the organization doing neither really well. It also may not be possible to achieve real breakthrough innovations in this way.

Strategy 6: Creative Combinations

With the previous strategy, both goals were slightly watered down to find a workable in-between solution. This strategy aims to integrate two opposite poles in their original, uncompromised form to see how they could reinforce each other and generate a creative tension. The exchange between two seemingly mutually exclusive worlds could give rise to all kinds of new initiatives that benefit both worlds.

A well-known example is a tech company that allows its staff to only work four days on the project portfolio of the organization.

On the one remaining day, people are free to work on their own projects, using the company's infrastructure. All they have to do is share their progress and results with their colleagues. As a result, the innovative spinoff for the company of this one day is far greater than of the four days of more traditional work. "Agile" product development is another way of bringing innovation and operation together: developers and business people each have their own roles but work closely together as part of one team, in short-term cycles.

In Strategy 6 opposite poles can be combined in different ways. Take "freedom" and "control": "Within the broad but well-defined boundaries of the scope, local teams are totally free to innovate and to take entrepreneurial risks." A variation could be: "Feel free to bring forward any new ideas, but once one of these new ideas has been chosen, its implementation will be strictly adhered to."

Strategy 6 can deliver great benefits but is also demanding. It requires high level communication skills to enable the exchange between both worlds and to bridge possible gaps. It specifically needs people who are passionate about their work; if this inspiration from within and the creative exchange between both parties are lacking, it may get bogged down in a bureaucratic box-ticking exercise.

Strategy 7: Synthesis

In Strategy 6, the two opposite poles coexist side by side. In Strategy 7, they are merged into something completely new. For example, "servant leadership" doesn't mean serving their staff two days a week and leading them the other three days. The point is to lead by serving.

On the one hand, the opposite poles are still unmistakably and fully present, but on the other hand, they can no longer be clearly identified as individual components, and their original forms certainly are not recognizable. This may give rise to something different, something that is more than just the sum of its parts, such as disciplined empowerment or autonomous alignment. To avoid getting tangled up in contradictions or dilemmas, it is imperative that we look beyond the superficial form in which the opposites appear and examine their deeper essence.

In our example, Strategy 6 clearly delineated roles and functions, and formal performance indicators were still required, but in Strategy 7, people have fully integrated innovation and efficiency into their DNA. It has become second nature to consider both values in everything they do. In this way, the innovation process feeds efficiency and the operation is continuously seen through an innovative lens. The two goals coincide, in the same way that a line manager doesn't consider caring for his staff as an incidental HR activity alongside his operational task but as essential to achieving his operational objectives.

People are empowered to take mixed developmental/operational initiatives and to determine for themselves the exact moment of transition from exploration to exploitation. It requires professionals to have a high degree of self-knowledge, self-confidence, initiative, situational flexibility, and communicative skills.

Synthesis may look like the ultimate way to combine the power of both sides, but it also has its limitations. It will take considerable energy, creativity, and inspiration to develop and maintain a state of synthesis, and there is always the risk that the newly created form gets disconnected from its original purpose of bringing both sides together. There is a time and a place for every one of the seven strategies.

The Polarity Wheel can be used for any polarity to consciously determine the desired and achievable level of integration. It is especially useful when looking at the key polarities that are driving the organization.

Although the Polarity Wheel is presented here as a menu from which you can choose according to the situation at hand, it can certainly also be used as a growth model. You could start carefully by creating a small and well-defined oasis for the neglected pole because any strategies focused on integrating both poles would for the moment clearly be a step too far. For example, a rather conservative organization can start with a small innovation unit developing controlled and isolated experiments. Based on small successes, innovation can start playing a more important role within the organization and spread from a separate department into the core business, to be in a later stage fully integrated into all activities.

3.4 Principles of Practice

How do you bring these fundamentals of both/and thinking and paradoxical leadership into practice? It's good to keep the following principles of practice in mind:

1 To change the world, **start with yourself**. We need first and foremost to take responsibility for our own personal polarities, before getting on with the polarities in the systems around us. We are ourselves an inextricable part of these systems, and the relation with our own polarities – including biases and blind spots – will directly or indirectly impact the balances that we want to "install" in our team or organization. Keep in mind the Greek aphorism: "Know thyself." It requires us to have the courage to seriously question ourselves and our own values and beliefs, and to check in with ourselves to feel and then adjust for the right balance. It's no use thinking that "Both/and thinking is a great concept for my team or organization, but I don't have time to apply it to myself." As a leader, you first have to apply the "both/and" perspective to your own opposing values and motives so that you can immediately set an example to others.

2 Whenever we do work with the polarities outside us, we should focus on those within **our own circle of influence,** where we are the **polarity owner.** Start with the relationships with our colleagues or with our team and not with the entire organization/world.

3 Both/and thinking is not a "management trick," but a **way of looking at the world and at ourselves**. Creating balance is not a one-off or a detached technical operation but requires the continuous effort to live and inspire this balance **from within**. If a system is not upheld by inner motivation, it turns into a dead format and automatically evokes its countermovement. We can merge a retirement home and a kindergarten, but if there is no motivation to keep the connection alive and continually renew it, this combination will lead to irritation and polarization rather than to synergy.

4 Paradoxical leadership is not about learning to cope with one or a few familiar polarities but about becoming competent in effectively **balancing polarities in general**.

5 The challenge is always to **dig below** the surface: "What are the polarities underlying a dilemma or a conflict that you face?" "Which values are colliding and causing tension?" "What is your relationship with both sides?" Find appreciation for "negative" values because they, too, have a function. What is the underlying positive power that they can bring?

6 Both/and thinking is not about trying to put even more things on our to-do lists and stretching our already overloaded schedules. It's not about the form ("I have no time as I have to rush to my yoga class") but **about the essence** ("How can I relax and fully be present in the moment?"). Maybe there are other much

more simple and less demanding forms to achieve the same goal (walking through the park on my way to the office or just talking a deep breath). It is certainly not about multitasking ("doing yoga while having my conference call"), which dilutes the essence of both tasks. Moreover, we don't have to be focused on balancing everything, as many things will balance themselves without any active intervention. Finally, it's also about listening to ourselves and striking the right balance between what we find important ourselves and what we think that the outside world expects from us.

7 Both/and thinking calls for **dynamic balancing,** not an ultimate solution. Every balance point that we achieve is a temporary state, a starting point for renewed calibration to reach the next balance point. Sometimes we must shift back from an integrated solution to separating both poles again, to bring them back together later in a new configuration. It's all about learning how to dance with polarities as the balance shifts continuously even though tension will always be there. The challenge is to become comfortable with tension and use it as a source of creativity.

8 This book does not prescribe what to do and what not to do. The aim is to **consciously handle** polarities, knowing what the consequences are of every choice we make. In principle all choices are fine – including black-and-white either/or choices – provided that we accept their consequences and take responsibility.

9 To make organizations paradoxically competent, consider deploying **a mix of levers**, on the one hand working on awareness, mindset, and competencies and on the other providing enabling structures and systems. Neither approach on its own will do the job.

DO THE PRINCIPLES OF PARADOXICAL LEADERSHIP
SUPPORT A PROGRESSIVE OR CONSERVATIVE COURSE?

One could think that the principles of paradoxical leadership are a plea for a politically progressive course, which would focus on fostering openness, diversity, inclusion, equality, participation, mixing of cultures, flexibility, continual change, innovation, and sustainable and ecologically sound solutions.

However, this reasoning misses the point. Paradoxical leadership is all about creating balance and transcends the concepts of progressive and conservative. An organization or society can be out of balance in different ways. For example, too much openness can lead to loss of identity. Too much tolerance and trust can lead to a disrespect of basic values and traditions and open the door to intolerant cultures. When there is chaos or a threat of civil war, a strong hand and stability will be needed to restore order and create a safe and secure environment.

The current polarization of society is strongly linked to globalization. It is in part a reaction to a cosmopolitan narrative that benefits some parts of society (personal and professional opportunities for highly qualified people, global growth for certain businesses, chances to travel the world and see other cultures), but very detrimental to others (jobs disappearing, competition with migrants who accept lower wages, loss of traditional values). The current polarization is probably a sign that we have gone too far in one direction, so that many people feel that they are threatened in their livelihoods, core values, and identity.

The solution will probably not be in building more walls or going back to isolationism or nationalism, but in acknowledging the legitimate underlying needs of identity, safety, security, shared values, and a sense of community and belonging. From there, a process can start to find new and positive ways to address these fundamental needs.

KEY POINTS

- Both/and thinking is on the rise in a world where boundaries are fading, the speed of change is ever increasing, and challenges in society and business are becoming more complex and ambiguous. However, the same trends have also sparked a strong countermovement toward the short-term clarity of either/or choices and single-minded leadership.
- Thinking in terms of paradoxes has always existed but has been overshadowed by straightforward either/or thinking. Interest in both/and thinking in management, academic literature, and in practice is now clearly growing.
- The key to both/and thinking is to give two opposite poles equal consideration and to not disregard a pole that may initially seem negative.
- The challenge is to look beyond the seemingly negative appearance of an opposite pole and to discover its positive contributions.
- By reframing the question from "'Do I choose for A or B?" to "How can I use and combine the underlying power of both A and B?" a range of new possibilities will arise.
- There are different strategies of combining and integrating opposite poles. I have described seven: (1) Either/or, (2) Exhaust valve, (3) Silos, (4) Situational, (5) Balance, (6) Creative combinations, and (7) Synthesis.
- All these strategies are valuable and have their pros and cons – maximum integration will not always be the best solution. It's about consciously choosing the strategy that works best in a particular situation and taking responsibility for its consequences.
- Both/and thinking and paradoxical leadership are a question of mindset, more than of technique or tools.

It's about consciously handling polarities, and it should
always start with ourselves and from our own circle of
influence.

- Paradoxical leadership transcends the concepts of progressive and conservative. The act of balancing may
  require both politically progressive and conservative
  measures.

HOW TO BALANCE BETWEEN OPPOSITE POLES

In this chapter, we will take a closer look at how to apply these principles to ourselves and to our teams and organizations. Following the principles of practice, we will start with the relationship with our own personal and professional polarities.

4.1 Handling Your Own Polarities

Learning to consciously interact with our own polarities entails several different steps. Most of these steps we already do naturally without any conscious effort. However, the steps become especially relevant as polarities become an issue:

1 **Recognize**: become aware of polarities and how they work
2 **Name and explore**: identify and get to know our own polarities
3 **Allow**: allow for tension as a productive force
4 **Value**: value both sides, exploring and fully experiencing the extremes
5 **Play**: switch back and forth between opposite poles
6 **Integrate**: experiment with combining and connecting opposite poles
7 **Communicate and connect**: engage others and reach out
8 **Serve**: contribute to a greater purpose

These steps combine the general principles and seven strategies of the previous chapter, specifically applied to the relationship with our own polarities. In practice the steps tend to be taken in parallel and are usually elements of an iterative process. Let's have a closer look.

4.1.1 Recognize: Become Aware of Polarities and How They Work

Sometimes we are trapped in a certain polarity without even realizing it. For example, a colleague who is always bursting with energy and optimism ("Of course we can!") may cause us to unconsciously adopt a cautious attitude, point out all the risks, and even step on the brakes. Another colleague who tends to see major roadblocks all over the place may stimulate us to automatically jump into action and go full speed ahead. Both colleagues can drive us up the wall because we find them either reckless or overly cautious. This pattern can lead to further polarization: the more one person is inclined to take risks, the more the other person applies the brakes. When we speak to our colleagues, however, we mainly talk about the specific content and issues at hand and not about the system we are part of and which unconsciously drives our behavior. We can only effectively deal with this polarity when we are able to recognize and articulate the pattern at a meta-level. Being caught in the process unconsciously, we will inevitably become frustrated. If we are conscious of this pattern, we can look for a complementary balance. After all, both risk-taking and caution are needed equally. Conscious awareness of polarities even allows us to play to the strengths and weaknesses of each extreme according to the needs of the moment, much like a "good cop, bad cop" routine; it allows us to deliberately switch roles and use them to our advantage.

As another example, we might be constantly swaying back and forth between two extreme positions without being aware of it. If we have an unbalanced relationship with one or both opposite poles, we might end up unconsciously zigzagging from one side to the other. For example, you have been appointed as the new head of a department that needs improvement. As the conceptually strong and decisive person you are, you first make a brilliant change plan which you then share with your team leaders. You succeed in convincing them and keep tight control during the development phase. You then delegate the implementation to your team leaders because you are convinced that they know best how to roll it out while you focus your attention on other strategic challenges. However, the team leaders are not used to enacting a plan like this without guidance, and nothing much gets done. In the meantime, you become impatient, and you return to micro-managing the entire process … You take full control, then you let it all go, and then you take full control again. Every time you take such a step, you have no trouble explaining why, but you don't realize that these steps form a pattern; not because you lack insight or intellect, but because you're in the thick of it.

The underlying and recurring pattern is often invisible to the "players on stage," and the ongoing discussions only focus on the concrete content in which the polarity appears: the conceptual advantages and disadvantages of each of the solutions. Becoming aware of this pattern is the first and most important step toward being able to change it and to tackle it at a more fundamental level.

It's useful to distinguish between the polarities that lie within ourselves (as in the previous example of control and letting go) and the polarities that the system, which we are part of, "imposes" on us (as in the example of how we might respond to our colleagues).

The polarities within ourselves are our personal themes, such as introversion/extroversion or adventure/safety. Maybe you have always been drawn to adventure, but at the same time you find it terrifying. You try something out, but as soon as you feel the slightest resistance or face even a minor setback, you quickly retreat into your comfort zone. As you're unable and unwilling to go all the way, you don't succeed in realizing your adventurous dreams. This pattern repeats itself over and over again, but you are not really aware of this because you see each specific "adventure" as a separate event, and you can explain very well why each "adventure" didn't work out, yet you fail to see the underlying pattern. It is therefore important to get to know our personal themes and patterns, to understand how they work and to recognize their impact. We can do this by self-reflecting and by consciously observing our behavior, but it is often even easier to accept and actively seek feedback from others.

Obviously though, we are not only self-contained individuals. We are part of various social systems and constellations, where we consciously or unconsciously play roles: in our relationships with our partners, our close and extended families, our teams at work, our clubs, our organizations, etc. At family parties, you always make sure that everything goes well. Others know this about you and assume that you will organize and manage everything to a T, so they automatically take on a more passive role. This may be a conscious choice, but sometimes it isn't. Sometimes, we are unconsciously forced by "the system" to take on a specific role: "Someone has to do it." Are you an authoritarian type of person who enjoys lecturing others? Not really, but over and over again you feel forced to play this role toward your rebellious teenage daughter, who drives you crazy. The same applies to the aforementioned example of adopting the role of the "driver" (pushing others into action) or the one who "sounds the alarm" (cautioning others about taking risks). What type of person are you really? You may be both, but you feel that "the system" is forcing you – whether you like it or not – into a certain role.

On the one hand, the system can also make us feel closer to a pole that we really like: your organization is going through a crisis and is crying out for a decisive leader, and decisiveness is one of your strongest qualities. On the other hand, the system can also make us take on a role that we feel less comfortable with and push us to such extremes that we end up feeling alienated from ourselves. This is why it is important to think about what role you are playing in the system and whether you really want to take on that role.

There are different strategies for coping with a situation where a system forces you into one side of a polarity. For example, if your role requires you to supervise and enforce strict rules and you feel narrowed down to this pole, there are several ways you could deal with it:

1 Give up your own preferences and learn to embrace your role, using the principle of "If you can't beat them, join them."
2 Adapt to the system but – for your own peace of mind – compensate yourself for this outside of the system by, for instance, pursuing a total sense of freedom when you're off work.
3 Accept what is being asked of you but do it your own way. Some people might be strict or authoritative when applying rules, whereas you might adopt a more understanding and empathetic approach.
4 Pretend to take on the role but continue doing your own thing behind the scenes.
5 Fight against the system and refuse to play along. In this case, you will remain true to yourself, but this will cost you a lot of energy, and you run the risk of losing your job.
6 Try to change the system from the inside. Instead of opposing your role, play ball. Start off doing what is expected from you and show yourself to be a reliable partner while simultaneously demonstrating the limitations of this approach and gaining commitment for introducing little by little your preferred approach.
7 Resign and leave the system.

In principle all of these strategies might be valid, depending on the situation. The important thing is to make a conscious choice. The first step is to make this often unconscious polarity explicit, both to yourself and to the system.

It is often very difficult to change our role in a system because all the other players in the system will have to change with us, which they may resist. For example, if you are no longer willing to clean up someone else's mess, then they will be forced to clean it up themselves, which they may not like doing. They might start to apply pressure by confronting you about your "irresponsible and disloyal" behavior, or by cleverly appealing to your sense of guilt and responsibility, or by simply assuming that you will continue to clean up after them because you can't stand the mess. In short, systems have a strong tendency to stay intact, but if we are explicit and persistent, we can break free from the polarized role that the system expects of us. If you are a crucial player in the system, you might be able to set off a process of change within its entirety.

4.1.2 Name and Explore: Identify and Get to Know Our Own Polarities

Being more aware of your polarities and how they work, and recognizing them when they surface, will enable you to examine them more closely. The questionnaire below (see text box) can help you get started. In appendix A, you will find a list of example polarities which you might find useful. Using neutral terms to indicate both poles will help you to look at both sides with an open mind, less distorted by value judgments and biases. For example, the polarity "Structure" and "Flexibility" works better than "Order" and "Chaos."

DISCOVER YOUR POLARITIES

Use the questions below to make a list of the polarities that play an important role in your life and work. You can use the list of polarities in appendix A for inspiration, but try to use your own words and don't hesitate characterize yourself with polarities outside the list.

1 In which polarities do you often find yourself swinging between the extremes of the two opposite poles (all or

nothing)? For example: "Sometimes I'm tremendously social and outgoing, but afterward I strongly feel the need to
be on my own."

2 With which polarities do you feel a strong positive connection with only one of the two poles? Do you find it
difficult to positively connect to the other pole, or perhaps
even feel repelled by it? For example: "I always need to be
in control and can't stand people with a laissez-faire attitude." You might have so much trouble recognizing this
pole that you can't even name it properly, or you might
have absolutely no association with it whatsoever, neither
positive nor negative. For example: "I'm always friendly
and find it difficult to get angry."

3 With which polarities do you feel a strong positive connection with both poles but experience them separately
from each other, usually in totally different contexts?
When you are in one pole, you find it difficult to connect
to the opposite pole, and vice versa. For example: "At
work, I'm very organized, with contingency plans for
all possible situations and get annoyed when my time is
wasted. When I'm on vacation, I just 'go with the flow';
just the idea of having to plan something makes me feel
stressed."

4 Which polarities occur regularly in your relationships with
your partner, family, friends, and colleagues? For example: "My colleague works very carelessly, so I'm having
to do all this extra work to sort out details and correct his
mistakes."

5 With which polarities do you have a strong positive connection with both poles and expertly switch back and forth
when needed? For example: "In some situations I enjoy
broad philosophical explorations, in others I am very practical and results focused."

This questionnaire is only meant to be a starting point. We are all capable of drawing up a clear and rational list of our own polarities. Sometimes though, we're so caught up in one that it's hard to notice and actually name something that is right under our nose. Or maybe the polarity is so threatening that we would rather not face it. However, the thing that hampers us most when compiling this list is that we "think" instead of "feel." We can only get to know our own polarities by tapping into our inner selves and by trying to name them from a concrete sensation, not by analyzing them as abstract concepts. The rational approach (and the questionnaire) can certainly help us discover and demarcate this area, but the crux is then to actually experience these polarities. The list we believed to have completed with an intellectual clarity and lucidity will most likely look completely different later on.

This is why it is important to explore our opposite poles from the inside. The constellation exercise below (see text box) may be very useful. In this exercise, you place two opposite poles in different places on the floor and physically stand in both places to feel the effect that each pole has on you. It may sound a bit spacey, but it has proven to be an extremely powerful exercise that will work for anyone who is willing to try it out.

EXPLORE OUR POLARITIES BY DOING A CONSTELLATION EXERCISE

The aim of this exercise is to explore and sense all the different aspects of a certain polarity at a deeper level. This is an exercise that you can do together with a colleague or friend who acts as your coach. While doing the exercise, you tell your coach what you sense and experience in each position. This will help you name and pinpoint underlying driving forces. Your coach can ask you questions to make your conclusions more clear and concrete. You have to be careful to stay close to what you feel and not start talking about it in an abstract or general way. It is important to stay in the moment. Follow the steps below:

Step 1: Take the polarity questionnaire you filled out and choose one of the polarities that you would like to explore further, e.g., quiet/hectic. Name the two poles and write each one down on a separate sheet of paper.

Step 2: You are now going to give this polarity a spatial dimension by placing each sheet of paper (each pole) in a different place on the floor. You can make this even more visual by placing an object on the floor that symbolizes the pole, for example your smartphone to represent "busy" and a round stone to represent "imperturbable peace and quiet."

Step 3: You are now going to start exploring the two extreme positions. You can start by standing on the pole that you are most familiar with, such as "busy" (represented by the corresponding sheet of paper or object). By simply standing on this pole, all sorts of thoughts, images, situations, feelings, emotions, etc. that you associate with this pole will start to surface. It can remind you of a recent situation in which you were trying to listen to someone on the phone and simultaneously checking your schedule to see what you still had to do. You will often feel this physically in your body. For example, at the "busy" pole, you unconsciously start moving and shuffling your feet, all sorts of ideas start racing through your mind, you feel light-headed or have the sensation of a knot in your stomach. Then you walk over to the other pole to see what happens there. You might start feeling much heavier, as if your body is being pulled down to the floor, or your breathing might start to slow down. This could feel

very pleasant or extremely uncomfortable, evoking a sense
of resistance (such as a tightness around your diaphragm).
Helpful questions for the coach to ask:

- What are the strengths and limitations of this familiar pole?
- What happens when you make this pole even more
  extreme?
- What are the strengths and limitations of the other pole?
- What resistance do you experience? How do you deal with
  that?

Step 4: You explore the space between the two poles. Go
step by step along the axis between the two extremes
and see how they feel as your proportional relation with
both changes. What images, thoughts, sensations, and
emotions do they evoke? How does your body or posture
change? Where do you feel resistance? Where do you feel
comfortable?
Helpful questions for the coach to ask:

- Where do you feel most at home on the line between these
  two poles?
- Can you shift slightly toward one or the other? What would
  help you do that in your everyday life?

Step 5: You finally step back from the axis between the two
poles and stand where you can see them both, but you are
no longer "squeezed" between them. Although you look at
them from a little distance, it is not a position of a detached
observer. You are still connected with both poles, just like
a charioteer holding the reins of two horses. What do you
experience here, and how does this differ from how it felt

in Step 4? You might feel more space, freedom, and choice with respect to the two poles or even a sort of synthesis such as "peace and quiet in a world of turmoil."

Helpful questions for the coach:

- What happens if you step back from the line and observe the two sides?
- How would a specific situation in your life or work look from this position?

Figure 4.1 shows what these positions on the floor might look like when seen from above:

Figure 4.1. Different positions in a constellation exercise

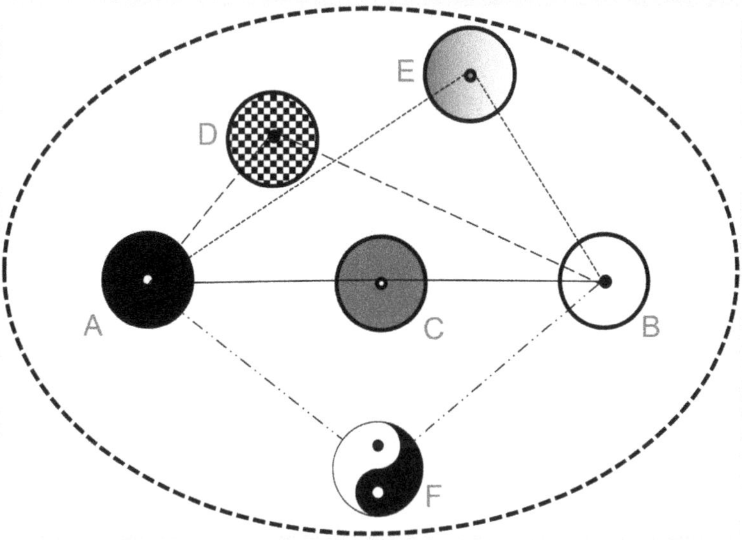

- Positions A and B are the extremes. If you choose to stay in one of these positions permanently, then you are opting for Strategy 1 (either/or) in the Polarity Wheel. You may also feel comfortable with both, although experiencing them

separately or in different contexts, such as at work and in your personal life. This corresponds to Strategies 2 (exhaust valve), and 3 (silos) in the Polarity Wheel.

- Position C represents an equally balanced in-between solution, but there are also other balanced solutions along the axis between the two extremes which vary depending on the ratio you choose. This corresponds to Strategy 5 (balance) in the Polarity Wheel. You also may find yourself alternating between Positions A, B, C, and other positions along this axis, depending on the situation. This corresponds to Strategy 4 (situational switching) in the Polarity Wheel.
- Positions D and E represent different ways of creatively combining the two opposite poles (corresponding to Strategy 6 in the Polarity Wheel: creative combinations). The boundaries between the two poles may be clear cut in one position (D) and more fluid in another (E).
- And finally, Position F represents a possible synthesis solution. This is Strategy 7 in the Polarity Wheel.

This exercise is not about getting concrete results ("Good! I've managed to bring that polarity back into balance. Now for the next one.") or forcing yourself to find solutions ("I have to find a way to create a good synthesis here.") but rather about exploring and feeling how these mechanisms really work. It will help you to clearly see how you relate to both poles, what the underlying positive power could be of a neglected, unknown, or suppressed pole, how difficult or easy it is to get to grips with this pole, which feelings of resistance you associate with it, and what actions could help you in transforming your relationship to this polarity. It will also make it easier for you to recognize this polarity in your daily life and work and to deal with it more consciously.

By doing this exercise, you will learn much more about a certain polarity than by just talking about it. Sometimes during the exercise a fundamental polarity might emerge from beneath the polarity you thought was the main issue – a polarity that you might not have expected at all and one that you would never have thought of by using plain logic. You might start with the tension between "always busy" and "doing nothing" and experience in the exercise that on a deeper level it's all about a core theme in your life and work: the tension between "I need to prove myself" and "I'm fine just as I am." This exercise is often the biggest eye-opener in the workshops I give on paradoxical leadership.

While you are drawing up your list of polarities, quite a large number of them may seem to be equally important to you. It is interesting to ask yourself whether there are a few "core polarities" that lie beneath all the other polarities and form the overall theme in your professional and personal life. For example, the polarities "lazy and workaholic," "alone and together," "personal and distant," and "risk and safety" might all stem from the more fundamental polarity of "authenticity and compliance." This underlying theme may be an important common thread in everything that you do. If you can deal with this core polarity in a more balanced way, then it will also be much easier for you to deal with all the other polarities associated with it or originating from it. You might have several core polarities, not just one. Unveiling these core polarities is not something you can do by forming logical clusters and making logical deductions. They are patterns that will reveal themselves while you experience and explore the tensions. All you have to do then is recognize them and look for the most accurate words to describe them.

4.1.3 Allow: Allow for Tension as a Productive Force

In order to really engage and work with our polarities, we will first need to allow for tensions. We often experience tensions as something troublesome that makes life complicated, and we tend to avoid or try to resolve them. The challenge is to turn this around by accepting tension as an intrinsic part of our life and work, not as a necessary evil we must endure, but as a generative force which we can use to our advantage. If we embrace this discomfort, new and unexpected insights can break through.

I personally experience this quite regularly when writing. I have a "brilliant" solution to a conceptual or literary hiccup in my book, and I just want to write it down and then move on to the next thing as I'm quite impatient and results focused. But then, in the back of my head, a feeling of unease arises, as I feel that there are some flaws in this solution. In the past, my first reaction would have been to try to justify my original solution and move on, but in the long term this always failed. I have learned to fully accept this frustration and even to embrace it, to slow down, to let go of all quick fixes and leave it to my unconscious to come up with something new, without any clear expectation. In this twilight zone, often a new idea arises that is far superior to my original solution. In this process, the tension itself is the generative power. I don't have to do much, except allow this tension to exist and work its creative magic.

4.1.4 Value: Value Both Sides, Exploring and Fully Experiencing the Extremes

We have met our own polarities and accepted the tension they generate. With some polarities, we may be extremely nimble at switching back and forth and striking the right balance. With others, there might be asymmetry in the way we know, value, and embody both poles, which makes it difficult to freely explore them.

Reasoned logic is one way of dealing with that. We intellectually understand what each pole is about, and we can see that both poles are necessary. So we immediately want to come to a workable compromise, a creative combination, or a powerful synthesis. But by doing so, we're skipping an essential step: we can only play with or connect opposite poles once we have tapped into each one separately and explored how they affect us in their purest form. We need to go to a deeper level and experience the value and limitations of each pole individually. In other words, in order to bring together, we first need to differentiate.

It boils down to courage because this can be tremendously scary or overwhelming. The pole that we have trouble associating with usually evokes negative emotions inside of us: fear, hate, guilt, or shame. Perhaps we have been taught from a young age that this pole is disgraceful or taboo; perhaps a bad experience has caused us to have negative associations with it. If you are constantly told that you should always think of others and that it is selfish to think of yourself, then you probably will feel guilty when you spend time on yourself. You may also have a hard time accepting support from others or receiving compliments. If you have always been told that crying is weak, you may feel deeply ashamed to show emotion and have trouble allowing yourself to grieve, even if this is part of the healing process after loss. When we reject a pole entirely and do not allow ourselves to connect to our true feelings, we are missing a piece of our authentic selves.

Sometimes, we impose this "self-censorship" ourselves. We're always aiming to be a top performer, going far beyond all expectations, striving for perfection and proving that we're the best. How are we ever going to be satisfied with a "good is good enough" solution, even if this may be all that is required in a given situation?

When such a negative association blocks the free flow between both poles, the challenge is to explore the positive core of the pole we considered malicious. This helps us regain possession of the parts of ourselves that we've lost and become a more complete and authentic person. It can be a tremendous relief to realize that something we've always wanted to sweep under the carpet is allowed to exist, that it's an integral part of who we are, and that it can even give us positive strength and be a useful tool. A lot of the energy that we've spent on keeping this pole under control or suppressing it is suddenly released, and we can now use it in a positive way.

Getting rid of these negative emotional charges and judgments can be quite a process. We can't always do this on our own; we may need external guidance – a professional coach or therapist – to make a breakthrough. An important first step in such a process is to explicitly name both poles in a neutral or even positive way. It might help to give the seemingly negative pole a positive or at least neutral label: "caring for yourself" instead of "selfish," "sensitive and empathetic" instead of "cry baby," "careful" instead of "cowardly." However, not all unfamiliar poles are so negatively charged. We simply might not have known them very well, or we may feel inexperienced with them, or perhaps we didn't even realize that they are part of who we are.

Once we feel more neutral about a pole, and the greatest barriers have been broken down, we can start to explore this pole further. What is its underlying power? How can it help us? How can we use it in a positive way in our personal lives and at work?

It's good to have a safe place to practice or experiment in; a type of laboratory setting that is, for the time being, not connected to the rest of our lives. This approach corresponds with Strategy 2 in the Polarity Wheel (exhaust valve/sanctuary). For example, you could attend an interpretive dance workshop and let yourself go uncontrollably wild for once, even though you don't feel at all ready to do this in your normal life. Once outside again, you can return to being 100 per cent in control of yourself. Practicing and experimenting together with people who share the same challenge can be extremely powerful and encouraging.

Role play can also be a safe way to experiment with certain poles that you're not very familiar with. It's "just" a role you are playing; you don't identify yourself with it at this point, so you can distance yourself from it and at the same time get the full experience. As an actor playing a role you have the license to go completely over the top, without putting your identity and self-image at risk. A safe and experimental setting allows you to explore both the positive and negative aspects of the unfamiliar pole, to get to know it better and to experience what the extremes feel like. The more you do this, the less threatening this pole will feel and the easier it will become for you to take advantage of its power and beauty.

This experience in an enclosed environment can be a start to allow this pole into other parts of your life. But perhaps just having a safe place to "let it out" now and then is already enough for you, and you don't feel like changing anything in your life. That is an illustration of how the exhaust valve/sanctuary strategy can be very useful: you have at least opened up parts of yourself and created more inner balance.

A nuance regarding this step of valuing both poles: you don't have to become some sort of Renaissance person who has developed every inner aspect and who is good at everything. With some poles, you may simply have less affinity or lack the talent and skills to be able to develop them further. You could spend a lot of time and energy tapping into these poles, but it might be more useful to let other people compensate for these. For example, if you are the kind of person whose focus and strength lies in seeing the bigger picture, you could learn to appreciate the power of detail and move slightly in this direction. But perhaps it would be even more efficient to work with someone who is a natural at filling in the details, thus bringing this aspect into balance. However, we can only speak of a true balance when we work together on equal terms and not when we – explicitly or implicitly – regard the ability to see the bigger picture as being superior to the ability to fill in the details.

If we skip this step and jump straight into finding a compromise or in-between solution, we may be able to move to a more balanced position between the two extremes, but this approach has its limitations. We don't get the opportunity to learn how to play with them, to switch from one to the other, or to combine and connect them in new ways.

4.1.5 Play: Switch Back and Forth between Opposite Poles

We have now experienced how both opposite poles feel separately and can accept them both as part of who we are. How can we now go to the next step and learn to switch flexibly and consciously from one to the other?

It is often relatively easy to situationally switch between opposite poles on a mental or behavioral level. For example, you might naturally switch between the roles of contributor to the discussion and facilitator of the process, between abstract vision and concrete solutions, between showing empathy and keeping professional distance, or between speaking and listening. You can learn this in all sorts of training courses, but also by simply being aware of it while doing it.

But polarities that are deeply embedded in our beliefs, fundamental values, feelings, emotions, personality traits, and even in our body systems and genetic programming are not as easy to summon up and control. When we feel sad, we can sometimes cheer ourselves up a little by thinking of something positive, but at other times the grief is so strong that this just doesn't work. Someone who is experiencing clinical depression is not at all capable of influencing their mood. We might also have trouble altering feelings of anger or fear.

However, there are methods, such as Neuro-Linguistic Programming (NLP), that can help us to evoke and activate these more fundamental aspects of ourselves by, for example, relating these aspects to specific triggers. These triggers can be physical, such as an object, piece of clothing, or part of our body, or nonphysical, such as a thought, gesture, or word. Triggers in our bodies can influence our mood. By standing up straight, you already feel more confident; by forcing yourself to smile even if it feels completely fake in the moment, you start to feel happier. Triggers can help you summon up deeper parts of yourself. Putting on your motorcycle gear makes you feel like the wild adventurer that you used to be; a sharp professional outfit makes you feel different about yourself than a floppy sweater and jogging pants. You can also choose a specific stimulating context: a walk in the woods relaxes you, or the view of the sea and the sound of the rolling waves cheer you up.

The same mechanisms influence, often unconsciously, our behavior in day-to-day life: an environment can make you feel gloomy; driving to the airport recalls relaxation on vacation; the physical position we assume in a meeting, like sitting on a lower chair, can make us feel inferior to our discussion partner. The upside here is that you can consciously choose the triggers and the contexts, giving you the freedom to reveal or conceal parts of yourself, depending on the given situation. This doesn't just happen to you anymore; you are now more in control.

The next step would be to no longer need external triggers but to be able to summon up these aspects without any help from outside. You become less dependent on the specific context or tools at hand and are more free to determine your course of action. For example, you may have integrated some triggers in parts of your body ("By placing my hands on my stomach and taking a deep breath, I can stand more firmly on the ground again.") or you can evoke them up through a small gesture or simply by thinking of something. Perhaps you have completely internalized and programmed them in your subconscious mind so that switching becomes a natural process, just like breathing.

The approach outlined above is based on a quite straightforward way of thinking: If we need more of A, then we simply summon it up. That's why this approach may seem a little strange, if not paradoxical, in a book about paradoxes. Assuming that opposite poles evoke each other, we can of course also turn this around: If we want more of A, then we could also start welcoming, embracing, and stimulating not-A. Instead of trying to conjure up cheerfulness, you can allow yourself to feel complete sadness so that your emotional system corrects itself and flips over. Through bitter tears, the sun starts to shine again. This is called a paradoxical intervention, and I will describe it in more detail in part 2, section 6.4.

Christian Ankowitsch's book, appropriately entitled *Mach's falsch, und du machst es richtig*[1] ("Do It Wrong to Get It Right") provides a wonderful example of how this approach can work. The author suffered from insomnia. He tried everything, but nothing seemed to help. He tried to calm down, relax, and think of good reasons to convince himself to fall asleep ("you need to be on the ball for the important meeting tomorrow morning"), but this was of course counterproductive; the more he wanted to sleep, the harder it was for him to relax and the longer he lay awake. Finally, Ankowitsch came up with the idea of trying to stay awake for as long as possible. And then, of course, within no time at all he was fast asleep.

This doesn't change the fact that there will always be aspects that we cannot or can hardly evoke. If you get stuck in a certain pole and can't do much about it, the most important thing to remember is this: don't try to fight it because this will only make things worse. It's best just to observe it and accept it for what it is. If you feel nervous, for example, and there's nothing you can do about it, then you may start worrying about this ("If I stay this nervous then I'm really going to make a mess of my presentation"), but this will only make you panic even more. If, on the other hand, you adopt a neutral attitude and simply observe how nervous you are and can admit this to yourself and allow it – and perhaps even mention this to the people around you – then a lot of stress will evaporate.

4.1.6 Integrate: Experiment with Combining and Connecting Opposite Poles

The more we've been able to experience what the two opposite poles feel like and what their underlying positive cores are, and the

---

1 Christian Ankowitsch, *Mach's falsch, und du machst es richtig: Die Kunst der paradoxen Lebensführung* (Rowolt: Berlin, 2011).

more we've been able to become familiar with them in their purest and most extreme forms, the more we will be able to combine and connect them in new and unexpected ways.

The challenge in this step is to allow elements to flow from one pole to the other so that they reinforce each other and offer a more powerful solution than each pole on its own. "When I'm at work, I would love to feel more carefree and relaxed, like when I'm on vacation, so that I can be more myself, and consequently work more effectively. How can I do that?" "How can I show more of that sensitive and empathetic side of me that is so visible at home, even when I'm doing my work as an auditor?" "How can I give my people all of my trust and still maintain control?"

As I explained in the fundamentals of both/and thinking, to make new or creative combinations, we have to get to the essence of each pole and look beyond its superficial form of appearance. It's more than just putting two things side by side or mixing them into an uninspiring mash. To stick to the cooking metaphor: If you want to give your child something "extremely tasty" as well as "extremely healthy," you don't necessarily have to split the plate in two, placing the delicious but perhaps slightly unhealthy food (like French fries and a hotdog) on one half, and quinoa and brussels sprouts on the other half. It also doesn't mean that you have to mash everything together (like with a compromise) because then the combination would lose both flavors and textures. Instead, you have to ask yourself: What do "tasty" and "healthy" actually mean? This will open up a broad range of creative possibilities. Maybe you can prepare and present one type of food the same way as you prepare the other, such as fast food with healthy ingredients. Or you can use herbs and natural seasonings to make the healthy dish spicier and richer in flavor and swap out spaghetti for zucchini noodles. These represent the creative combinations of Strategy 6 in the Polarity Wheel. Or perhaps you can make a completely new recipe, which is irresistibly delicious and extremely healthy at the same time (the synthesis solution of Strategy 7).

When trying to find ways to bring opposite poles together and experience both simultaneously (in creative combinations or synthesis) we are directly confronted with our inner tensions and contradictions. This forces us to find our sense of self and our identity on a deeper level than mere identification with one of the poles. We are apparently more than only extroverted or introverted, progressive or conservative, conceptual or practical. We then start to realize that we are more than just sets of opposite characteristics, and that we can actually oversee the total array of options and make different choices and combinations. If this were not the case, we would have a perpetual identity crisis. We come to realize that, although we embody all of these opposite poles, they don't define us because we can distance ourselves from them and choose to go in a different direction. This means that we can be extremely adaptable without feeling that we are constantly losing our identity.

WHAT ABOUT OUR "TRUE SELVES"?

The paradoxical view on identity boils down to the fact that "the real me" does not exist. The challenge is dealing with a multiplicity of selves. But what does that really mean? We do have the impression that we have a clear and undivided identity and that we know what we stand for. Is that just an illusion? Are we chameleons without any identity? Or do we, in the manner of accomplished Zen masters, need to systematically destroy all identifications in order to step into a blissful state of emptiness? No, the challenge is to connect and identify with all the different aspects of ourselves, but without letting them define us.

The metaphor of the bus – based on the work of the Italian psychiatrist and psychotherapist Roberto Assagioli and widely used in the therapeutic context of Voice

Dialogue – can shed some light on this question. In this metaphor, you are not one person, but a busload of sub-persons. One sub-person – whom you experience as your conscious self – is in the driving seat, and all the other sub-persons are scattered throughout the bus. Regularly, one of those sub-persons (e.g., "overprotective me") steps forward and takes over the wheel, steering the bus in a different direction. There are primary sub-persons who sit at the front of the bus and very regularly take over the wheel. In some cases they are "protectors" who may have been useful in the past, but who can also get in the way. These sub-persons take the wheel so often that your conscious self may not even notice them anymore, and your identity starts to align with them. Others sit in the middle of the bus, and a few have their place at the very back, even in the trunk ("disowned sub-persons"). But they can also abruptly take over the wheel at unguarded moments. How the dynamics between those sub-persons develop and how aware the "conscious self" is of this process will differ from person to person.

The good news is that we carry that diversity of styles within us, and it allows us to adapt to the changing environment. The bad news is that this is often an unconscious process that just happens to us. Any given situation can immediately – as an automatic reflex – trigger a certain sub-person, even though this sub-person may not be the most suitable for that situation. But we do it because we are programmed that way. Someone insults us and immediately the ferocious Viking within us arises, or the venomous serpent, or the withdrawing hermit crab, or the crying child …

Back to the question of who we actually are. Of course we are both the savage Viking and the hurt child. But we are also the stage manager who is above all this and who can choose which one of our many selves can come and take the wheel and which self needs to move to the back of the bus. We can associate with these different sub-persons to a certain extent, but we don't entirely identify with them. We can always go to a slightly broader state of self-observation, being aware of which sub-person is currently driving.

This is also the essence of many meditation techniques: the process of always being able to distance ourselves from limiting identifications by observing ourselves on a meta-level. We don't have to do anything specific for it, except to be aware and to know that this is only a part of ourselves and does not define us.

The word "stage manager" is perhaps somewhat misleading, as it suggests that everything could be planned and masterminded and that you just have to shout "Action!" for the right actor to enter the stage. This is of course not the case. Sometimes you can steer this process to some degree, for example when consciously choosing specific roles, positions, approaches, or perspectives. But other times, such as when it comes to emotions, there is hardly any way of directing or guiding their natural flow. You can only observe them as a witness, acknowledge that they are there, give them the space they need, live and feel them, and examine their role and meaning in your self-regulating mechanism. In short, you observe them with mildness and curiosity until they go away by themselves or transform into something else.

4.1.7 Communicate and Connect: Engage Others and Reach Out

For the sake of clarity, in the previous steps I focused on the process within the self and may have given the impression that we do all this in a vacuum. But of course we're always in close interaction with others. This means that we need to engage the people around us in our inner process of exploring and balancing, not just at the end, but at every step along the way.

Especially in a leadership role, it's crucial to communicate about your dilemmas and balancing maneuvers as they will have a significant impact on others. If you are switching back and forth between opposite poles, this can be extremely confusing for those around you. If you don't provide any context, it may seem like you don't know what you want, or that you're opportunistic and have no principles. You may be seen as flippant, unreliable, or outright crazy.

That's why it is crucial to explain why you make different choices in different situations. When you communicate, you have to switch to a meta-level by not only conveying content, but by clarifying context to those around you. The first challenge is to explain that you're not relating to unilateral values but to polarities. You are not someone who either stands for change or sticks to tradition but someone who tries to balance and reconcile these two aspects because they both carry necessary and powerful attributes. You then need to be transparent as to the specific dilemmas and tensions you face and how you decide the balance of elements in each specific case. As the environment and context changes, you will also need to clarify how these changes will impact the balance between both poles.

It may take a few more words, but it is something that everyone is capable of understanding. The fact that you can go absolutely wild at a party and still be a conscientious person at work should make perfect sense: you're still the same person, right? The ability to adapt is the essence of human existence.

Reaching out to others also means making connections to people who adhere to completely different values or radically opposing views. The challenge will be to avoid polarization and to enter a process of constructive dialogue, by putting yourself in the position of the other and trying to understand the positive drivers behind someone's (seemingly negative) behavior or views. As you have learned to value the positive sides of your own "weaknesses" (step 4), you are in a good position to be mild and empathic toward others. More about ways to avoid and overcome polarization in section 6.3.

4.1.8 Serve: Contribute to a Higher Purpose

Particularly in a leadership role, it's not just about your own position, but about making the best possible contribution to the organization or the system that you serve. This means that you have to be able and willing to transcend your own ego, position, and personal interests for the greater good. It's about admitting mistakes and misjudgments, being able and willing to abandon a set course if it doesn't bring the expected value, or even stepping down when other leadership competencies or styles are needed. Authentic and vulnerable leaders build support and loyalty, not by pretending that "everything is under control" in a world that is inherently volatile, complex, and unpredictable, but by explaining the context of continuous tensions and trade-offs, by naming and recognizing collective struggles, and by invigorating an organization-wide dialogue to instill the right balance. More on this in the next section and in part 2.

4.2 Working with the Polarities of Your Organization

Having first looked at our own polarities, we now focus on how we can use their generative power at an organizational level. What are the overall preconditional steps that are required to stimulate and integrate both/and thinking in a team or organization? Once we have laid the groundwork, part 2 will give a detailed description of how we can apply the both/and perspective to specific business and management challenges and how we can make organizations paradoxically competent.

Introducing both/and thinking in an organization involves the following steps:

1 Make explicit the organization's polarities in a joint exploration.
2 Embrace the power of opposite poles.
3 Create a common language and develop paradoxical competence.
4 Allow opposite perspectives to exist and stimulate the exchange.
5 Demonstrate that both/and solutions work.

4.2.1 Make Explicit the Organization's Polarities in a Joint Exploration

Within every organization, there are several critical tensions which have to be constantly juggled, like the tensions between quality and cost, long term and short term, or profitability and social responsibility. These are often recurring themes on the strategic management agenda.

In addition, there are also a number of dominant polarities which organizations oscillate between without consciously managing them, like the balance between central management and local autonomy. These cycles and pendulum movements often take place over longer periods of time, making them less visible.

First, identify and make explicit all the important polarities of the organization. This will reveal the realm of opposite poles that the organization must take into account at all levels. This is not just a task for the management team but a collective process. A team or organization can only learn to switch flexibly between poles when every person in the organization understands

- which tensions the organization needs to balance;
- that these tensions cannot be resolved and can therefore never have a definitive answer; and

- that it is therefore necessary – not just for the management team but for everyone in the organization – to switch between the opposite poles and find the right balance in every situation.

Just like the mission or core values of an organization, the core paradoxes should be known and shared in every corner of the business.

Start by making a long list together. An open brainstorm will reveal many different tensions at different levels in the organization. To have an overview and to be able to prioritize them, you will need to structure and cluster these polarities. In figure 4.2 you'll find an example of a way to structure and cluster the organizational polarities that came out of a brainstorm session with the teachers of a secondary school for children with disabilities.

The two upper quadrants are about the mission and purpose of the school: what is our social contribution and what do we want to bring to our students? The bottom two are mainly about its internal working: what tensions do I experience in my role as a teacher and how do we want to work together? The braces attempt to cluster polarities that are related and may derive from the same deeper polarity.

The external contribution of the school and its internal functioning are of course interrelated. But in this concrete example, it seemed logical for the team to first start a dialogue with each other about the upper left quadrant regarding the social contribution of the school. Everyone on the team agreed on the same key question: "How do we cope as an organization and as professionals with the tension between following the officially prescribed curriculum and taking care of the specific needs of our students?"

Clustering organizational polarities is just a means to create some structure for us and provide an overview, not to pull them apart and put them in closed boxes. Beyond any structure, all organizational polarities stay very much connected and knotted.

Figure 4.2. Clustered polarities of a secondary school for children with disabilities

In relation to its mission

- Follow curriculum – Start from student experience
- Focus on content – Focus on how to manage own life
- Learning objectives – Well-being and care

In relation to its students

- Protect – Learn from making mistakes
- General rule – Personalized approach/exceptions
- Focus on the group – Focus on the individual
- Creativity/possibilities – Limitations due to disabilities
- Cognitive developement – Emotional resilience

In relation to the role of the teacher

- Dedication/passion/high workload – Resilience/boundaries/self care
- Teaching – Administration
- Explicit appreciaton – Intrinsic motivation
- Own vision – Loyalty
- Democracy – Leadership

In relation to ways of working and internal processes

- Ad hoc/action oriented/quick fix – Helicopter view/reflection/integrated approach
- Artistic/chaotic – Structured
- Preserve – Innovate

There are of course many different ways to categorize and cluster organizational polarities. Wendy K. Smith and Marianne W. Lewis for instance distinguish (1) performing paradoxes (such as mission and market), (2) learning paradoxes (such as short-term and long-term), (3) organizing paradoxes (such as centralization and decentralization), and (4) belonging paradoxes (such as global and local).[2] There is only one criterion in how to cluster the organizational polarities: they should make sense to the people in the organization and enable their understanding.

In addition to the polarities that apply to the organization as a whole, there may be polarities that specifically apply to a certain division, team, or function, such as speed and accuracy in the finance department, employer's interests and employees' interests in the HR department, or collaboration with suppliers in the long term and pressure on prices in the short term in the procurement department. It's interesting to explore whether there is a relationship between these departmental polarities and the overall polarities of the organization. After all, a division is simply part of a whole, so it is worthwhile to discuss the departmental paradoxes in connection with the core paradoxes of the organization.

4.2.2 Embrace the Power of Opposite Poles

We could see polarities as unavoidable obstacles that make our work difficult. But we can also highlight their innovative power: both opposite poles are essential ingredients for an integrated solution. The creative tension between them and even their constructive collision can give rise to new solutions. Paradoxes force us to think beyond the obvious, to formulate sustainable solutions for the longer term

---

2 Wendy K. Smith and Marianne W. Lewis, *Both/And Thinking. Embracing Creative Tensions to Solve Your Toughest Problems* (Boston, MA: Harvard Business Review Press, 2022), 238.

and to be more creative when looking at our options. Switching flexibly between opposite poles make us more agile, as organizations, teams, and individuals.

But merely broadcasting that this is valuable is not enough. You also need to walk the talk by actively seeking and appreciating critical feedback, and by involving people with opposing opinions rather than avoiding them as "difficult." It takes some courage to open up, to put ourselves in a vulnerable position, and to invite others to question us, but the outcome of this confrontation will probably be more solid and enjoy broader support.

However, blowing your trumpet on the benefits of paradoxical leadership does not take away from the fact that dealing with polarities is quite difficult and sometimes frightening. Tensions between opposing visions and values stir up uncertainty because there is not just one right answer, and you can never be sure that you are on the right path. This can cause paralysis because no one wants to make the wrong decision and fail. It takes a lot of trust and self-confidence to deal with polarities. It doesn't help to say in a reassuring tone, "it will all work out, just trust me," or to force people out of their comfort zone. It is particularly important to first identify and acknowledge this fear, to share your own personal fears, and to show that expressing these fears does not make you a coward. Heroes are all the more heroic for being afraid.

You can also try to reduce the anxiety by boosting others' self-confidence and creating a general atmosphere of tranquility, serenity, and stability. It is a paradox in itself that the more stability we create, the more people are willing to initiate change and take risks (see also section 6.1 on change). When you give people the confidence and space to make their own situation-based choices while navigating between opposite poles, this will further reduce anxiety. It implies that you accept the risk that people might draw the wrong conclusions and make mistakes (see also section 8.1 on paradoxical dialogue).

4.2.3 Create a Common Language and Develop Paradoxical Competence

A "common language" is the terminology that everyone shares when talking about polarities and paradoxes, such as the concepts and models mentioned in this book. It allows everyone in the organization to understand one another when they talk about a polarity, synthesis, or the difference between synthesis and compromise. Creating this common framework only takes a few hours. In a creative company of about eighty people, for example, it only took me one session of two hours to briefly illustrate the concept, do an exercise in which people could really experience their polarities, and hold a wrap-up session in small groups to share insights. In the weeks and months that followed, completely different conversations were taking place during the project and appraisal meetings, where people were suddenly talking about the polarities they experience in their work and in their project teams.

The next step is to improve and broaden the skills required for dealing with paradoxes. I will elaborate on the paradoxical skill set in section 9.2. In order to develop these paradoxical skills, different methods and tools are available. Since paradoxical leadership always starts with the self, there are two important steps involved: giving people the tools to cope effectively with their own polarities and then giving them strategies for dealing with the polarities of their teams or of the organization. For the latter, various methods can be used: role plays with alternating roles, individual or collective constellation exercises (you'll find the instructions for a collective constellation exercise on p. 254), or a bilateral debate with two groups being asked to support radically opposed views and then to switch positions. A game with a competitive element is both highly educational and lots of fun. In my training sessions and workshops, I often use a paradox game in which the teams are confronted with a series of dilemmas. The team that formulates the best integrated both/and solution wins the round. It is also interesting to see what happens when you interrupt the competition between the battling teams and ask some people to switch teams.

In addition to providing people with a safe learning environment, it is obviously important to get them to integrate what they have learned in their day-to-day work. It is useful to allocate some time in your team sessions to examine the effects of the polarities on the team and its performance and to explore new strategies to cope with them in future; likewise, you can challenge people to come up with creative both/and solutions for dilemmas that tend to repeat themselves in daily practice can be helpful.

4.2.4 Allow Opposite Perspectives to Exist and Stimulate the Exchange

There are many different ways to create space for opposite poles in an organization: by letting people play around and experiment in an otherwise tightly managed organization; by allowing space and time for people to express their concerns, feelings, and emotions; by getting team members to take on completely different roles inside or outside of the organization; by stimulating people to challenge each other and to come up with different perspectives; by being open to proposals that go completely against the status quo, etc. It's all about the stimulation of true diversity and inclusion by not only actively hiring employees with a different background and way of thinking but, above all, by giving the floor to these "different perspectives" (and not by letting them drown in the sea of uniformity). I will describe this in more detail in part 2, section 7.2 (How Diversity Can Help Achieve Better Results).

At first, it might be a good idea to create free spaces to experiment with ways of working that are opposite to the mainstream, separated from the rest of the organization in order to prevent assimilation and dilution. In the long run though, it is obviously not productive to keep these opposite poles isolated from each other. We need to find ways for both allowing the successes in the playroom to grow and ripen in an undisturbed way and to gradually let them seep into the ongoing business.

The biggest challenge is to keep focused on making connections, because before you know it, paralyzing polarization can start to take

place instead of a stimulating dialogue. There are certainly supporting structures to facilitate such a dialogue, such as regular meetings
between divisions, between people in different roles, or between
management and people at the shop floor, in which the different
points of view and interests are openly discussed. It is also useful to
systematically examine any major issue from a number of different
perspectives in order to gain a clearer picture of the causes, consequences, advantages, and disadvantages of different approaches.
After a first exchange of views, one could even challenge the participants to put their own points of view aside, to fully empathize
with opposing opinions, and to question their initial position from a
"devil's advocate" perspective. The point is to pluck the benefits of
all options and to jointly come to a more integrated solution.

But it is clearly not the meeting structure or the discussion format itself that leads to a fruitful dialogue. Such a dialogue can only arise from
the inspiration of those who are conducting and facilitating it, those
who passionately believe that we can reach a higher level by confronting divergent and opposing views. It helps to demonstrate in practice
that changing one's point of view and adopting that of others is not a
sign of weakness but rather of great openness and self-reflection.

4.2.5 Demonstrate That Both/And Solutions Work

Challenge people to look beyond the obvious solutions and the gray
compromise, to refrain from seeing each issue as a zero-sum game
or as the classic problem of allocating scarce resources and making
tough choices, where choosing always means losing. By seeking synergy, new resources and sources of energy will appear. Show how
saving costs and improving customer service do not have to stand
in each other's way but can actually reinforce each other. Make sure
that all Strategy 6 (creative combinations) and Strategy 7 (synthesis)
solutions are widely shared with the rest of the organization. These
are the inspiring examples that give people a sneak preview of what

the future could look like. Consider setting up a contest for the best both/and initiative of the month.

However, a transformation toward "both/and" doesn't always mean directly achieving tangible outcomes. It can already be a great achievement for people to start to think and act in a different way, even if this may not initially be in the interest of the organization. For example, a valued employee could end up leaving to become an independent entrepreneur or travel the world. Encourage people to believe more in themselves at work and to develop all their different sides and qualities. People who are recognized for what they are and feel free to be themselves in all their aspects will also be motivated to give the best of themselves.

KEY POINTS

- First learn to play around with and balance your own personal polarities before focusing on the polarities around you and in your organization.
- Whatever choice you make when coping with a polarity, remember to be observant, choose consciously, and be aware of what the effects may be.
- Don't be tempted to go directly for a compromise or synthesis. Have the courage to explore both poles in their extreme and purest forms.
- We are not capable of managing and balancing at will all polarities within ourselves, but what we *can* do is consciously observe and understand what is happening inside of us from the position of a neutral observer.
- Make explicit both your personal polarities and those of your organization and open up the dialogue.
- People best learn to effectively work with polarities in their daily work practice, stimulated by examples, dialogue, and dedicated space and time.

PART 2

AT WORK

This part of the book will show you how to apply the both/and perspective to a number of well-known management and business challenges, which I have grouped together under a few broad topics:

- setting the strategic direction and steering the business
- change
- where people and organizations come together
- conducting the paradoxical dialogue
- paradoxical competence

SETTING THE STRATEGIC DIRECTION AND STEERING THE BUSINESS

How do you apply the both/and perspective to challenges regarding the direction of the business? This chapter addresses various fundamental questions, each with their corresponding polarities: How can we flexibly switch and find balance between opposite directions (left *and* right) without getting stuck in the middle of the road or creating confusion and chaos? How can we divide up tasks, roles, and functions without losing connection with the entire value chain (the chain as a whole *and* the individual parts)? How can we give a clear direction to the business without putting it in a straitjacket (from the top *and* from the bottom)? How do we know when we're on the right track in achieving our goals, and how do we steer around dimensions we can't quantify (objective *and* subjective information)?

5.1 Strategic Agility

We are used to defining a good leader as someone who can plot a steady course and steer the business in a clear direction – the clearer and steadier the course, the better the leader. But, as I mentioned, this straight course is in most cases only temporarily straight; when the leader's term ends, the successor often sets a radically different course. Over a longer period of time, you will notice that organizations tend not to follow a straight course but move in an erratic zigzag pattern (see 2.3.1 A Wobbly Course).

"Steering" actually means balancing between opposing forces and navigating between opposite directions. These opposing forces keep each other in equilibrium and are vital for a healthy and well-functioning organization. In their renowned book on organizational strategy, Bob de Wit and Ron Meyer[1] identify a number of primordial polarities that recur in organizations and that essentially cannot be eliminated:

- logic – creativity
- deliberateness – emergence
- revolution – evolution
- markets – resources
- responsiveness – synergy
- competition – collaboration
- compliance – choice
- control – chaos
- globalization – localization
- profitability – responsibility

There are various ways of balancing these polarities. You can paddle for a long time on the left side, until your canoe is almost at right angles to the current or even starts to swing around its own axis, but then you will have to paddle like crazy on the right side in order to get back on course. You can also try to go in a more or less straight line by alternating left and right strokes. Although it seems illogical and has been proven to be an inefficient waste of resources and energy, many organizations (unconsciously) adopt the first approach. The organization only corrects its one-directional course when it has

---

1   Bob de Wit and Ron Meyer, *Strategy: Process, Content, Context* (Boston: Cengage Learning, 2010).

gone too far one way and has become dysfunctional; at that point, a "one-directional" course in the opposite direction seems to be the only solution.

5.1.1 Steering in Two Directions without Getting Tangled Up

But how can we steer in two opposite directions, and how do we make sure that the organization doesn't become paralyzed and enter a state of chaos? Here are a few tips.

ALLOW FOR BOTH FORCE AND COUNTERFORCE

The first step is to recognize the fact that steering in one particular direction also requires steering in the opposite direction. This doesn't mean following a moderate, mediocre, or "neither fish nor fowl" course. As leaders, we constantly need to shift between different goals and priorities, depending on the changing context and environment. For example: a director of a social enterprise feels the need to push for more result orientation and a business-like mindset as the culture has become a little too relaxed and production is declining.

Balancing explicitly means paying attention to both force and counterforce. It's not about replacing one with the other. After all, although the social enterprise's focus is now temporarily on performance, it should also carefully watch over its clear social purpose and strong social core.

When we set course in a certain direction, it may be necessary to actively steer in the opposite direction at the same time. For example: Your main focus might be on a business-like approach and achieving results, but you should invest to the same extent in creating a warm and pleasant working environment. Or, you can reduce costs by letting your customers do their basic transactions in an online application, but you should invest simultaneously in personal customer service for more complex questions.

UNDERSTAND HOW BOTH COURSES RELATE TO EACH OTHER

It is sometimes difficult to distinguish between the main direction and the opposite direction. The main direction may be so obvious and so deeply embedded in the DNA of the organization that we no longer have the necessary distance to see it. As a result, it might *seem* like we're only focusing on the opposite, less important direction when we're actually just trying to mitigate the risks of the main direction. For instance: After years of efficiency programs, staff may have completely internalized the focus on speed and production volumes. To keep everything in balance though, it might be necessary to focus on improving quality and customer service. If we took an outside-in look at the organization's documents, the frequent use of the words "quality" and "customer focus" might give us the wrong impression that this organization must be an ace in these areas while in fact they are the ones most in need of improvement.

This can give a distorted picture of the real situation. Consider some more philosophical examples. Is the world becoming increasingly unsafe, given all the conflicts and terrorist attacks that we see on the news every day? Or has the world just become much safer and all conflicts more noticeable because they are an exception to the rule? Are dictators and fundamentalists returning us to the Middle Ages or is this simply a rearguard action against a much larger mainstream movement toward emancipation and modernization?

In organizational terms, is the organization still extraordinarily social and compassionate but now shifting to become more business-like, or is the organization becoming hard and impersonal as the last remnants of social and human care are systematically broken down? It depends on whether we see the glass half full or half empty. And there is always enough evidence to argue both ways. Therefore we always need to see this from a little distance, taking the broader context into account. It is also important to explicitly name both aspects and their antagonistic interaction in all communication (in this case, the tension between the business and social aspects) so that it is clear to everyone that both of these play a crucial role.

A SCHIZOPHRENIC GOVERNMENT?

From 2010 to 2020, there were two trends within the Dutch government, taking place at the same time and in opposite directions: centralization and decentralization. The police, for example, were working hard toward building a single national corps with regional units and a general service center for all supporting tasks. This makes sense, because criminality does not stop at the municipal or provincial borders, and it is more effective to join forces and resources.

Child protection services, on the other hand, were being decentralized from the central government to local municipalities. The logic was clear: the central government had not been in touch with the needs of the individual citizens; the municipalities know the local situation better, can offer better solutions, and can use the resources much more effectively and efficiently.

The Dutch government was therefore going in two opposite directions at the same time. Is it then right to conclude that it was inconsistent or even schizophrenic in its strategic choices? That certainly doesn't have to be the case. After all, both sides of the coin are important: becoming more effective by bringing efforts, resources, and information together as well as benefiting from local knowledge about specific problems. The two aspects need to balance each other within both departments. If they become imbalanced by too much focus being placed on one of the two and allowing it to go too far, this will automatically lead to a corrective movement in the opposite direction. Of course, the wider context and trends in society also determine which pole should (temporarily) be given more attention. In the case of the police, this is the (inter)nationalization of crime. With respect to child protection services, this is the prevention of unnecessary medicalization, the search for integrated solutions within the immediate vicinity of the persons concerned, and the increasing focus on activating and strengthening their own social networks.

In both cases, it's all about finding a creative combination and mixture where both aspects are taken into account to obtain a good balance: a national police force that combines large-scale efforts with local initiatives; child protection services that can link local expertise to a coordinated national approach.

PINPOINT THE CORE POLARITIES

How do we apply situational agility without creating confusion and chaos? How do we do this without giving the impression that we are contradicting ourselves, going wherever the wind blows, or being an opportunist without principles?

A crucial step is to make clear to the organization that strategy is not about making straightforward choices and sticking to them, but about continuously balancing opposite directions. We need to balance self-organizing teams with a clearly defined overall direction or combine innovative initiatives with a structured delivery agenda.

The challenge is to formulate the strategy in terms of core polarities, always including both sides of the coin. Every organizational strategy can be described in terms of several core polarities or crucial areas of tension, which form the essence of that organization.

The core polarities for a large city might include these:

- economic growth and quality of life;
- tourists and residents;
- rich and poor;
- the center and the periphery;

- local initiatives and a citywide plan; and
- small experiments and large programs.

An industrial firm might juggle the following polarities:

- following the market and defining the market;
- compliance and creativity;
- specialization and diversification;
- flexibility and predictability; and
- top-down plan roll-out and bottom-up initiatives.

And an NGO might constantly be navigating around these areas of tension:

- long-term vision and opportunism;
- fast mediagenic interventions and labor-intensive lobbying behind the scenes;
- providing emergency aid and increasing self-sustainability;
- strengthening its profile and collaborating with partners; and
- being critical of regimes and cooperating with the authorities.

CONDUCT THE STRATEGIC DIALOGUE AT ALL LEVELS OF THE ORGANIZATION

Once the strategy has been defined in terms of polarities, it is vital to make all stakeholders understand that these are the organization's fundamental axes of tension and development, and that the amount of focus on each of these depends on the situation and the life cycle of the organization. Everyone in the organization – and not just management – should understand that, depending on the context, different choices and combinations will have to be made. This way you can involve all levels of the organization in the constant balancing act and stimulate people to find creative combinations. It's not just about making the polarities visible and transparent but about

experiencing them together. It will be helpful to initiate and maintain a broad dialogue throughout the organization, in which the following questions are addressed:

- What is the organization's current choice – implicit or explicit –
  regarding the two poles of this core polarity? How does it relate
  to the environment and context?
- When do these two poles complement and/or reinforce each
  other? When do they clash? Where in the organization is the
  tension mainly felt, and who is struggling with that tension? For
  example, in a company, the clash between general standards and
  specific business unit needs is particularly notable in the finance
  department. They put in extra effort to provide customized reports for the various business units and then manually consoli-
  date these different formats into one consistent general report for
  the company as a whole.
- What creative solutions might reconcile both poles (Strategies 5,
  6, and 7 on the Polarity Wheel)? How can the need for standard
  reporting, for example, be combined with the request for customized reports for the various business units? Is it possible to
  offer customized solutions by combining standard modules?

I will explain more about how to shape the paradoxical dialogue
in section 8.1. If you have shared with your managers and colleagues
that the organization needs to constantly navigate between opposite
poles, it's easier to understand a change of direction. It's less abrupt
and confusing than announcing that you are suddenly going to go
right when you've been going left for the past few years.

BUILD AN UNDERLYING, SHARED VISION

Switching from one direction to the other is much easier when
the underlying vision, mission, and purpose of the organization
are broadly shared and lived through. When people are well-ac-
quainted with the organization's purpose and ultimate goal, it is

easier for them to understand and accept that they will sometimes have to row a little to the left and then a little to the right. It's all about making a clear difference between the means and the end: the end should be relatively stable, while the best means to achieve this will frequently change depending on the context.

This underlying vision explains why an organization does what it does. Its values and beliefs form the profound identity and the living core of the organization. Leadership thinker and author Simon Sinek emphasizes the immense importance of the *why* aspect.[2] He argues that we can only really inspire and make a difference as an organization once we have been able to clearly answer the question *why*.

The underlying vision of a school could be, "to encourage students to fully develop their own special talents and shape their own lives." To achieve this objective, very different and even contradictory approaches may be necessary. Some students will need to be closely supervised while others will need to be left to their own devices. As long as the ultimate goal is clear to everyone, there is nothing wrong with switching between different approaches as the situation requires. This strong sense of identity allows us to be more agile; I will explore this concept further in section 6.2 (Adaptability, Versatility, and Identity).

However, it is important to bear in mind that this underlying vision is not set in stone either. A vision or mission can last for some time but sooner or later it will evoke its opposite. For the school, the vision in a few years' time may be "to develop the knowledge and skills required for the major economic and technological challenges of the future." Although more stable, a vision is therefore also a temporary beacon.

Any vision must be regularly renewed, updated, and kept alive. Especially when a new situation arises, the organization will need to ask itself: what does our vision actually mean in this new context and what are the consequences? What does "shaping their own

---

2 Simon Sinek, *Start with Why: How Great Leaders Inspire Everyone to Take Action* (New York: Portfolio/Penguin, 2009).

lives" actually mean for students who, due to a global pandemic, only have online classes? How does this crisis affect the balance between the various aspects of "shaping one's own life," such as knowledge, social contact, self-management, and mental health? To keep this vision alive and to prevent it from becoming just another hollow statement, it must be a recurring topic in an ongoing dialogue.

5.1.2 What Is the Shelf Life of a Leader?

An organization will inevitably be required to make a strategic turn, and it is more versatile when it is aware of its core polarities and the need to strike a balance. Can a leader – or an entire management team – also make a strategic turn, without losing credibility or causing great confusion? Let's imagine that you've taken on the position of chief executive in a period of deep crisis. You feel that your main role at this stage is to restructure the company, including harsh measures like cutting costs and jobs. Suppose you've also succeeded in doing this, and the company can start to grow again after a few years. Can you then reposition yourself in a credible way and become a connector and driver of innovation? Or will others always see you as the cost-cutting crisis manager and not be able to recognize or trust you in this new role? Would it not be better to find someone to replace you, someone without a specific reputation and label? In short, can a leader develop together with the organization as it reinvents itself from one stage to the next, or does each leader have a limited shelf life? Would it be better to simply acknowledge that limited shelf life and ensure that long before this expiration date there is a suitable successor warming up on the sideline who can step in and bring the organization one step further?

In this case, we are of course assuming that you are willing and able to transform, that you are able to adopt a completely different role and actually enjoy it. This is certainly not self-evident. There are many leaders who feel particularly comfortable in one specific role (as crisis manager, connector, organizer, or innovator) and who want to focus on their trademark style. When the job is done, they switch to another job where they can again apply their unique talent. This is, of course, fine. But even when you are capable of change and eagerly want to reinvent yourself, will your transformation be accepted?

This question is difficult to answer in general terms, but there is one important prerequisite. To avoid confusion, it is essential that you take a helicopter view in order to explicitly state the organization's current (or next) stage of development and the type of leadership that this stage requires. You must clearly define and mark those stages of development. For example: "In the past two years, we have made tremendous headway in achieving the necessary cost reductions. As a leadership team we have been steering the organization restrictively in order to make this happen, but we are now in a position to start growing and innovating again. We can now provide our teams with the necessary space, responsibilities, and resources to develop and drive new initiatives, with the leadership team in a more supporting role in the background."

This is quite a challenge because a change in the context or the start of a new stage of development is usually a gradual and almost imperceptible process. You may not notice this new phase until you have already entered it. You may already be unconsciously working in your new role, which can lead to bewilderment and confusion. Or you may still be happily humming away in the role of the previous phase and won't realize that a new approach is required until serious problems start occurring. You have to be self-reflective, receptive, and willing to act on signals and feedback from your surroundings. But even if you are a little late, clarifying and marking the stages of the organization's development, and the required leadership styles for each stage, will still be very helpful for the organization's ability to change.

5.1.3 The Strength of Connected Dual Leadership

A more structural way of dealing with contradictory requirements and unexpected situations is to establish co-leadership with a complementary duo. For example, someone with in-depth content expertise and vision could work well with an efficient organizer, or a results-driven change manager could be paired with a people-oriented connector. This basically means connecting opposite poles – which can sometimes be water and fire – at the highest level of the organization. If the directors are at an equal level, then it is dual leadership. This construction is often found in the healthcare sector, where there may be a business director and a medical director. A more common variation is when two directors actually run the organization together but only one of them is ultimately responsible. The co-leadership duo might comprise a CEO who, as the external representative of the company, is more focused on the market and stakeholders, and a COO who deals more with the internal organization and business operations. There may even be a trio if the co-leadership also includes a CFO who focuses on the financial course.

Dual leadership is nothing new. In their book *The Corporate Tribe*, business anthropologists Danielle Braun and Jitske Kramer write about dual leadership in tribes where the chief runs the ongoing "business" and the shaman guides the community in change processes and ritual transitions. Even today, some royal couples form complementary partnerships as "mother" and "father" of the nation.

I talked once to a private equity firm that demonstrated to me how effective dual leadership can contribute to financial success. An analysis of the portfolio showed that the most successful start-ups in many cases consisted of a creative, entrepreneurial CEO and a strict, bottom-line-oriented CFO, provided they worked closely together. It was the combination of equally valued and opposite but complementary talents that led to significantly better business results. With this new insight, the private equity firm then applied the same principle to the way they allocated nonexecutive board members to the companies in their portfolio. Each start-up was allocated a supervisory board member with a complementary profile who often had a very different view of the business in a number of aspects. While respecting roles and responsibilities, the nonexecutive board member was in a good position to constructively challenge what seemed to be self-evident within the company.

Dual leadership in its various forms can be successful if everyone understands the common goal and the complementary mutual relationship between the different approaches. Even if there are two people at the helm, they need to speak with one voice, especially when the initial views seem to be different or even contradictory. This requires both leaders to engage in deep mutual dialogue, to transcend their individual positions for the greater cause. These fierce discussions do not necessarily have to be covered up for the rest of the organization. In fact, it's important for the organization to be aware of the need for both roles and to understand why this complementary setup is so important. It can serve as a good example to the organization of how you can build on each other's strengths and how you can deal with the inevitable tensions and conflicts that may arise.

However, if there is no mutual connection, no common language, no recognition of the need for different points of view, no acceptance of each other's talents, and no willingness to engage in continuous dialogue, this can also be a recipe for disaster. Then dual leadership becomes dualistic leadership; the two leaders are played off against each other. The gap between the two visions can and will be abused.

Dual leadership requires self-reflection. Both leaders need to have a good idea of their strengths and limitations and be willing to admit to themselves and to others that they are not competent in everything. Sometimes egos can get in the way. Dual leadership also requires everyone to recognize that both leaders are fundamentally equal, as are their individual qualities, perspectives, and contributions.

You can read more about how to make opposing styles work together effectively in section 7.2 (How Diversity Can Help Achieve Better Results).

5.1.4 Being in Balance with the Whole Ecosystem

The organization's ultimate goal should be the reference point for any new direction. However, the organization's goal is only a part of an even broader societal or ecological perspective. That is why it is important for the organization's goals to be in balance with the overarching goals of society. This is the essence of corporate sustainability and social responsibility. In order to create this balance, an organization sometimes needs to invest in initiatives that counterbalance and compensate for the impact of its business operations.

Let's say you are a soft drinks manufacturer, and your goal is to sell as many soft drinks as possible around the world. Soft drinks may be tasty, but they are definitely not healthy; frequent consumption leads to obesity, diabetes, and all kinds of health problems. The occasional glass, however, can be tempting and delicious. If you want to be in line with the societal goal of allowing healthy people to enjoy a nice drink now and then, then it is your responsibility to also contribute to the awareness of a healthy diet and lifestyle. You could take care of this yourself (by including in all your communication a caveat such as "enjoy but drink in moderation") or, as an organization, you could sponsor health information campaigns. The challenge is to find effective ways to balance your own mission with the greater whole.

The extent to which you will need to counterbalance and adapt your mission depends on the context. When consumers already live healthy lives and make sensible choices, you will not need to make changes to your business model and marketing strategy at all; the context will automatically ensure this balance. You may even be able to afford to market tastier and less nutritious products because you know that there will be little or no risk of over-consumption. This of course does not apply to a market where problems with obesity and diabetes are the order of the day.

Support for the countermovement can also be used to polish up your image and brand. In principle, there is nothing ethically wrong with that strategy since business interests and social responsibility can go very well hand in hand. Doing the right thing does not necessarily need to be a burden or a cost. In fact, taking an interest in societal challenges and needs can lead to new market opportunities.

However, it can also be used as a cheap cover-up, like when a highly polluting company sponsors a local tree-planting initiative or provides mediagenic birdhouses and bee hotels on its corporate HQ to improve its image. Or when a company that is responsible for massive deforestation of the tropical rainforest supports small projects for those whose natural livelihoods have been destroyed. This may be good for PR, but the business goals and opposing societal goals are clearly not in balance with each other. Fortunately, we live in a time of transparency when ethical window-dressing and greenwashing are rapidly uncovered. Informed and outspoken citizens and social media activists can act as a healthy counterbalance.

KEY POINTS

- Steer in one direction while keeping an eye on the opposite direction.
- Make the core polarities of your organization transparent and tangible.
- Be clear about your ultimate goal so that you know where you want to end up as you meander toward it.
- Clearly state when you're changing course and mark the turning points.
- Support an ongoing dialogue about the organization's current position with respect to its core polarities and ultimate goal.
- Combine and connect complementary competencies and visions through co-leadership.
- Use the counteracting forces outside of your organization to keep the whole ecosystem in balance.

5.2 Specializing while Working Together

Almost every organization struggles to find the balance between the organization as a whole and its individual parts. How do you ensure that everyone remains focused on their part of the process without losing sight of the overall goal?

If you are self-employed, then you are not only the managing director but also the manager of sales, marketing, production, logistics, finance, IT, and administration. You might outsource some of these tasks, but you remain responsible for all of these domains. That's a lot of work, but at least you have short lines of communication! Nevertheless, you will occasionally find yourself in a pickle because you will have to weigh up conflicting interests: "Should I invest in a marketing campaign or in a larger warehouse?" "This renowned company would be an exciting new client, but will investing in this relationship also lead to substantial revenue?"

5.2.1 Silo Formation

When an organization grows and becomes more complex, its separate functions and organizational units professionalize: the sales department focuses on landing new contracts, the finance and control department on keeping track of the costs. These departments have a clear focus, set targets and expectations, formulate measurable performance indicators, hire professionals, and install managers to ensure that the targets will be met. Of course, the managers of these organizational units want to excel in achieving their own goals. Their professional pride is largely associated with the importance, impact, and performance of their functional unit, and their aim is to make their unit stand out. And before the company knows it, it has created a fragmented landscape of silos.

If the organization is lucky, the silos will work well together and meet up regularly to align their work; mistakes due to insufficient cooperation will remain negligible. If it is less fortunate, each unit will go its own way; there will be minimal exchange, mutual rivalry, missed opportunities, and fierce battles between assumed competencies. When things go wrong, the units will point fingers at each other and sometimes stand in each other's way.

This is a logical development because functions and units may have goals that seem contradictory. The sales department wants to sign off a new contract immediately, but the legal department wants to ensure that the risks are covered, delaying the negotiations. The departments can very easily lose sight of what it's all about, which is working together to achieve the overall organizational goal. All parts may be fully optimized on their own while the construction as a whole teeters. Only general management feels ownership for the overarching goal.

When the scale and complexity of organizations increase, the issues with this type of compartmentalization will become more acute. Where management may previously have focused on dividing up tasks and activities among specialized units, it must now counterbalance this by strengthening the interconnection and cooperation among specialized areas. Management might start by creating new liaison and coordination roles, such as that of a "value chain manager," an "integration manager," or a "process owner." However, this tactic might lead to an additional level of organizational and managerial complexity and to confusion about roles and responsibilities: does the integration manager have a supporting or a leading role, or a bit of both? And will this one person have enough weight and impact to match the dynamics emanating from well-established organizational units with their own focus and logic?

5.2.2 The Organizational Structure: Choosing Means Losing

The solution is too often sought in a change of structure. An organization can be structured around different dimensions: type of product, area of expertise, region, market segment, channel, customer, etc. To find the most suitable structure, we look at which parts of the organization can best be put together to maximize focus, efficiency, communication, and cooperation and to avoid fragmentation as much as possible. However, we shouldn't forget that there is no "best" way to structure an organization. Choosing means losing; by choosing one particular structure, we will always create a deficiency somewhere else. For example, if we divide by product specialization, we will lose the overall view of a customer or region. If we divide up by customer or region, on the other hand, we will lose in-depth knowledge of our different products or areas of expertise. There are so many relevant dimensions; one structure can never cover them all.

We can try to solve this by building a matrix organization with cross-functional teams, by, for instance, combining product specializations and regions, but this may lead to a splintered capacity or an extra level of complexity. It may become unclear who is in charge. Is it the person who is responsible for the client or region, or the person who is responsible for the area of expertise? To solve this, one could think of practical solutions. The account manager, who is responsible for a client, could ask the content expert to participate when the client has a specific issue. But should the account manager then step aside as soon as the client has been brought in contact with the expert? Or should the account manager remain the client's first contact person with the expert in a back-office role? And when it comes to a deal, how is the revenue allocated?

It is without doubt useful to choose an organizational structure. This immediately creates focus and establishes direction and clarity. However, there really is no "best" structure. Each one is imperfect and temporary. Dividing up the organization in a client-centered way is in itself no better than by service channel or even by product. The structure that works best depends very much on the situation, and it is important to opt for the least imperfect structure at a given time.

An organizational structure becomes problematic when it is permanent and absolute, which leads to rigid compartmentalization and paralysis. This happens all too often. Organizations rightfully replace a rigid and dysfunctional structure, but the new structure is often introduced as "The Solution," and it too becomes rigid and impermeable. History repeats itself: employees who have been working for the organization for some time will ironically remark that they are back where they started ten years ago. There just aren't that many different options.

Any division leads sooner or later to the formation of silos. A structure should be nothing more than a temporary form of support which can easily be altered when the situation changes. It should never grow beyond its original intention, so that the organization does not lose the natural osmosis between all its parts, nor the connection of its parts to the greater whole.

5.2.3 How Can We Keep Everything Running Smoothly?

To return to the key question: How can we balance the individual parts of an organization with the greater whole? The eternal dilemma between specialization and integration is unsolvable and requires a constant balancing act. There are a number of things you can do to facilitate this.

PUT THE SILO EFFECT ON THE AGENDA

Clearly state what happens when you create functions and units. Mention the positive aspects, such as creating focus, building in-depth knowledge, and professionalizing, as well as the ingrained limitations, such as disconnection from the greater whole and paralysis. Discuss the challenges involved in specializing and integrating as one of the core polarities of the overall strategy. Ensure that staff and managers are sufficiently aware of the risks. Place "silo formation" at the top of the strategic agenda and make it a standing topic of discussion. Encourage staff and managers to identify silo tendencies at an early stage. This will help you make timely adjustments and ensure that the structure does not become completely dysfunctional before you finally realize that you need to take action.

EMPHASIZE THE INSTRUMENTAL AND TEMPORARY CHARACTER OF ANY SUBDIVISION

In your communication to all stakeholders, introduce new structures only as temporary solutions with built-in restrictions. You will feel less need to justify why you used to advocate for the old structure and now feel passionate about something entirely new. This doesn't mean that you are contradicting yourself: circumstances have changed. Or if you made a mistake with the previous structure, be open enough to admit this. "It was just a tool that we thought would work well, but it didn't. That is the risk of any type of structure. Let's now give this new structure a chance while critically monitoring how it will work in practice."

CONNECT THE INDIVIDUAL PARTS TO THE ORGANIZATION AS A WHOLE

As the process of partitioning in specialized subunits is self-reinforcing, it does not need to be additionally encouraged. Conversely, it is often necessary to explicitly invest in a strong feeling of connection with the whole organization. Each individual in every unit should be well aware of how their work is related to the overall goal and the entire value chain: not only to the previous and next links in the chain but to the chain as a whole. Everyone should understand the work and challenges of colleagues in other departments and their ultimate impact on the customer, and of course they should get to know colleagues and customers on a personal level. Spending a day or week working in each division can make big difference. You will experience firsthand how your distant colleagues depend on your contribution and what their dilemmas are, and you will expand your network so that you can quickly get into contact if something goes wrong.

It is also important for the units to have a balanced mix of departmental goals and organizational goals, each carrying the same weight. You could think of valuing how well a department contributes to preventing hitches or helping to solve problems in other parts of the value chain, or how it brings up and openly discusses issues that arise between departments in day-to-day collaboration.

Finally, it can be useful to have a "value chain manager" or "process owner" to oversee and coordinate the whole chain. However, it may be better not to make this a permanent role to prevent this extra structural layer from getting stuck in pursuing its individual goals. You will need to prevent the additional polarization of our department versus the process management department. It is better to rotate this role among the various organizational units involved, which would make each feel more engaged in the overall organization.

ENCOURAGE A LAYERED IDENTITY

On a deeper level, it is important to encourage people not only to identify themselves with their team or division but also with the organization as a whole. To use a metaphor, they should see themselves as belonging to their hometown, their province, their country, their continent, and the world, all at the same time. I give more details on a layered identity in section 6.2 (Adaptability, Versatility, and Identity).

TURN AN "I PROFILE" INTO A "T PROFILE"

People with an "I profile" are specialized in only one specific area (with their in-depth knowledge being represented by a vertical line, as in the letter "I"), which makes them more difficult to deploy in other areas. They will have a problem if the organization shifts: for example, if it decides to bend more toward the market, investing heavily in gaining insight into clients' needs and outsourcing all noncore business specializations. They may also be laid off if some specializations become superfluous through technological break-throughs. But pure generalists (represented by a horizontal line, as in a dash), who only have a broad profile without any specific in-depth knowledge, are also vulnerable. The market increasingly requires very specific competencies to make a real difference.

People with a "T profile" have both broad and in-depth knowl-edge. On the one hand, they have a wide range of generic skills, which makes it relatively easy for them to familiarize themselves with new domains, but they are also specialized in a certain field, which makes them unique. Their area of expertise may be of a tem-porary or more permanent nature, but if it is no longer required, their broad generic background makes it easier for them to spe-cialize in something else. People with a T profile can more easily adapt to a changing context, and organizations will benefit from encouraging staff members to develop a T profile. Of course, it is up to the individual to determine which type of profile they want to develop.

ENSURE FLEXIBLE SUPPORT STRUCTURES AND SYSTEMS

Support structures and systems should always be easily adaptable. You could, for example, create a single talent pool of professionals with different capabilities and deploy them flexibly in projects or temporary teams, depending on business needs and priorities. This is also the essence of the Agile organization model that many project organizations (like those in IT development) have adopted. In this model, people work in "tribes" and "squads" and can be flexibly de-ployed according to the priorities and the workload. However, here too, tension arises between flexibility and stability, both for the in-dividual and the organization. Too much flexibility can create chaos and unrest. Pragmatism is extremely important in the application of Agile principles, as such a model can also become a dogmatic straitjacket with prescribed formats preventing people from doing what is really needed.

Organizations rely more and more on the systems they use. Make sure that these systems are set up so that they don't become a limiting factor when the organization needs to change direction. Systems should be quickly and easily adaptable to a new process and organizational structure. A modular approach, allowing for a wide range of combinations, might be useful. However, as already mentioned, creating a balance between specialization and integration is more a matter of mindset than of technology.

KEY POINTS

- The ultimate organizational structure does not exist; structure is always imperfect and temporary. It is important to explicitly state this with each organizational change.
- Make sure that all structures remain flexible and do not become rigid. Make silo formation a standard agenda item.
- Always link the individual parts of the organization to the organization as a whole. Ensure that there is a good balance between departmental goals and organizational goals.
- Encourage staff members to develop a T profile: a broad orientation in addition to specialization in a certain field.
- Ensure adaptable support structures and systems.

5.3 Directing an Organization without Putting It in a Straitjacket

Once you have decided on the direction you want to take, you need to ensure that the organization also moves in that direction. You can do this by setting ambitions, principles, values, rules, norms, goals, targets, performance indicators, and the like, and steering the organization along these lines. However, this is very much a balancing act. The crux lies in finding balance between a number of polarities. They are often formulated as dilemmas:

- **Freedom and/or control**: Do you want to empower people with the risk that everyone goes their own way and things get out of control? Or do you want to keep tight control, with the risk that the organization will become passive and inert from too many procedures and rules?
- **Integrated and/or focused**: Do you need to steer toward a wide range of balanced goals? A well-known tool for this is the Balanced Scorecard, in which direct, short-term financial results need to be in balance with the long-term growth and innovation targets, and in which customer-oriented and market-oriented objectives have to go hand in hand with equally important internal operation objectives. Or you could think of balancing goals related to *profit, planet, and people*, as in the philosophy of corporate social responsibility. You know that this broad and complementary palette will guarantee an integrated perspective, but do you still have an eye on all of your dashboard gauges at the same time? Or do you prefer to keep everything simple and focused, with the risk of later having to balance all kinds of things that have gone off track?
- **Objective quantification and/or subjective qualification**: Should all your goals be SMART and measurable, with the risk of ending up with all kinds of artificial and practically useless quantifiers? Or should you keep some of the objectives a bit general and vague, with the risk that they will not be taken seriously?
- **Absolute and/or relative standard norms**: Can you set goals based on your own ambitions or do you always have to relate these goals to external benchmarks? Can you shape the world and set new standards, or do you just have to keep up with the mainstream as best you can?

- **Uniformity and/or space for exceptions**: Do general rules apply and should everyone comply with them, with the risk that these rules may in some situations be irrelevant and even be absurd? Or should you allow exceptions to the rules and risk inconsistencies and a sense of injustice? For example: Should a large corporation allow its newly acquired innovative start-up to retain its autonomy and entrepreneurial character so the corporation can benefit from its ability to quickly adapt and innovate? Or should the corporation try to integrate the start-up into its own processes in order to create as much synergy as possible with the existing business?

Without aiming to be exhaustive, the following sections zoom in on two important leadership polarities from the above list. The first section takes a closer look at the polarity of freedom and/or control. The second one explores the polarity of objective quantification and/or subjective qualification.

5.3.1 Freedom and Control

Consider this real-life example: A global pharmaceutical company was struggling with high travel expense claims. To keep spending under control, it introduced stringent approval procedures. Staff members first had to justify their travel with extensive application forms and approval from various superiors before they could book their business trips. This kept travel costs somewhat under control, avoiding some clear excesses, but did not lead to any significant overall reduction. It also took a lot of time and caused major irritation because even people who booked their trips at the lowest cost had to follow a procedure that assumed everyone was a potential fraud. At some point, this approach was completely abandoned and replaced by a system where everyone was free to book trips without prior approval. The only type of control was making travel costs transparent on the intranet so that everyone could see how their travel costs compared to others'. And as a result, total travel costs decreased significantly.

The fundamental tension between freedom and control exists in every system. Organizations have a tendency to go for one of the two extreme poles, each with their obvious downsides. That a control-based system can flourish is demonstrated in the Chinese political model: it achieves incredible results in terms of growth, transformation, and policy deployment. However, this comes at the expense of individual freedom. In a control-oriented organization everything needs to be reported. As a consequence, staff members will be careful not to make mistakes, won't take any risks, will strictly stay within their own area of responsibility, and will document everything they do. They often won't take any initiative beyond what they have been instructed to do and will rely on top management to resolve the overall issues of the organization.

At the other extreme, in organizations with a "laissez-faire" attitude, everyone does their own thing without much cohesion. Entrepreneurship flows through the veins of the organization. Those who come up with good ideas and are able to sell them with convincing arguments get the chance to realize them and inspire others; cooperation is voluntary and based on enthusiasm, not on coercion. Sometimes brilliant ideas arise, but it's very difficult for the organization to prioritize among the abundance of initiatives and to create a clear company strategy. Some great ideas may not be fully explored and implemented because attention has shifted to new and more exciting things, interest is rapidly fading, or there is no driving "owner." Unsuccessful initiatives are not systematically analyzed to gain insights and learn from previous mistakes. This free and entrepreneurial approach is typical for organizations structured as networks of knowledge workers or independent experts.

An organization can sometimes tip from one extreme to the other. Before the banking crisis of 2007–8, the control mechanisms within financial institutions were applied quite loosely, and exceptionally smart professionals had the opportunity to develop exotic products and conduct market transactions without much thought or concern for the potential impact and risks. As long as there was money to be made, all was right with the world. After the banking crisis ("Never again!"), financial institutions became heavily regulated and inundated with rules and control mechanisms to put an end to this kind of unbridled proliferation. This immediately caused the opposite extreme, a bureaucratic and risk averse approach. However, many of these regulations did not impact the underlying mindset. When you, as a client, want to buy shares or invest in a financial product, you have to fill out loads of paperwork and risk assessment forms to officially document that you know what you are doing and what the specific risks are. This is not an in-depth discussion about risks but rather another burdensome tick-the-box formality that needs to be handled in the most efficient way ("we'll get through these regulations quickly so you can sign").

5.3.2 Disciplined Empowerment

Is it not possible to achieve a synthesis or a creative combination of the two poles? Can we not allow a high degree of freedom, entrepreneurship, and empowerment on the one hand, and instill a strong sense of control on the other? Take disciplined empowerment, for example: there could be many different ways to achieve this. An obvious approach is to establish a limited number of clear and undisputable boundaries and to give people within these boundaries all the freedom and space they need to develop their own initiatives. Another way could be to have very clear corporate values that people internalize and use as guiding principles to make their own judgments.

The travel costs solution above could be another interesting path to explore. It provides a new perspective on how to combine these two poles: Everyone books their travel costs without prior permission or approval, yet there is an incentive to exercise self-discipline and take responsibility. Through the process of comparison and benchmarking with peers, a natural range of what is acceptable and what is not arises without having to define it in advance. You can use the outcomes in a traditional top-down way by asking people to explain why they have deviated from the average, or you could let the system regulate itself because no one likes to stand out without a clear reason.

However, there is also a danger to this approach, as it incorporates lateral steering through social control and peer pressure. In my personal view, this comparison with the group average should always be anonymous to avoid blaming and shaming. Instead of comparing everyone's results out in the open, one could opt for personalized reports showing someone's results compared to an anonymized list of the others. This would be a more ethical way of instilling ownership and self-management.

You can apply this mechanism to all kinds of challenges where sectional interests have to be aligned with collective interests. For example, an organization may eliminate internal budgeting and invoicing for communication and HR projects in its business units to avoid unnecessary bureaucracy, with the side-effect that the internal shared service center that provides these services is always over budget. In this situation, the organization could use the travel costs solution above by making each unit's expenditures transparent and comparable. This creates a basis for self-steering and also allows management to intercede when one unit regularly over-spends, putting too much pressure on the shared service center.

The comparison between peers is not about eliminating deviations, but about having an open dialogue on why people or organizational units deviate from the average: there might be very good reasons for doing so. Trust rather than distrust should be the underlying attitude driving this way of working. Therefore, it doesn't have to be in the rather confrontational form of publicized comparisons. Just raising these questions in advance with colleagues or in team meetings can help professionals weigh the pros and cons and make well-informed decisions in certain cases ("Can I make an exception for this customer?"). It allows organizations to avoid all kinds of nitty-gritty if-this-then-that rules or extensive approval processes at the front end. More about this when we talk about paradoxical dialogue in section 8.2.

5.3.3 Lateral Control: Stifling or Stimulating?

Peer-to-peer comparisons, lateral steering, and social control might look like attractive ways to combine the strengths of personal responsibility and top-down control. However, these mechanisms have strengths and downsides.

The more social control mechanisms are in place, the less central management we need to keep everything running smoothly. Close-knit villages and neighborhoods where there is a lot of social control require less policing. By contrast, in neighborhoods where there is little social cohesion and control, authorities have their hands full. Self-regulating social control mechanisms are more effective than centralized control as they are less polarizing. Applying an external force to keep everything under control automatically leads to a dichotomy between the local community and central authority. In neighborhoods with a strong and visible police presence to fight crime, tensions with the police increase, and instead of bringing order and peace, it often provokes more polarization and violence.

Social control has its merits, but it can also be restrictive, repressive, and stifling. If someone deviates even slightly from the implicit social norm, they run the risk of being explicitly or implicitly forced to conform: laughed at, ignored, bullied, ostracized, or even outright banned. Instead of peers uniting to challenge central authority, polarization alienates groups of peers, usually resulting in a majority versus minority setting. Social media can have the same negative effect, pressuring people to conform to implicit but completely unrealistic social norms. On a daily basis people see how happy, beautiful, and successful their peers or idols appear to be, inviting comparisons. Social control mechanisms lead to the strange paradox that the more we are free to be ourselves, the more we want to look and be like everyone else. Pressure to conform to social norms can undermine individual self-esteem and collective tolerance for diversity and innovation.

I am not advocating that repressive central authority be replaced with a form of equally repressive lateral control. The point is that both can be just as lethal to personal freedom, self-initiative, and entrepreneurship. In the travel expenses example, I don't mean that everyone has to have an average score. Travel expenses can be high or low, depending on the context, and most deviations can be easily explained. If sharing this information results in people traveling less when they actually need to travel in order to conform to the social norm, then this approach has completely missed its aim (although it might win points for meeting climate targets).

The principle of social comparison should work as a means of self-steering rather than as an instrument of repressive social control. Therefore, it can only work in combination with an open dialogue free of judgment. The rules of this dialogue should be clearly defined and guarded by leadership, to avoid an insecure and paralyzing culture of dog-eat-dog.

You could argue that public comparisons have a positive effect: a race to see who can achieve the greatest reduction in costs and a race to see who can generate the highest income and sales. No one wants to be at the bottom of the list, and some people are extra motivated to be among the top three. But this system only works for people who have a strong competitive attitude and – bearing in mind the principle of diversity – not everyone does. For less competitive people, this is more likely to bring on additional stress and reduce productivity. They may start to panic and become obsessed with the figures, their energy going down the drain. They perform best when they can just calmly focus on their work. In short, it depends very much on the types of people involved whether you want to compare individual results out in the open or more discretely to offer greater safety and less stress.

We can conclude that self-steering is more effective and costs less energy than top-down management. Peer-to-peer comparisons could be an important ingredient, but social control should never be allowed to devolve to social policing, which causes all kinds of dysfunctionalities and undesirable effects. The essence of self-steering is and remains the responsibility and judgment of the individual, preferably supported by an open and nonjudgmental dialogue with peers and management. It is also important to keep a close eye on whether self-steering really is self-steering or simply a well-camouflaged form of top-down control.

KEY POINTS

- Stop swaying between either bureaucratic control or a laissez-faire approach and explore ways to combine freedom and entrepreneurship with accountability and control.
- Explore different paths to combine the strengths of both. An interesting option is to explore is how you can stimulate self-steering by creating transparency.
- Make sure that lateral steering mechanisms don't turn into a stifling form of social control and peer pressure. It's all about having an open and nonjudgmental dialogue, based on trust and clear rules of conduct, carefully guarded by top management.

5.4 The Obsession with Measurement and the Limitations of KPIs

An example: An NGO supports structural, social, and economic de-velopment by adopting a long-term perspective and step-by-step approach to influence policies in developing countries and bring different parties together. This may be extremely useful, but it's a long haul behind the scenes, and it doesn't immediately yield visible results. Sponsors are increasingly critical. They want to know what their financial support has achieved in the short term. Otherwise, they'd rather invest in something where they can make a tangible dif-ference, something as measurable as possible, with attractive images of relief supplies being delivered to an area of famine. The NGO faces a dilemma: Should they try to quantify something that is difficult to measure, renouncing part of their overall goal? Or should they play the long game but watch sponsors' funding dwindle even further?

The management world is obsessed with measurable results. Standardized and repetitive work is clearly measurable; there are figures and clear targets for production volume, sales, delivery reli-ability, and error rates. However, not everything can be quantified. What do we do with long-term development goals, such as innova-tion or penetration in new markets? Are we going to try to quantify these too? This section will explore the polarity of objective quantifi-cation and subjective qualification as supportive instruments.

5.4.1 Going Overboard with Quantification

With hindsight, everything is measurable; we can see if an inno-vation has actually led to an increase in turnover or a reduction of costs, and we can see how much turnover and profit have actually been made in a new market segment. However, these results only become visible in the long term; they can't be used as indicators or benchmarks to see if we are doing the right thing in the moment. This is why the overall goal is often split up into sub-goals, and indicators of the final desirable *outcome* are translated into more tangible indicators that measure *output* or *input*. For instance, if the desirable outcome is "a higher level of objective and perceived safety in the city," then the desirable output for the police might be "an increase in the number of criminal offenses that are brought to justice or prevented." This desirable output can in turn be translated into an input indicator such as "an increase in the number of hours of police patrol on the street."

Innovation targets could be translated into an "X number of improvement proposals" or a "Y number of publications in top journals." The target for penetrating a new market might be an "X number of new contacts with decision-makers," the "organization of a Y number of seminars," or "a Z number of product presentations with at least Q number of participants."

It's logical that we want to quantify these intermediate goals through KPIs (Key Performance Indicators) because they break up the final goal into manageable chunks and create clear focus points for the short term. However, there are limitations.

DEVIATING FROM THE OVERALL GOAL AND CREATING PERVERSE EFFECTS

People tend to zoom in on their own objectives and lose sight of the overall goal. For example: a government agency with the aim of helping as many people on social welfare as possible to rejoin the work force has two departments. One places candidates directly with employers, and the other offers an intensive training program to candidates with gaps in their skills so that they can later be placed more easily. A conflict arises between the two departments because the direct placement department was able to fill a vacancy with someone who was still in the trainee pool of the training department, but the training department didn't want to let this person go because it meant they wouldn't meet their production quota (to deliver X number of people who have successfully completed the training program). Achieving a sub-goal can therefore prevent achieving the overall goal.

A sub-goal can also have a counterproductive effect. For example: A government agency wants to reduce their total costs and translates this into "fewer civil servants." The agency lowers the number of civil servants everywhere by outsourcing many of the services, ultimately leading to an increase in total costs. Another organization wants to save costs by drastically cutting back on consultancy services. As a result, several programs that were aimed at structurally improving efficiency and reducing costs lost momentum or never got off the ground.

THERE IS NO LINEAR CONNECTION BETWEEN INPUT, OUTPUT, AND OUTCOME

Sub-goals and their measurable indicators are often very artificial. There is often no linear correlation to the overall goal. Achieving the sub-goal of "X number of new contacts" will not automatically lead to accomplishing the final goal of "conquering a new market." It's often a matter of luck. Which would you prefer: someone who diligently and dutifully ticks off all their sub-goals, or someone who puts all these sub-goals aside and passionately goes their own way to reach the overall goal? How would you assess these two people: one doesn't achieve their sub-goals for two years in a row but still manages to penetrate the market in year three by following their own instinct while the other meets their sub-goals every year but fails to have a real breakthrough? This also applies to reward and appreciation: should someone who has won a small but highly innovative contract in a new market receive less appreciation than someone who has sold a large bulk assignment in an existing market?

5.4.2 A Quantitative and Qualitative Approach Hand in Hand

We should therefore accept that many things that are crucial for the health and growth of an organization simply cannot be measured. The traditional approach of using quantitative performance indicators might be perfectly okay for the more standardized and repetitive activities, but it should certainly not be the standard mold into which all aspects of the business are made to fit.

This does not mean that the less measurable activities should be carried out in a noncommittal manner; nor does it mean that targets cannot be set or performance assessed. Here too, establishing and maintaining an ongoing exchange and dialogue process would be very helpful. What is it that we ultimately want to achieve? Are we still doing the right things? What works well and what is less effective? An ongoing appraisal, which allows for some adjustments along the way, is preferable to the traditional annual or half year appraisal process. Regular discussions along these lines can also be held in a team of co-workers as a continuous inter-collegial professional review process.

For the outside world, we still need a plausible and truthful explanation. For this purpose, a convincing qualitative analysis with anecdotal "evidence" could also work well. It's at least better than trying to demonstrate something with artificial statistical figures that may be disputable or even arouse skepticism and cynicism ("They can find numbers to prove anything").

KEY POINTS

- Use quantifiable indicators for standardized and repetitive processes.
- Accept that not everything is measurable and don't try to force quantifiable KPIs onto things that cannot be measured.
- Establish and maintain an ongoing qualitative exchange and dialogue process about nonmeasurable goals.
- A good, qualitative, and even anecdotal explanation can be just as strong as hard figures.

CHANGE

In this chapter, I will lay out a number of typical challenges for organizational change from a paradoxical perspective. The first question is the desired balance between the new and the existing situation, and how we can achieve it. The second is how we can make an organization more adaptable and flexible without losing its identity. The third section is about the social process of change: How can we manage the confrontation between supporters and opponents in a productive way? Finally, in the fourth section, I will look at paradoxical interventions as an unusual and counterintuitive change strategy. In all these challenges, I will explore how a both/and perspective can lead to better results.

6.1 Change and Continuity: The Old and the New

The model of radical change is still very popular in the world of management. This change model emphasizes and maximizes the difference between the old and the new. All old values are replaced by new (opposite) values. Who has never seen the commonly used models depicting all the "as is" values and principles on the left and the opposite "to be" values on the right, with an arrow showing the transition from left to right? From "fragmented" to "aligned," from "bureaucratic" to "client-oriented," from "reactive" to "proactive," or from "silos" to "chains." In this model, everything from the past belongs to the "old way of thinking" and is rejected from the outset. Any criticism about the new way of thinking indicates clinging to the past and is regarded with suspicion. The key question: Is this popular approach also an effective one?

6.1.1 Making a 180-Degree Turn

Radical change involves fundamentally breaking with the past; since the old course wasn't working or even failed, there is nothing left to do but to throw everything overboard and take the opposite direction. The old approach was part of the problem, so it can't be part of the solution. For example: "The power of the unions and employee participation have been so strong that we have only been focusing on our own staff at the expense of our business purpose and clients. Now it's time to put our clients and organizational goals first."

At the top management level, such a change is usually accompanied by the arrival of a new management team, one that is not tainted or bound by the past. It often also means a shift in the power balance throughout the organization: factions supportive of the old course lose their influence and are pushed aside by advocates of the new course. This way of viewing change corresponds with the model of dialectical change (thesis and antithesis) and the shock-wave development brought on by revolutions, which plays a central role in Karl Marx's thinking.

The radical change model has a number of major advantages:

- **Clarity**: It is very clear to everyone what the new direction is and what needs to be changed. This is easier to communicate than a complex story full of nuances.
- **A fresh, new start**: It seems like all the problems of the past will finally be tackled and solved. The promise that everything will be completely different and better has a strong energizing effect.

- **No other option**: By breaking with the past, doing things the old way is no longer an option. Everyone needs to go along with the change; all doors leading to the past are closed. This radical break provides the momentum and drive to change, and without it, everything would remain the same.
- **Restoring balance**: The previous course went too far and for too long; it must be drastically corrected to repair the worst damage. The canoe that went completely off course when it was only paddled on the left must now be steered back by intensely paddling on the right.

Is it an inevitable part of human nature to swing from one direction to the other? Maybe we need to fully experience the positive and negative aspects of both opposites before we can take on a more moderate position somewhere in the middle. For example, after the fall of the Berlin Wall, the caricatured East German police state was replaced by the free market with cheers of joy. Only later did the downside of freedom become clear: unemployment, individual responsibility, uncertainty. Many began to feel that the "good old GDR" was not so bad after all, with its full employment, safety, security, and state care. Is it inevitable to go through a period of absolute anarchy after a long period of a dictatorship before a balanced approach can be taken? And have we not been extraordinarily naive in the West to think that with the Arab Spring or the fall of the Taliban in Afghanistan a bloody dictatorship could be seamlessly replaced by a democratic regime? In short, isn't it necessary to first fully experience thesis and antithesis before we can achieve a new synthesis?

6.1.2 The Downside: Waste of Energy, Depreciation, Uprooting

At the same time, this radical change model has serious drawbacks. As I explained in section 2.3 (Why Doesn't the Either/Or

Approach Work?), it leads to massive destruction of value and of capital. First, many old processes and tools that worked are discarded along with the ones that didn't. Moreover, there's a big chance that the new approach will also go on too far and for too long, requiring another radical change to restore balance. This cycle fuels cynicism: "We're going back to where we were ten years ago."

From the perspective of staff members, a radical change will often feel very disruptive and destabilizing and thus evoke a lot of resistance. "What we were doing before was apparently not good enough." The methods, values, and principles that people have been applying and to which they owe part of their professional (and even personal) identity and pride are suddenly of no value at all. People can feel a loss of purpose ("It doesn't really matter what I do.") that only makes them cling to what is familiar and reject everything that's new. When people have to let go of everything they've stood for, it can often feel like a matter of "all or nothing," which can lead to an escalating and energy-draining battle.

Staff members will be forced to reinvent themselves. For the forerunners and advocates of the new way of working, it will mainly mean building further on what they had already started. The more agile staff members, the ones who have formulated their professional identity on a deeper level (i.e., the purpose or "why" of the company) and can thus more easily break free from the concrete nature of the current situation, will also have fewer problems with the change. But for many staff members, being forced to break with the past will still be an extremely uncomfortable and sometimes quite traumatic experience. Some will be able to take this opportunity to reinvent themselves; others will withdraw into themselves; still others will continue to fight the change either out in the open or behind the scenes; some will just leave.

Managers often don't realize the full impact of such a transformation and unrealistically expect that people, after feeling uprooted from the familiar and replanted elsewhere, will immediately start growing new roots again. Managers sometimes see this as an ideal opportunity to shake things up, to get rid of a number of people and bring in new blood. However, this all takes a tremendous amount of energy and resources, which also could be spent on other priorities.

6.1.3 In Search of a New Synthesis: Enriching the Old with the New

It is more effective from a both/and perspective not to replace but to enrich "the old" with the new. You can value the power of the existing in addition to the new in the following ways.

PRESERVE THE THINGS THAT WORK WELL

Be critical in what you throw away and what is still useful. Specifically mention, value, and keep the things that were working well. Not everything has to be broken down or discarded; some rooms in the house are still in good shape and may only need a new coat of paint.

EMPHASIZE CONTINUITY

Don't try to sell the change as something completely new or as a "challenging, radically new way of working." This will only appeal to a small group of "early adopters"; most people will feel unsettled and uncertain. Instead, emphasize the things that will continue to exist, probably in a slightly different form. Is everything completely new, or are some things still recognizable when you "put on your old glasses"? Which old and trusted values still live on in a slightly different form?

For example: Does everything become impersonal if you place your services at a physical distance? Or does this distancing mean that extra attention will have to be paid to empathy and a personal approach? Shouldn't the continuing importance of empathy and personal attention be given a prominent place in the communication about the change? Rather than positioning it as a radically new way of working, consider: does the essence of the work really change, or just its form?

Let's consider a concrete example: Big data analytics and machine learning will yield patterns and connections that could previously only be produced by people with years of professional experience in this field. This will mean a major change in the role of subject matter experts. However, the interpretation of these big data results will require even more in-depth professional expertise and practical experience as well as intuition. In other words, the core skills of the expert will be in even more in demand. Emphasizing that something is brand new feels threatening to many and provokes a reaction of resistance; it is often more engaging to explicitly connect the new element to what people are already doing today.

UNDENIABLY DIFFERENT BUT UNMISTAKABLY FAMILIAR

When it is necessary to create an irreversible change, for example by introducing new systems and processes, some external coercion may be necessary. These changes should be realized swiftly, without arousing more unrest than necessary. Once this irreversible initial change has been made, all emphasis can be placed on establishing the links with the old way of doing things, on recognizing "the old" in "the new," and on giving meaning and importance to the new by referring to familiar values. For example, we're still providing customer service, just no longer through face-to-face contact but instead by telephone or chat. This means that we will have to focus on the *essence* of our staff members' competencies (i.e., listening, understanding, providing workable solutions) and not get stuck on their specific *form* (face-to-face, phone or chat). It's important to reaffirm the value of these competencies in the new context.

EIGHT PRACTICAL TIPS TO BREAK
THE PENDULUM MOVEMENT

Here are eight practical tips for leaders to avoid the traditional zigzagging between extreme positions. By adjusting the organization's course smoothly and fluently, anticipating the moment when policies and practices become dysfunctional and outmoded, you can lessen and even avoid sudden, radical shifts.

Let's return to and expand upon the figure presented on p. 45 with the example of an internal service organization, providing support services to the core business, that oscillates between a

Figure 6.1. How an organization oscillates between the two poles of a core polarity, revisited

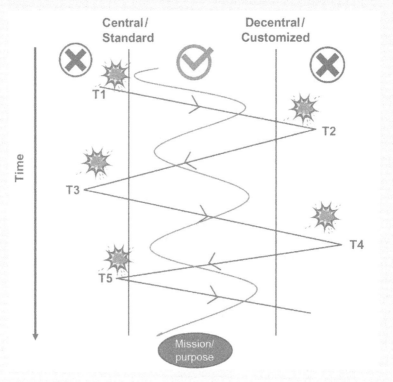

centralized model – with the focus on economies of scale, efficiency, and standardization – and a decentralized model – with the focus on customer intimacy and customized solutions.

The following tips combine the different principles and tools of paradoxical leadership into one integrated approach.

1 **Explore and identify**. Find out together which pendulum movements tend to repeat themselves in your organization and which polarities are involved. You can get a good idea by talking to people who have been working for the organization for a long time. They form the collective memory of the organization and can often tell you in full color what the recurring patterns are. For example, if you enthusiastically proclaim that the internal services will need to be decentralized because they have become too bureaucratic, someone with a long career in the organization might be able to tell you that this was how the organization was run ten years ago, before the call for standardization and synergy.

When the recurring polarities of the organization are an explicit topic in the strategic debate, they become more manageable. As part of the management team, you can include both aspects when formulating a dual strategy or a paradoxical challenge for the organization. How can the strength of both of these aspects be used? For example, how can short and personal communication lines with customers be combined with the efficiency of standardized processes and economies of scale?

2 **Make the overall goal of the organization clear** and always use it as the ultimate point of reference. Polarities such as "centralized" – "decentralized" are only means to achieve the overall goal. For the internal service provider

this goal would be "enabling our colleagues in the core business to do an excellent job" (the "Mission/purpose" oval at the bottom of the figure). Always ask yourself: How does the course we're on contribute to the ultimate goal? What is the most suitable approach in the current situation to achieve this goal? See also section 5.1 on strategic agility.

3 **Explore together the power and the limitations of each pole** and determine together the desired range between what is effective and what is dysfunctional. This discussion is best done at the level of operational teams (due to size and similar field of work) using concrete examples and cases. For example, in which cases and contexts do we want to provide centralized standard services and when and where are decentralized and fully customized services more appropriate? How far do we want to go in either direction? In most cases, you will fairly rapidly agree on what is completely unacceptable on both ends of the spectrum. The "gray zones" and the "borderline cases" will prompt the most heated debates. These will not necessarily lead to unanimous conclusions. There will always be a certain level of dissent within a team, as different views clash. That's not a problem as long as communication lines are kept open and people know where to find each other for peer consultation when such gray zone cases present themselves. Through this dialogue on specific cases, it also becomes clear that abstract terms such as "customization" or "standardization" can mean completely different things to different people. This alone provides great insights and makes this dialogue worthwhile. Making these notions concrete and sharing them with each other will help you to understand why others do what they do, and it will stimulate

you to make more conscious professional considerations. For more details on how to conduct this paradoxical dialogue see section 8.2.

4 **Listen to signals** from people in your organization and from your clients and actively seek their feedback. They are often the first to feel the limitations and disadvantages of a particular course in daily practice. For example, by steering toward more uniformity and standardization, those on the shop floor might be burdened with more central reporting and administration, ending up with less time to spend with customers. Or they will be confronted in practice with absurd situations, making it clear where these wonderful new operating procedures contradict each other.

5 **Make time for reflection and critical evaluation and dare to make adjustments.** This certainly takes guts because you need to be willing and able to abandon a direction that you have wholeheartedly defended if it is in the interest of the organization, without seeing this as a personal failure or a loss of face. You need to be able to take a vulnerable position and rise above your own ego and personal interests for the greater good. For example, as a leader, dare to admit that you might have underestimated certain effects of the path you chose to follow and have thus made errors of judgment, instead of forcibly and unconvincingly trying to show that you have always been consistent. Gaining new insight is part of life and a sign of a highly developed learning capacity. See also section 9.2 about paradoxical skills.

6 **Organize counterbalance with diversity.** Make sure that your teams include people who have different perspectives.

Invest in getting to know each other's differences and in
seeing the underlying positive intentions. This is not about
stating "that everyone has their own truth" but about actively seeking a new and connecting perspective through
dialogue. This requires a different way of speaking: not in
terms of a judgmental "us" versus "them" but in terms of
underlying polarities, where both sides are valued. Appreciate and reward those who adopt a constructively critical
attitude and be open and inquisitive when opposing views
arise. See also sections 6.3.2 on constructive confrontation
and 7.2 on diversity.

7 **Explain clearly why it is necessary to make a turn** at a
certain moment. You will need to explain how the new
course fits into the overall picture, the changing context
and the organization's goals, and also how it incorporates
successful elements of the current way of working. For
example: "We are now entering a new phase in our development. Our internal customers face new, more complex
challenges, which in turn have a profound impact on what
they expect from us and our work. We will continue our
standard approach for the more straightforward issues. The
more complex challenges require us to team up with our
clients and work across our different areas of expertise."

In addition to communicating what the change will be,
it's important to be transparent about the decision-making
process and your own deliberations during this process. Be
open in expressing what you find difficult and share with
others any struggles and tensions you may experience. People will feel recognized as they experience similar struggles
and tensions in themselves.

8 **Appreciate what already exists** and don't discard the
things that work. Refrain from using words such as "right"
and "wrong" or "old" and "new." The existing course has
brought you where you are now. You may have gone a little
too far in one direction and now face its negative aspects,
but this doesn't reduce the underlying value of this pole.
Show how the new can enrich the current way of working
and look for ways to connect the power of both poles rather
than stating a replacement. For example: "Thanks to our
huge efforts and investments in centralizing, standardizing,
and automating the bulk of our services, we are in a great
position to now work closely with the core business on
complex, multidisciplinary, and nonstandard challenges."
Broadly sharing the experiences and insights that are gained
in combining both can help and inspire all. By valuing both
poles and making a clear connection between them, you
also explicitly show your appreciation for all the good work
in the past. This will reduce the resistance created when
people feel unappreciated, as in "we were apparently doing
everything wrong and now we need to be fixed."

6.1.4 And in Case of a 180-Degree Turnaround ...

A radical change of course and extreme corrective measures in the
opposite direction may nevertheless be inevitable in order to regain
balance. In this case, the following aspects can be considered:

CONTEXT AND INTERPRETATION
Describe the broader context, for example, as a necessary but temporary correction of a one-sided course in the past that was useful

for a while but finally derailed. Emphasize the fact that this is a temporary measure – a phase of transition in order to restore balance.

MOURNING

You can expect a period of mourning when breaking with the past. Letting go of something familiar involves grieving, and sometimes people will have to leave a piece of their previous professional identity behind. We can only welcome something new when we have had the opportunity to say goodbye to the past. This goes without saying in our personal lives, but many change processes skip this phase, usually due to time pressure. There's a tendency to immediately start building the new world in the hope that people will have something to focus on. Foreseeing a period of mourning means creating time and space for people to express feelings of sadness and anger without expecting productive results. It's counterproductive to respond to these emotions with counter arguments about the necessity of change, or by downplaying them by trying to shed a positive light on everything. Listen and allow these "negative" emotions to exist. Mourning shows respect for the achievements of the past. Managers are used to taking action and finding solutions; allowing time to grieve is not often the first reaction. They often fear that the "moaning and groaning" will only spread and last even longer. This is not usually the case in practice: people who have been given the necessary time and space to share their feelings of anger, grief, or disappointment will be quicker in coming to terms with their loss and adopting a more neutral attitude from which they can start building again. If you don't allow time for mourning from the start, the latent grief will continue, slowing down and frustrating the process of building something new.

CHANGING COURSE IN TIME

Don't wait until things become dysfunctional and the disadvantages take their toll before you change course. For example: Let the "start-up CEO" phase out in time and find a good replacement at an early stage (a "consolidation CEO") so that this person can take over with a smooth transition. Ideally, you could let the two work together for a while, with the former CEO moving more into the background (for example, by focusing on a limited and decreasing number of remaining tasks) and the new CEO taking on a more prominent position in the foreground. You could also apply the strategy of dual leadership, using two leaders with complementary skills, as described in section 5.1 (Strategic Agility).

6.1.5 No Change without Stability

In his 2012 article in the *McKinsey Quarterly*,[1] Colin Price writes about the importance of creating stability to promote adaptability. Price states:

> Constant or sudden change is unsettling and destabilizing for companies and individuals alike. Just as human beings tend to freeze when confronted with too many new things in their lives, so will organizations overwhelmed by change resist and frustrate transformation-minded chief executives set on radically overturning the established order. Burning platforms grab attention but do little to motivate creativity ... Paradoxically, therefore, change leaders should try to promote a sense of stability at their company's core and, where possible, make changes seem relatively small, incremental, or even peripheral.

He writes about the relentless flow of change projects that drives managers and employees absolutely crazy. His example is a company that decides to break up this endless flow of changes into explicit, well-prepared, and manageable quarterly change packages. This was less unsettling and created more trust and commitment from both managers and staff. This way of structuring change also made the individual "change packages" more balanced and coherent.

---

1 Colin Price, "Leadership and the Art of Plate Spinning," *McKinsey Quarterly* (November 2012).

An organization and its people can grow tired of constant change and improvement. The challenge is to find a balance between periods of change and periods of stabilization, processing, and "digestion"; only after a good "digestion" is the mind open and free to take steps in a new direction. In a change process, it is therefore important to create "islands of stability" between well-defined periods of change. Focusing on familiar and reliable anchor points in some areas can also make people more willing to change in other areas. You could think of a number of familiar traditions or iconic "rituals" that reflect the deeper identity of your organization and give a strong sense of common ground and belonging; things that, regardless of what the future holds, will never disappear because they are the essence of the organization and hold it together. These can be simple things like a daily start-up session, a weekly blog or cartoon, a communal break-fast on Thursdays, or an after-work drink on Friday afternoons.

6.1.6 Incorporate the Benefits of the Current Approach in the New Approach

When we want to change, we often focus on the aspirational goal or target. However, even if we are all convinced of the new approach and we make a comprehensive transition plan, the desired change may not actually happen.

There may still be many advantages to the previous way of working. For example, you may need your organization to work in a more multidisciplinary and integrated way instead of continuing to focus on separate professional disciplines. However, there are significant benefits to working in disciplinary silos: it is more efficient without the endless meetings and discussions with other disciplines; experts of the same discipline understand each other and speak the same professional language; specialists are trained in their standardized and proven methodologies; individual experts are valued for their visible contributions.

If there were no benefits to the current method, it would have been abandoned long ago. To bring about successful change, it is thus crucial to include the benefits of the existing approach in the new approach. An organization could ask itself: How can we work in a multidisciplinary way but maintain speed and efficiency? How can we focus on a team result while valuing the specific expertise and contribution of the individual expert? If we are unable to include the key benefits and drivers of the current approach, change is unlikely to happen; many people may be in favor of the principle of "multidisciplinary work" in words, but in practice fail to change their approach.

All problems that really matter – in our lives, organizations, and societies – are of a complex nature. A complex problem has, by definition, different and seemingly contradictory sides that need to be balanced, such as a good mix of preventive and curative measures, a combination of empathy and clear boundaries, or a balance between clear direction and an openness for new developments. Complex issues can never be solved in a one-sided and linear way. If they could, they would have already been solved and would not reappear time and time again.

KEY POINTS

- Don't throw away everything old to replace it with something new but *enrich* the old with the new.
- Draw parallels between the existing and the new so that people can relate to new things with the aspects that feel familiar.
- Encourage change by creating stability.
- Include the drivers and benefits of the current approach in the new approach.
- Complex problems need solutions that address and balance both sides of the coin.

6.2 Adaptability, Versatility, and Identity

Stepping back from single change programs, we can ask ourselves: How can we enhance the adaptability of an organization? How can we reinvent ourselves as an organization without losing our identity? First, some iconic examples.

Nokia started up by making wood pulp. Then it moved into generating electricity and producing rubber boots and telephone cables, growing into what undoubtedly became the global leader in telecom infrastructure and cell phones … at least until the rebirth of another company. Apple made its breakthrough in the 1980s with the easy-to-use Macintosh, which had an intuitive graphical interface and did not require any knowledge of complicated programming language. For a while, this was a revolutionary and unique concept, until Microsoft introduced Windows in the 1990s. As Microsoft grew to become the number one market leader, Apple led a marginal existence for more than a decade, focusing primarily on niche applications in the graphics industry … until it resurfaced in the mid-2000s with the iPod, the iPhone, the iPad … wiping the then market leaders Nokia, Research in Motion (Blackberry), and associates off the shelves within just a few years and growing to become one of the largest technology companies in the world.

Versatility is not about managing a specific transformation from A to B. It goes much further than that. It's about implementing "adaptability": embedding the ability to change in the DNA of its people. A versatile organization can handle change well and can adapt quickly to new circumstances. An organization can go in many different directions during its life cycle, with different products, markets, clients, technology, working methods, people, and management, and still keep its identity. The trick is to constantly reinvent while retaining a recognizable core. The examples of Nokia and Apple show that companies don't always succeed in doing this. Sometimes organizations spend too long riding the waves of success and believing too strongly in their untouchable position, losing their self-reflecting capability and their connection to their core purpose and values. They can get stuck in a heavy and cumbersome structure they have set up to keep on doing more of the same thing (only better and faster), the primary goal of which is to maintain itself.

6.2.1 Many Different Types of Versatility

There are various degrees of versatility. An organization could have the ability to switch smoothly between two directions along one axis, to find balance in multiple directions, or to reinvent itself in all directions, which I refer to here as biversatility, multiversatility, and omniversatility, respectively.

A BIVERSATILE ORGANIZATION

This type of organization can move quickly in two directions along one axis and thus easily adapt to its environment. An insurance company has a direct sales channel and a channel through brokers, a publishing house produces traditional paper books but also provides content in digital formats, a manufacturer offers both standard and tailor-made products. Depending on the situation and changes in demand, one direction may be given more focus and weight than the other.

Sometimes, the organization is split into two subdivisions that operate independently from each other. In this case, not much is expected of management and staff in terms of their ability to switch; both subdivisions simply follow their own courses.

There is more involved when both directions exist within one organization, and especially when individual people have to switch between them. They may have to work on standard products one day and focus on customized products the next. Some people might find the diversity fulfilling, but it also means that they need to be able to consciously switch between one set of values and operating procedures and the other, and probably master multiple sets of competencies. Chapter 9 (Paradoxically Competent) explains what this requires from people and how you can stimulate this as an organization.

In either case, this duality should also be reflected in the mission, values, and strategy of the organization. Basing the identity of an organization on either Operational Excellence ("we produce high volumes at low costs and are fast and efficient") or Customer Intimacy ("we listen very carefully to our clients and use our expertise and creativity to come up with unique solutions") is not enough. In order to reflect both aspects, the direction of the organization should be formulated as a paradoxical challenge, e.g., how can we optimally combine efficiency and low costs with unique solutions for our customers? Both "standard" and "customization" could be the inseparable core values of the company, or both aspects could be integrated in a combined value, such as "standardized customization," with concrete examples of what this means in daily practice. The organization could also try to look for an overarching value that incorporates both aspects. This could be something like "modular solutions for every target group." However, formulating this value in terms of what both aspects have in common does not emphasize the field of tension and the difference between them, making the value more abstract, less appealing, and perhaps even meaningless.

MULTIVERSATILE ORGANIZATIONS

Many diversified multinationals and conglomerates try to be versatile in many directions by using the traditional formula of a broad portfolio of activities: from vitamins to high-performance plastics, from medical equipment to financial services, from meat processing to underwear. It is the same principle as spreading risk in an investment portfolio: if things go well in one sector, that sector will be expanded; if things go less well in another sector, that sector will be phased out. In this way, the Dutch company Royal DSM has transformed from a Dutch state-run mining company to a fine chemicals company, and

Royal Philips from a light bulb factory to a supplier of medical solutions. In principle, these types of organizations do not have to be managed very differently from traditional (one-product or one-service) organizations. Activities are assigned to autonomous business units that operate independently from each other and have their own focus even though they are part of one holding. What they have in common is often limited to financial reports, top management, a shared pool of managers and professionals, and perhaps shared support services. Some nice-sounding but rather vague "corporate" values might be formulated to make the conglomerate's deeper binding factor (which is often predominantly financial) sound more appealing. It's the organizational structure that is versatile (the business units, which can either grow or decrease in size or which can easily be acquired or sold); agility does not necessarily have to be practiced at the deepest level of the organization where the work is done.

OMNIVERSATILE ORGANIZATIONS

These are organizations that are able to constantly renew and completely transform themselves, like the Apple example and for a limited time the Nokia example, without feeling that their core or essence is lost. This kind of agility goes one step further than just having a flexible holding structure with traditionally operating units. In omniversatile organizations, agility is embedded at the deepest level: in the DNA of the organization and its people.

6.2.2 Stimulating a Matryoshka Identity

The level at which an organization determines its identity is crucial. For example, a car manufacturer in this day and age could formulate its identity at the following different levels:

- Level 1: "We make awesome, energy-saving cars."
- Level 2: "We offer environmentally friendly mobile solutions."

- Level 3. "We provide sustainable energy solutions for today and tomorrow."
- Level 4: "We set the pace for a world worth living in."

The more concrete and specific the identity, the more difficult it becomes to switch to other activities, both on a collective and individual level. For people who have worked in a car manufacturing company for years and whose professional pride and identity are deeply connected to the beautiful cars they make, their world would collapse if car production ceased, and the company switched to another activity. Some would get over it and switch over to a new mindset and competencies after a professional and sometimes also personal period of mourning. Others would have more trouble getting past the crisis or never really would.

A broader identity allows much more freedom of movement because it articulates the essence of the organization. This broader identity corresponds to the three levels that Simon Sinek distinguishes: "what," "how," and "why." An identity only really makes a difference to the success of an organization if it is deeply rooted in a vision that provides answers to the "why" question: "Why do we exist, what is our purpose, and how do we contribute to the world?" Such a vision is inspiring and touches people deeply. However, many organizations define their identity only at the level of "what" ("we make furniture" or "we are a law firm") or "how" ("we make designer-like furniture for an affordable price" or "our legal advisers are both masters in their profession and sector specialists who fully understand your business").

However, a broadly formulated identity can also become so abstract that it no longer has any content or emotional value. A combination of different identity levels works much better. Just as you can be a neighbor, a member of a local community, a citizen of a city, province, state, country, continent, and of the world, all at the same time, you can also build up this kind of matryoshka identity for your organization. It is important to apply the both/and principle: Being a world citizen doesn't mean that you can't identify yourself with your neighborhood, town, or region. In the past, it sometimes seemed to an open-minded cosmopolitan that identifying yourself with your country, region, city, or neighborhood was narrow-minded and parochial and therefore *not done*. In the past, countries also promoted standard national languages and discouraged regional dialects. Fortunately, we can now feel at home at all these levels. It is yet another sign of self-awareness and pride that we can now allow our local accent to resonate in our native language or in the international English we speak with people of other countries. In short, the both/and perspective allows for different, even seemingly contradictory, identities to coexist.

Organizations can also build up different layers of identity. The first layer is that of the concrete *here and now* (product, client, process, team, colleagues, etc.). This gives that basic feeling of security and familiarity that most people need in order to have a sense of purpose and belonging: the feeling of tribal membership, as it were. You could think of some activities, rituals, and the like to enhance this feeling, but if you encourage this local identity too much, it may become inward-looking and narrow-minded and lead to "us versus them" thinking.

6.2.3 Outside Our Comfort Zone: A Journey to the Challenges of the Future

To help people form a broader identity, it helps to take them away from their immediate surroundings, to allow them to fully experience visions and images of the future. Telling a story on a rational level is not enough; it will go in one ear and out the other, and people will simply think "interesting" or "we'll see when the time comes," and then they'll return to the order of the day in their familiar environment. To have any impact, you will need to touch people on a level of personal experience. You can do this, for example, by organizing a kind of company "vision quest." In a traditional vision quest, an individual stays for a few days in isolation, with only the bare essentials and without any distractions, means of communication, or contact with the outside world. With proper preparation and coaching, this confrontational strategy can make people ask themselves fundamental questions about their habits, convictions, values, and beliefs.

You could apply the same principles in a collective process, in which the familiar world is left behind and everything is exposed for questioning. What are the external trends and developments and what could they mean for us? What are the possible scenarios? How could these affect my activities, my role, and my position? What will this mean for me as a person? Do I want to go along with this? Do I feel enthusiastic or am I more afraid and uncertain? What do I need to be able to take these steps, and who or what can support me? It's important that people can share their experiences and feelings openly without any judgments; all reactions are personal and therefore valid. The purpose of such an immersive experience should be to make people more aware and reflective of what might happen if the world as we know it fundamentally changed. In this context serious gaming and simulation exercises could be helpful for experiencing different scenarios.

6.2.4 Nourishing the Soul of the Organization

Another way to foster a broader identity is to build strong underlying values that remain the same for years and decades, even though the organization may change beyond recognition in all other areas. These values may be elusive, but they remain totally familiar and define "the soul" of the organization. For example, the quirky, ironic, and playful writing style and the typically absurd humor of the popular Flemish television magazine, *Humo*, which has existed since 1958, are unmistakably present in every edition, although the specific form has evolved over time and different generations of journalists have succeeded one another. Apple, too, has always been known for going against mainstream developments and putting user experience first; these have been Apple's constant elements of identity throughout all phases of its development. The same principle applies to many great artists who reinvent themselves in very different themes, styles, or genres while keeping their unmistakably unique signature.

The trick is to nourish this unique core identity and at the same time to renew its meaning and reshape its form at every phase. The soul of an organization is not something static; it's a bonding, shared, and living "feeling." It's necessary to regularly and with the whole organization redefine what the organization's core identity is and how it should be understood in the current context. By consciously facilitating this process of ongoing renewal and revitalization, you can create a stronger and more relevant identity instead of getting stuck in abstract and meaningless mission statements or worn-out traditions. It goes without saying that this cannot be accomplished with a one-off event; this is an ongoing, almost ritual process that the company needs to experience on a regular basis. This requires permanent attention and a significant investment of time and resources from the leadership of the organization. This is not an easy task, as in every organization our attention is drawn to the daily operations and the realities of the here and now.

We can gain a lot by developing a broader identity in addition to the concrete here-and-now identity. If a specific process or product needs to change, people will feel less uprooted when they can resort to a familiar core identity. This will enable a smoother and less bumpy transition. By regularly changing, we get closer and closer to the pure essence of our shared identity.

6.2.5 It's Not Just about Willingness but Also about the Ability to Change

The previous section was mainly about the willingness to change. This is a major prerequisite for agility, but it doesn't say much about the actual ability to change. At an organizational level, we need flexible structures, adaptable systems, a limited number of generic roles (instead of lengthy and detailed job descriptions), and so on. At an individual level, we need to be able to combine specific competencies with a set of broad competencies that can be used in different situations. I will come back to this in section 9.1.2 (Multiple Careers), where I talk about T and M profiles.

KEY POINTS

- Build up the identity of your organization in layers, like matryoshka dolls that fit inside one another, with both very concrete layers ("what" and "how") and deeper and more abstract layers ("why").
- Work together on nourishing a strong and deep core identity for your organization that will enable it to change without the feeling of losing its soul.
- Make sure that people are connected to this living core identity so that it becomes easier for them to let go of the concrete layers of "how" and "what" when necessary.
- Also ensure that more people not only have expertise in one specific area but can master a broad range of generic competencies to adapt to new situations.

6.3 Polarization and Tribal Wars

Change is not an abstract process that settles evenly over the whole organization like a blanket. On the contrary, it usually manifests itself very noticeably in a struggle for power and influence between rival groups, with each group defending its own point of view and agenda. For example: traditionalists versus innovators, or those who believe in quick action versus those who foster thorough preparation.

In some cases, these cracks appear within the same team or occupational group. In other cases, they occur between different organizational units: finance versus marketing, sales versus operations, etc.

The relative influence of these groups can change, with one group taking up a more dominant position, depending on factors like the economic situation, the political context, recent successes or failures, and the development phase of the organization. For example, at a global car manufacturer, for a long time the power and influence were with production; during an economic crisis, this shifted to finance; as the economy recovered and competition increased, it moved to R&D for a while (innovation!). Later, procurement played a prominent role since the costs of manufacturing a car largely depend on the costs of external suppliers.

6.3.1 United through Division

The battle between factions is not necessarily just a struggle for power, and the parties involved rarely experience or present it that way. All factions may be genuinely convinced that they are right and that it is for the benefit of the entire organization that their vision becomes or remains the leading one. The emergence of factions can be useful because an idea can materialize within the closed circle of a faction without being diluted through compromise. These ideas are strengthened through opposition to the visions of other factions.

Every faction looks for a counterforce to keep itself sharp and focused, and to strengthen the like-mindedness within the faction. Every in-group needs an out-group. If there is no opposition, there is a good chance that the faction will splinter and fall apart due to divided visions. Having a common enemy is still the strongest binding factor. The system as a whole also works like a polarized magnet: if a piece of metal is magnetized, both a north and a south pole are created. North and south cannot exist separately. Therefore, every movement creates its countermovement, and in this way the overall balance of a system is maintained.

The tension that arises in this process can take on various forms:

- Tension can be **constructive** if both parties are open-minded. By exchanging ideas and challenging and questioning each other, they are forced to examine their ideas and become more creative. They might come up with a new and better idea together, combining the best of both worlds.
- Tension can also be **pointless** if everyone sticks to their guns, and no one is prepared to budge. This leads to fruitless discussions between believers and nonbelievers. Rational arguments don't help either, when each side has a fundamentally different view of reality embedded in their beliefs or even in their characters. Do you believe in nature or nurture? In trust or control? In individual heroic achievements or in the silent coercive power of the system? In rational thinking or in intuition? All of these fundamental convictions are to some degree true, but generalizing them into absolute claims also makes them false. There are examples to back up every side.

  In short, such exchanges are often a waste of time. Since there are no possible connected solutions, one vision will prevail over the other at a given time, depending on the context and climate. In a stable and predictable environment, the "blueprint design gang" will be in charge. In an uncertain and volatile environment, those in favor of "going step by step and seeing where we end up" will determine the rules of the game. If there are numerous cases of abuse of trust, the faction that attaches more importance to stricter control will take the reins.
- Finally, tension can be **disruptive** and lead to further polarization. Both parties might dig in their heels and become even more convinced of their views. People will avoid each other or come into open conflict. Positions tend to become increasingly extreme.

Each party will gather their ammunition in the hope of finally convincing the undecided, crushing the opponent, and winning the battle. However, this will only result in both positions growing even further apart, making dialogue virtually impossible. In the meantime, this struggle will absorb everyone's energy and the organization as a whole will suffer. In some cases, the chasm between the parties will be so wide that a neutral mediator will have to be called in to bridge the gap, without any guarantee of success.

6.3.2 The Constructive Confrontation

In short, a confrontation of opposing visions can be beneficial or destructive. It just depends on how it is handled. The following steps can help to stimulate constructive dialogue and avoid polarization.

BRING THE UNDERLYING TENSIONS TO THE SURFACE

In many cases tensions are under the surface and not in the open. They are rarely mentioned, but they are strongly felt by everyone. They often literally divide groups: Do you belong to the inner circle or not? Are you in the progressive or the conservative faction? Addressing these underlying tensions requires energy, effort, and courage. It's easier and more convenient to avoid a real dialogue and stick silently to your own position, but the power struggle will nevertheless continue under the surface and will go on with its destructive work.

It takes courage to open this discussion and make the positions explicitly clear. Perhaps at first, people will deny that a power struggle is going on, especially those who are actively playing the game. There is even a risk that it will explode in your face, and all involved will close ranks against you as the bringer of unwanted and uncomfortable truths. But the first person to mention the struggle may also be able to count on recognition and a sense of relief from those who have unwillingly become drawn in and would rather focus on being productive.

Uncovering the fault lines and conducting an explicit dialogue does not mean that reconciliation and compromise need to be immediately sought. Sometimes, a deeper and sharper discussion needs to take place first: not about superficial manifestations, incidents, and symptoms, but about fundamental principles. An open confrontation is often preferable to simmering tensions.

CREATE A COMMON LANGUAGE

People can have entire conversations and not understand each other at all because they think differently and use different vocabulary. To a person of emotion, abstract terms such as "structure," "system," "KPIs," "management model," or "implementation" may evoke a feeling of resistance. A person of emotion might talk more about "seeking connection," "making a journey together," and "touching the soul of the organization" – phrases that sound vague and incomprehensible to more analytically minded people.

It may be that we mean the same thing with different words and even agree with each other, but it may feel like we come from completely different planets and can't communicate with each other. Knowing what personality type you are or what style of communication you prefer can help. There are many different management typologies, including color categories. They all refer to a number of fundamental perspectives from which someone can view reality. These perspectives differ greatly, but they can also be surprisingly complementary.

Most importantly, these typologies aren't meant to put you in limiting boxes or reduce you to an archetype. Categories can sometimes be an excuse to stay in your comfort zone and not reach out ("I'm blue [rational], so emotions are not my area"). They should instead make you aware that there are different perspectives and help you to understand these other viewpoints and their associated concepts and vocabulary. This may not always work. In some cases, a "multilingual" interpreter will be needed to clear up the confusion and get the parties talking to each other.

GO TO THE UNDERLYING NEEDS AND CRITICALLY SELF-REFLECT

It is important to distinguish between the concrete form and the underlying need for its existence. Perhaps the concrete form in which an opposite pole appears feels objectionable, reprehensible, or even repulsive, but that should not prevent you from investigating the underlying and often legitimate reason for its existence.

For example, in the narrative of globalism and multiculturalism, the attachment to local cultural traditions and to national or regional identity has been often labeled as parochial, narrow-minded, or even xenophobic. Many "broad-minded people" considered cultural identity as outdated, ridiculous, and even morally reprehensible as it fuels "us" versus "them" thinking and a feeling of superiority of one's own group. These "broad-minded people" think this way often without noticing that this reaction is exactly the same: stating their own moral superiority over another group, now with "broad mindedness" as an identity feature to differentiate "us" from "them."

Instead of denying the existence within ourselves of these motives that we find archaic and dubious and attributing them only to others, it is better to be self-critical and to accept that they are also part of who we are. Thinking in terms of "us" and "them," for example, is deeply engrained in us as humans. It is linked to our basic needs for security, familiarity, stability, uniqueness, and recognition. Only by recognizing the same tendencies and patterns in ourselves can we connect with others, taking them seriously and entering into a dialogue. It helps us to recognize the underlying needs, concerns, and fears that drive attitudes and behaviors, even despicable ones such as xenophobia or different forms of supremacism. We can strongly oppose and condemn the form while still exploring and acknowledging its deeper roots and looking for socially acceptable forms to channel it.

Focusing exclusively on fighting the manifestation will only strengthen it and fuel further polarization. If people feel their underlying needs, concerns, and fears are not recognized and heard from the start, these needs will become increasingly extreme in their manifestation. For the other side, this radicalization provides the reassuring confirmation that they were right in their initial rejection. As a consequence, polarization grows as a self-propelling dynamic, with people who formerly took a more neutral or moderate position also tending to one of the extremes.

It should also be clear that acknowledging the underlying needs will seldom help to open up the dialogue with people who have completely identified themselves with an extreme course. Letting go of their extreme position will mean for them nothing less than loss of face. They often thrive by stirring up polarization as it provides them with purpose, status, and recognition by the group they represent. Therefore, it is not really in their interest to find a sustainable solution for the underlying problem as it will mean giving up all these. However, it's good to realize that these extremes are only in a small percentage of people in any given position. It's therefore more important and fruitful to focus your attention on starting the exploratory dialogue with people who are more in the middle ground. They share the underlying issues but not necessarily the extreme solutions. Addressing the underlying needs of this group will also help to reduce the number of people holding extreme positions on this issue in the long term.

6.3.3 How to Find Common Ground: A Practical Model

I would like to introduce here a practical model based on the mutual gains approach,[2] which will enable you to take systematic, exploratory steps toward the underlying needs, concerns, and values in your search for common ground.

---

2 Roger Fisher, William L. Ury, and Bruce Patton, *Getting to Yes: Negotiating Agreement without Giving In* (New York: Penguin Books, 1983).

This model is especially relevant when two parties have become stuck in radically opposed positions, creating a seemingly unsolvable conflict. Your aim is therefore to gain a better understanding of both poles by shifting the dialogue away from positions and opinions and taking it to the deeper level of underlying needs and values. The model is depicted by two overlapping triangles as shown in figure 6.2. The overlapping area is called "The golden triangle."

The two triangles represent the positions of the two parties in conflict. They are transected by three levels of exchange: (1) on positions and opinions, (2) on needs and concerns, and (3) on values and goals. The entire process can be divided into six steps.

At the surface and most visible level (positions and opinions), the parties are completely opposed to each other, and the triangles do not overlap at all. The more they try to persuade each other, the more convinced each becomes that they are right, and the more they drift apart. **Step 1** is to articulate this tension and to pinpoint the areas of difference and disagreement, using neutral terms: "Which points do we seem to totally disagree on?"

Once you have accepted the opposing positions of the two parties for what they are, the next step is to explore the needs and concerns that drive both positions. This is **Step 2**, where the parties ask: "What is this divide really about?" "What is at stake?" "What are the underlying needs and concerns of each of the parties?" The answers should explore what the positions and opinions from Step 1 actually mean to each party. These can be very personal, like a need for recognition, a desire to be heard, or a concern with personal gain or status. The strong personal nature of needs and concerns makes them different from the more moral and abstract categories, values, and goals, that are on the next level down.

In the figure, you can see that at the level of needs and concerns, the triangles are starting to overlap: there is a common area in which solutions can be sought that can meet the needs and concerns of both parties. This is **Step 3**, which can be started by

Figure 6.2. The golden triangle

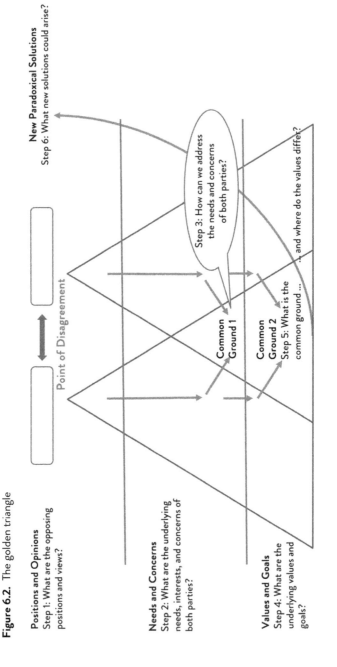

Positions and Opinions
Step 1: What are the opposing positions and views?

Needs and Concerns
Step 2: What are the underlying needs, interests, and concerns of both parties?

Values and Goals
Step 4: What are the underlying values and goals?

New Paradoxical Solutions
Step 6: What new solutions could arise?

Point of Disagreement

Step 3: How can we address the needs and concerns of both parties?

Common Ground 1

Common Ground 2
Step 5: What is the common ground ...

... and where do the values differ?

asking: "How can I reformulate or broaden my own position in such a way that it also accommodates the needs and concerns of the other party?"

Step 4 takes you to another level: that of the values and goals that the two parties uphold. The questions are "What values and goals are at the root of each party's views on this issue?" and "Which do they share and where do they differ?"

At this level, the overlapping section of the triangles becomes even larger, which is where you will find **Step 5**. Both parties should ask themselves: "What is the common ground from which we can look for a suitable solution?" In this step both parties can define the specifications and boundaries for a suitable solution, without the need to restrict themselves to a single option.

From these specifications new paradoxical solutions may be created that could look very different from the two initial positions: **Step 6**. You should ask yourself: "What new or even out-of-the-box solutions can be found to meet the commonly shared specifications?" The paradoxical solution chosen will be a new tangible manifestation of the shared values and needs. It is a both/and alternative to the initial two conflicting positions and therefore returns to the top of the diagram.

CASE STUDY: FRANK AND ESTHER

This process of digging deeper can be illustrated in a professional conflict. This example is about the working relationship between two individuals, but the same approach could be applied to two groups, teams, or organizations.

Frank heads the policy department of the city council. He is new in this role, and he has just received an important assignment from his director to investigate the impact of upcoming national legislation on both the community and the city council's processes. Frank asks Esther, a senior adviser in his team, to make an initial impact analysis of this major legislative change and to write an advisory report with a clear recommendation on what to do. The report needs to be finalized in three months.

Esther energetically sets to work and starts talking to the different stakeholders: officials at the ministry, experts from the city council and other government agencies, companies, and citizens. Her conversations bring up a whole series of new questions, and it becomes increasingly apparent that no one knows exactly how things will work out. The parties involved become more and more engaged in this topic and feel the need for further clarification and discussion. Since Esther has become the linchpin, they invite her to prepare and organize a roundtable. But what about that advisory report? Everyone agrees that it's far too premature for that; it is more sensible at this moment to clarify the matter further in a professional exchange process with all stakeholders.

Esther enthusiastically updates Frank, but he is not happy. This project is going completely in the wrong direction. "What do you mean by 'professional exchange process'?" He had clearly asked for an advisory report, and now one and a half months have passed with no progress. Esther is disappointed with this response. She lets it rest a few days before she tries to explain everything again to Frank, but she comes up against a brick wall; Frank is now clearly irritated and impatient. The more Esther talks about setting up a dialogue and building a forum, the more Frank focuses on the output of an advisory report. Esther is convinced that a report doesn't make any sense in this exploratory phase with so many unknowns. She strongly believes in the value of a dialogue process, both from a content and an engagement point of view. She tells her story to her stakeholders and is reinforced in her conviction that she is on the right track.

All further attempts to come to terms with Frank fail. All Frank and Esther end up doing is trying to convince each other that they are right. This only leads to more misunderstanding, distancing, and tension. The whole situation is deadlocked. Both admit that outside help is needed to get the conversation going again. They ask Gabrielle to act as mediator.

Step 1: Positions and Opinions. Gabrielle immediately realizes that no form of reconciliation or compromise is possible at the level of personal views and positions. The conversation has narrowed itself down to "we need a report" versus "we need a collaborative brainstorming process." It's important to leave behind this level of positions and take the discussion to a deeper level.

Step 2: Needs and Concerns. Gabrielle proceeds to the level of underlying needs and concerns and asks Frank why he thinks the report is so important. After an open conversation, the picture is clearer. Frank has a somewhat "blue," results-oriented style. He has been a successful project manager for many years, and the trademark of his success has been always delivering on time. In this case, Frank has two main needs and concerns. First, he is relatively new to his role and wants to prove himself. The request for advice has come from his director, and he would like to make a good impression by delivering a tangible result. The second reason is that Frank likes to keep everything under control, and he's afraid that the process will go in all directions. "Before you know it, you're having good conversations with everyone, but nothing is happening."

Talking to Esther, it is clear that she sees herself more as a "connector." That was also her success formula in previous complex assignments. Esther is very empathic and feels the stakeholders' need to unravel this complex issue together and to avoid recommending a direction without carefully thinking through all the consequences. She also feels the strong appeals of all parties for her to take responsibility for this process and to step into the role of process facilitator. It's often her pitfall that she is reluctant to say "no" and she ends up with too much on her plate.

Step 3: Common Ground 1. This offers some openings to get the conversation going again. How can Esther reassure Frank's concerns while still keeping the essence and strength of her process-based approach? Frank doesn't necessarily need a report, but he needs something with which to score points with his director, and the assurance that Esther is doing the right thing and not wasting her time chatting with everyone. Since Frank prefers concrete results, the best outcome would be tangible. Perhaps Esther could organize a well-prepared and effective meeting in the short term with all parties involved, to which she also invites Frank. Perhaps they could make an attractive summary report of the results of that meeting, or even better: a short, flashy video that Frank could share with his director. Or maybe Frank could invite the director to be present at the meeting and take care of the kickoff. In short, one form (an advisory report) is abandoned, and new forms can then be sought based on underlying needs and concerns.

From the other side, how could Frank support Esther to clearly delineate the scope and the expected outcomes of this process and to protect her own boundaries, dealing with the soaring expectations of the different stakeholders?

Step 4: Values and Goals. Gabrielle goes to the level of underlying values and goals. In her conversations with Frank and Esther, she noticed that they both care a lot about the city they work for and are eager to do something to help improve the lives of their fellow citizens. They both want a sustainable and comprehensive solution for the long term. Frank mainly wants to achieve this with an expert-driven approach and quick visible results to create momentum, while Esther fosters a bottom-up approach, where the necessary time is taken to build consensus.

Step 5: Common Ground 2. Frank and Esther had lost sight of their shared passion for a sustainable and comprehensive solution that directly benefits the city. In a joint session Gabrielle helps Esther and

Frank to return to their shared values and goals. This forms a strong basis to reconnect and resume cooperation.

Shared values and goals lay a foundation that is even broader than simply acknowledging and reassuring the individual needs and concerns of each party. Unearthing the underlying values and goals can make it clear that differences are often more on the level of the "how" than on the level of the "why." The "why" should always determine the "how."

Nevertheless, it's important to point out the differences in values and goals as well as the similarities. Not all of the parties' values and goals will be useful for finding common ground. In some cases, the conclusion might become inescapable that there is not enough common ground to be able to work together on a given issue.

Step 6: New Paradoxical Solutions. Finally, how can Esther and Frank translate these shared values and goals into a new direction and create a joint project that transcends the obvious solutions that both parties initially put forward? For example: why not organize a broader meeting, involving many more city stakeholders? Perhaps they could achieve a concrete and widely supported result through a structured participation process with residents and other stakeholders … something that might even be of interest to the press? Perhaps this will become an example for other cities of how to deal with these types of issues in a contemporary way. "Let's set a date!"

The example process is shown in figure 6.3.

It's not always easy to uncover the underlying common ground because the opposing views and positions demand all our attention and energy. But if we're willing to dig deeper, we might discover that there is much more common ground than expected. This applies just as much to struggles in partner relationships or to political polarization as to the workplace. For example, the radical left and radical right may be miles apart in their views and concerns,

Figure 6.3. The paradoxical process for Frank and Esther

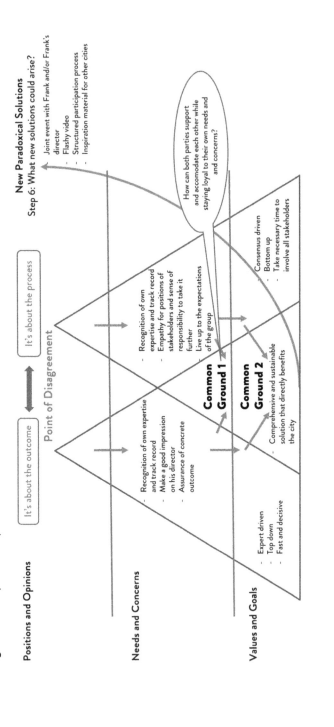

but at a deeper level they are driven by many of the same values, such as

- a sense of justice;
- the feeling that the hard-working citizen, who has to struggle to make ends meet, is not being heard by the political and economic elite;
- the need for a better quality of life and respect;
- the desire for moral revival; and
- a warm local community and sense of belonging.

It may be tempting to make the common goals and values more and more abstract so that they are acceptable to everyone. But in that case, they will remain meaningless principles with widely differing interpretations when put into practice. Everyone may want "peace on earth," "happiness and prosperity for all," "justice," and so on, but we all have a different interpretation of what these concepts mean. For example, for one person "conserving biodiversity" means more wildflowers in city parks, for another it means turning acres of cultivated land into a new wilderness.

A leader or coach should make those hidden polarities at the level of shared goals and values explicit, facilitating an incisive discussion based on concrete cases and examples. Once it is clear where the similarities and differences are, the process to recalibrate and reinvigorate this common purpose can begin.

KEY POINTS
- Every movement evokes its countermovement.
- Try not to cover up differences but hold an open dialogue about the heart of the matter.
- Be aware that you might need to translate from one "language" to the other.

- Recognize in yourself what you see in others, especially the things that you may not like.
- Focus your attention on conducting the dialogue with people who are more in the middle ground, who share the underlying issues but haven't yet completely identified themselves with an extreme solution.
- Go beyond the positions and opinions at the surface to the underlying needs, concerns, values, and goals in order to find common ground and a both/and solution.
- Sometimes it is difficult to facilitate this process while being a stakeholder in it at the same time. A neutral mediator can help formulate the underlying needs of the parties involved.

6.4 Paradoxical Interventions: Doing the Opposite to What We Want to Achieve

Many road accidents involving younger drivers are caused by texting and social media use while driving. In my home country, Belgium, all sorts of well-intended government campaigns have been launched to emphasize the dangers and discourage this behavior. Over the years, these campaigns have tried different persuasion strategies, from preachy messages to more playful but often cheesy slogans, but because these didn't really work, grim images and videos were subsequently being used to illustrate the harsh consequences of this behavior. The question remains whether all these dissuasive campaigns have the desired effect. They certainly don't work for me! Although I am well aware of the dangers of being distracted while driving, I'm convinced that I'm an exception to the rule and can definitely combine both activities at the same time without running undue risks; this message isn't meant for me but for everyone else.

So how could a campaign effectively change this behavior? As a campaign designer, you could think of using even stronger, more shocking images. Maybe an image of a ripped-off hand holding a smartphone with a half-finished message on the display saying "I can't wait to hold you in my arms again" would force people to change their behavior. Or would this also quickly slip their minds after the initial shock?

There's an excellent YouTube video about a Belgian driving school[3] that shows a completely different approach. In the video, you see a straight-faced driving instructor explaining to the novice young driver that nowadays, to pass your driving test, you not only have to be able to drive but to demonstrate that you can drive and text at the same time. We then see a number of young people at the wheel, with their smartphones in their hands, typing a text message as instructed by the driving instructor while steering between cones and doing all sorts of maneuvers. This is a total disaster, and the tension and fear in the faces of the young drivers is plain to see, until one of them indignantly exclaims, "But, sir, what you're asking us to do is completely irresponsible!" Exactly what the driving school was aiming for.

6.4.1 Increase the Imbalance

This is a typical example of a paradoxical intervention. Such interventions are paradoxical because the action seems to be the opposite of the goal. If a system is out of balance, the straightforward approach would be to restore balance from the outside by introducing the missing pole. The system, however, will often oppose this and, in a polarizing movement, will shift even more toward the dominant pole. Conversely, a paradoxical approach will make the imbalance even greater by reinforcing the dominant pole, with the expectation that the system will be forced to rebalance itself. The effect is similar

---

3 Responsible Young Drivers Belgium, "SMS au volant: impossible?," 6 May 2012, https://www.youtube.com/watch?v=p7RnH5W_NrY.

to a vaccine. Since the body's systems are self-regulating, it counter-acts the injected stimulus with new antibodies.

For an interpersonal example: You ask someone to do something for you, and even though they agree, they put it aside. You can get angry at them, but this might make them even more reluctant. But if you say, in a neutral tone, "Okay, no problem. I'll do it myself or I'll ask someone else," then there's a good chance that the other person will say, "No, that's okay. I'll do it."

Every change process involves resistance. Those who oppose the change will find lots of arguments for resisting it. Some arguments will make sense, and others will be beside the point, inappropriate, or just plain weak. Much of the resistance may be on an emotional level, not a rational one. We could enter into discussion with them, with the best of intentions, and provide counterarguments, but this approach has the opposite effect; the more we push, the more the other will resist.

Change management practice shows us that it is much more helpful to make the other person feel free to express their concerns and fears, to listen attentively without judgment and to take these concerns and fears seriously. But sometimes it may work even better to go along with their reasoning and take it even a step fur-ther. "Maybe you're right and this change is not a good idea at all, and the way we do things now is actually just fine." This often triggers the self-correcting mechanism, and the person will start to back down from their point of view: "No, the way we're doing things now is not good either." Suddenly, a real dialogue starts taking place.

In complex systems, processes are not always as linear as we would like them to be. Sometimes we have to steer to the left in order to end up on the right.

We are probably more familiar with the counterproductive effects of well-intended, straightforward interventions. For example, the more we impose strict control mechanisms out of lack of trust, the more people will look for ways to get around the rules. Fortunately, with a paradoxical intervention you can also use this principle to your advantage: the more explicitly we trust people, the more difficult they will find it to betray that trust.

There are many examples of this dynamic in daily life:

- The more stability we create, the more people are willing to change. Stability gives a feeling of safety, which is what we need in order to dare to step off the familiar path.
- The more we're not allowed to do something, the more we want to do it. As soon as something is allowed, it loses some of its appeal and can even become boring.
- The Streisand effect: the more we emphasize that news is very confidential, the more the message will spread.

6.4.2 Handle with Caution

Using paradoxical interventions doesn't come naturally, and it's sometimes even frightening because something might go wrong. If you encourage your teenager to light up another cigarette (rather than preach about how bad smoking is), this will not necessarily encourage them to think about their own health. Paradoxical interventions don't always work, and sometimes it's better to go from A to B in one straight line. When a house is on fire, the firefighters do not set more fires to encourage the blaze to self-correct. If you discover misconduct somewhere in your organization, you should not encourage the malpractice in the hope of instigating the self-correcting capability of your organization; you should intervene immediately. Sometimes we need to alternate between steering in a straight line and going in the opposite direction, or even combine the two, depending on what works best in a given situation. For example, to speed up the change process in your organization, you may have to juggle between pushing things forward and applying the brakes.

In any case, paradoxical interventions should be applied in small doses and with a certain amount of subtlety and caution. If you use them too frequently or too explicitly, they become transparent tricks and undermine your credibility. A paradoxical intervention clearly contains a manipulative and strategic element: I have a hidden agenda and am not completely open about my motives, which puts me on unequal footing with the other people involved. They can end up feeling manipulated and not taken seriously. If you choose a paradoxical intervention strategy, it's only fair to explain afterward what you were doing: "If I had tried to convince you, we might never have agreed, but when I sided with you, you concluded yourselves that change was needed. I admit that I was being a little sneaky, but it all worked out in the end."

6.4.3 Build in Self-Correcting Mechanisms

To prevent organizations from getting off track, we need to ensure a good balance between force and counterforce.

Here's a tip I received from a wise and seasoned government official: "It works best to have a liberal policy (for example: the provision of social services) carried out by more conservative officials (who will more strictly apply the rules and make sure there is no abuse of the regulation), and vice versa: to have a conservative policy (with emphasis on control and fraud detection) carried out by more liberal officials (who will uphold the policy with more feeling and empathy). This is an effective way to ensure that the policies don't go too far in one direction, causing unwanted side effects."

The idea is to build in a self-correcting mechanism. This method could work in any type of organization. For example, by having enough people with a background in humanities or social sciences in your big data team, you can make sure that the essence (i.e., providing insights) doesn't get lost amid all the awesome technical innovations. In an extremely operational and hectic environment, make sure you have plenty of thinkers in addition to the adrenaline-addicted doers; the thinkers may come up with structural solutions by which a number of the current pitfalls can be avoided. And enrich your research or policy department with passionate doers to keep things moving. However, give them enough space to take action so that they don't get swallowed up by the mainstream or become demotivated out of frustration.

6.4.4 Adopt Countercyclical Thinking

Steering in a single direction clearly has its limitations. Dare to think countercyclically. In times of economic crisis, many organizations start cutting costs, placing innovation projects on the back burner. They stop hiring new personnel even though this is the time when a lot more talent can be found on the labor market than in times of economic growth. As soon as the economy starts to pick up again, these organizations will not have a new range of products lined up with which they could seize a large chunk of the market, nor will they have people with the skills required for tomorrow's market. In fact, it's better to turn this logic around: invest when the market is going down and be critical of costs when things are going up. Warren Buffet became rich by daring to invest countercyclically. You need vision, courage and, of course, a good sense of timing. Many will think you've lost your mind when you do this, and you will need to be able to withstand the pressures of the mainstream, but the results in the longer term are often more favorable.

KEY POINTS

- Paradoxical interventions are strategies that use the opposite action to achieve the effect you want.
- Intervention 1: Instead of fighting against an undesirable attitude or behavior, push it even further to encourage the other side to self-correct with a balanced solution.
- Intervention 2: Sometimes you have to steer to the left to go to the right.
- Intervention 3: Strengthen the self-correcting capability of organizations by ensuring a good balance of force and counterforce.
- Intervention 4: Dare to think and act countercyclically.
- Combine linear and nonlinear approaches.
- Use paradoxical interventions in moderation and with care. Be open afterward about your paradoxical intervention and explain why you used it.

WHERE PEOPLE AND ORGANIZATIONS COME TOGETHER

In this chapter, I will explore how to help people thrive within an organization, and by doing so maximize their contributions to a flourishing organization. I will focus on three main questions: How can you convert something that initially looks like an undesirable dark side into something positive? How can you make diversity work to your advantage? How can you create space for creativity and innovation?

7.1 The Power of What Is Hidden in the Shadows

Self-doubt, envy, cowardice, shyness, superiority, passivity, greed, aggression, laziness, selfishness, anger, depression … These are all negative traits that we feel ashamed of, especially in our professional lives. We tend to deny that we have anything to do with them, even to ourselves. These are usually characteristics that we exclusively assign to others. On the outside we only show our shiny side: of course we are active, outgoing, confident, generous, driven, daring, energetic, etc. Even if we pretend that we don't possess any negative traits and even if we only show the bright and gleaming versions of ourselves, these undesirable traits are always looming in the background because they are an integral part of who we are as human beings. We call these unwelcome aspects of ourselves "shadow sides," not because they are sinister or evil, but because we keep them out of sight.[1] Growing up, we learned to keep these blemishes covered. We are encouraged to imagine that chaos and disruption would arise if these dark sides of our characters were given some leeway.

7.1.1 Personal Shadow Sides

However, it takes a tremendous amount of energy to try to deny or cover up these negative traits, energy that goes to waste and could have been spent more productively. It's like there is an elephant in the room demanding everyone's attention, but nobody wants to talk about it. These shadow sides are often fundamental driving forces that set people into action, so they're also important sources of energy that are not being taken advantage of. We must give this locked up energy some space and attention because completely ignoring it leads to stress, deep discomfort, self-alienation, and finally to burnout, illness, or depression. Inner tension can also build up so high that the volcano erupts uncontrollably now and then to release the built-up pressure, causing damage along the way.

Does this mean that we should let our shadow sides run wild? That would be out of balance in the other direction, but there are some good ways to deal with them. Here are two steps you can take:

RECOGNIZE AND ACCEPT THE SHADOW SIDES
OF YOURSELF AND OF OTHERS

A very liberating first step is to recognize that these uncomfortable, socially undesirable sides do exist and that every one of us struggles with them. Creating a safe atmosphere and space where

---

1 See also the work of Connie Zweig, who builds further on the Jungian concept of "shadow." For example: Connie Zweig and Jeremiah Abrams, eds., *Meeting the Shadow: The Hidden Power of the Dark Side of Human Nature* (New York: Jeremy P. Tarcher, 1991).

people can share what they really feel, without being judged or looked down upon by others, can give rise to a liberating sense of recognition. This is not so difficult to put into practice. If people who are highly regarded in the group or who act as role models put themselves in a vulnerable position and admit to, for example, sometimes feeling uncomfortable about recommending a new product to clients, to struggling with the workload, or to feeling scared when speaking in front of a large group of people, many others may recognize their own struggles. More and more books are being published that revisit and revalue qualities that were previously considered to be signs of weakness, such as sensitivity,[2] introversion,[3] imperfection,[4] vulnerability,[5] and slowness.[6] These books often become bestsellers because they strike a chord by bringing up aspects that readers recognize in themselves but haven't been able to own up to or exhibit.

People are nevertheless still afraid of admitting their shadow sides. They fear a negative reaction like rejection, ridicule, criticism, or even abhorrence. In practice, this fear is frequently unfounded. People are often praised for their openness, honesty, and vulnerability, which are valued as signs of courage and leadership. It takes guts to share your struggles. When admired role models do this, the effect is even greater. However, the reaction of course depends to a large degree on the level of openness and safety of a specific culture.

---

2 Elaine Aron, *The Highly Sensitive Person: How to Thrive When the World Overwhelms You* (New York: Harmony 1996).

3 Susan Cain, *Quiet: The Power of Introverts in a World That Can't Stop Talking* (London: Penguin Books, 2012).

4 Brené Brown, *The Gifts of Imperfection: Let Go of Who You Think You're Supposed to Be and Embrace Who You Are* (Center City, MN: Hazelden, 2010).

5 Brené Brown, *Daring Greatly: How the Courage to Be Vulnerable Transforms the Way We Live, Love, Parent, and Lead* (London: Penguin Books, 2012).

6 Haemin Sunim and Katy Spiegel, *The Things You Can See Only When You Slow Down: How to Be Calm in a Busy World* (New York: Penguin Books, 2018); Maggie Berg and Barbara K. Seeber, *The Slow Professor: Challenging the Culture of Speed in the Academy* (Toronto: University of Toronto Press, 2017).

People in charge are also often reluctant to allow the expression of strong emotions as they fear opening a Pandora's box and losing control; what has up to now stayed safely hidden in the shadows might spread. Anger, for example, is a very powerful emotion that can be frightening and threatening for many people. A manager confronted with anger after a reorganization may fear that this anger will be contagious, disruptive, and make the whole situation spin out of control. But perhaps it is the other way around: as long as these shadow sides remain hidden there's no way of controlling them. At least if they're out in the open, they can be discussed and addressed.

TRANSFORM SHADOW SIDES INTO POSITIVE FORMS OF ENERGY

A second step you can take is to give a positive purpose to these shadow sides and to use their underlying power in a constructive way. We tend to focus on their negative manifestations and use negative terms to describe these, but we need to find their essentially positive core. Doubt, fear, and cowardice are signs of caution; selfishness is an extreme form of self-esteem and self-respect; underneath aggression lies a fighting spirit, and so on. The challenge is to find a more positive, socially acceptable, and manageable form to constructively express the shadow side's powerful energy. For example, if you consider failure an opportunity to reflect and learn, it can be a rich source of personal and professional growth; hesitation can be a counterbalance to risky decisions or arrogant behavior; a big ego and the need to show off can be drivers of socially beneficial achievements.

7.1.2 Organizational Competence in Dealing with Shadow Sides

Let me first share an anecdote with you. For many years, I worked for an international consultancy firm. The culture was very performance driven, both financially and in delivering results for clients.

There was a strong meritocracy where there was no place for poor performance. This might sound like a ruthless and competitive environment, but it didn't feel that way. There was a pleasantly open and amicable atmosphere at the workplace. This was largely because it was very clear and transparent to everyone what was expected; hidden agendas and political games were rather rare.

I was also for some time a member of the supervisory board of an organization for personal and spiritual development. The culture there was the complete opposite: love, peace, harmony, no pressure, everyone could be themselves, and there was a lot of hugging. However outwardly caring, open, and gentle this organization might seem on the surface, it held some strong taboos. The first was money. Money was considered a necessary evil, to be disdained rather than desired. You were expected to make a voluntary financial contribution that felt right for you. The other taboo was judgment. Judging others was frowned upon. Instead, everyone should accept and value other people and things as they are. However, in this organization almost every discussion turned out to be about money ("hmmm, this voluntary contribution is not high enough" or "they make more money than I do"). There was also a lot of envy and competition below the surface smiles and hugs ("I'm doing more than they are" or "I'm spiritually much more developed").

The more explicitly we ignore or repress basic human drives and needs, the more influence they will have on organizational culture. They just go underground and become more elusive but no less real. It would be more effective to acknowledge them and find way to express them in a socially desirable way.

Organizations have to deal not only with the specific shadow sides of individuals but also with these collective shadow sides and taboos. In an organization where self-confidence and "being in control" are the norm, people tend to hide their feelings of insecurity and doubt, leading to undesirable outcomes. For example, people may think that it's better to make promises they can't keep rather than admit that they are unable to do something; that it's better to cover up mistakes with even graver errors rather than to report the mistakes right away; that it's better to stick to a certain course, even when they know it won't lead anywhere, rather than to admit they were wrong. Here are some suggestions for how to deal with collective shadow sides.

DARE TO NAME AND TALK ABOUT THE SHADOW SIDES OF THE ORGANIZATION

I write "dare" because it is taboo even to mention these hidden and forbidden sides. The unspoken rule is this: "In our organization this doesn't exist, and we don't talk about it." It therefore takes courage to speak up; by mentioning the taboo, you run the risk that others will distance themselves from you, even if they know exactly what you're talking about. True leadership is required to break that deafening silence and set an example. Speaking from your heart will often inspire others to come forward and follow your example, which can turn the culture around. The first step is to recognize that the shadow sides exist and can play a dominant role in the organization.

It's also not easy to identify these shadow sides because they are often disguised as their opposite. For example: What looks like a macho culture where everyone parades around and shows off is often a cover-up for fear. Acting tough and trying to appear invincible is in fact a way of dealing with fear. Here's another one: At schools where all students wear the same uniform to promote a sense of equality, students feel a greater need to distinguish themselves from others, even if this is simply by using small accessories.

It is best to speak about these hidden cultural features in a neutral but clear manner. Try to describe it in factual and behavioral terms so that everyone can recognize it, without charging it with emotions, playing it down with euphemisms, or making moral judgments. For example, "not giving clear feedback to each other on performance and behavior" instead of "soft" or "mushy." Finally, create a safe environment where staff members can talk freely without the fear that their honesty will later be held against them.

BE CAREFUL NOT TO CREATE OR STRENGTHEN ANY SHADOW SIDES

If we become too obsessed with eradicating the shadow sides, this will become counterproductive. It will create an atmosphere of fear and will further strengthen the impact of the shadow sides' energy. We can fight with all our might against a negative manifestation of a shadow side – such as integrity issues – and apply strict rules and strong moral taboos, but this will create an atmosphere of insecurity and suspicion for everyone (and not just the few for whom it was necessary). "Can I take the leftover food from the lunch meeting home for the kids, or would that be considered a breach of integrity now?" What we want to vigorously eradicate instead becomes an omnipresent theme of daily work life.

It is important not to approach a shadow side from a morally judgmental point of view; shame and guilt will make people try to cover up and repress their shadow sides even more, which lends them more weight. The only thing we can do is address the negative impact of certain *behavior* on other people, never the underlying *intention* someone might have had. People shouldn't be ashamed of their intentions either because that's often part of who they are. In the context of work, it is not up to us to morally judge the characters of people. We can only address the behaviors and the negative effects of the shadow side on others.

PROVIDE AN OUTLET FOR COLLECTIVE SHADOW SIDES

Knowing that each corporate culture creates its own shadow sides (as the repressed opposites of its values), you have to make sure that this shadow side's energy can also be vented within the organization. For example, if you demand a lot from people in terms of engagement, effort, and performance, you should also provide ways for them to relax or to step out and switch off while they're at work. You shouldn't expect them to take care of this themselves in their free time and justify that they are paid for working hard. As a good employer, you should at least think of ways to give the necessary space to this "just relax and be yourself" side, whether individuals need this space in the form of yoga classes, dance sessions, or leisurely activities during office hours.

FIND POSITIVE WAYS TO UTILIZE THE SHADOW SIDE POTENTIAL

Shadow sides are intrinsic and contain vital sources of energy. You should aim to channel this energy in a positive way by turning it into something acceptable, constructive, and even productive. For example, you can place a person in a role where their shadow side's energy can be released in a controlled manner, coaching this person on how to set boundaries for this energy and use it to their advantage. Fierce aggressiveness can help to conquer a new market; shyness can be converted into an approachable, unpretentious way of selling, putting the client and the client's needs first.

7.1.3 Being Authentic and Open

Shadow sides are part of being real and authentic. It's often hard for us to be open about our deeper motives and intentions because this makes us feel vulnerable. Fear is the primary motive here. We don't want to fully expose ourselves and fall prey to the judgment and criticism of others. We're also ashamed of our real motives and feelings when they don't conform to the socially desirable norms and values. As a result, we may construct narratives that burst with positive, highly regarded motives.

THE WHOLE STORY

Initially, it may seem comforting and safe to construct an embellished story to justify our plans, but that's only an illusion. Not being open and honest about all our motives is counterproductive because by avoiding talking about something, we draw attention to it and encourage resistance and cynicism. People tend to listen the most to what's left unsaid. When we hear such tales, we immediately sense that something is fishy, and we focus on what the storyteller is trying to hide. It's therefore much better to tell the whole story right away and to mention all our motives, both those that will be viewed in a positive light and those that may be frowned upon.

For example, the fact that clients or citizens are expected to do more and more themselves is not only based on positive motives, such as wanting to encourage empowerment, self-reliance, or participation; it's also based on the simple motive of saving money. Instead of only telling the one-sided, positive story about empowerment, it's also important to be open and honest about the money-saving side. People won't like hearing this message, but it is open and clear, so they can understand and process it, make up their minds, and even accept its rationale. They will often appreciate the openness and sincerity because this will make them feel like they're being taken seriously and are regarded as equal partners, not as children unable to cope with the whole story.

BEING DISARMINGLY HONEST

My banker once asked me at the end of December to postpone a transaction (transferring a significant amount of money to another bank) until January because "it would be better for his operational and financial targets." I found this an extremely forthright request. His openness made me feel like he was sharing his problem with me, and I could empathize with him and understand his situation. If he had made up some story about rescheduling this transaction to the next fiscal year as being in my best interest, I would have become suspicious. And if I had found out afterward, I would have felt manipulated and stopped doing business with him. However, a basic level of trust was needed for him to be able to ask me such a question.

This also means letting go of the myth that leaders should always be strong and determined and should never show any doubt. It can actually be useful for leaders to express their dilemmas and to share them with the entire organization. This openness can mobilize people into thinking along and taking ownership to tackle the problems together. Here, too, there needs to be a basis of trust. In a highly polarized situation, where every word becomes a weapon for the other side, this is of course not usually possible.

GIVING BAD NEWS

The same applies to giving bad news. Revealing small chunks of an ugly fact – with the aim of limiting the damage and avoiding the risk of a big shock – is destructive. If something has gone wrong somewhere, people will not rest to get to the bottom of the matter. And what is more detrimental to trust than to be forced to admit new revelations of an unpleasant fact under pressure from others? It's better to drop the bomb and let people start to come to terms with the damage immediately rather than to release bad news after bad news, leaving everyone wondering if and when it will ever end, damaging the trust that had once been built up.

KEY POINTS

- Admit that shadow sides exist instead of denying them. Identify, acknowledge, and talk about them openly and without judgment.
- Never judge someone's intention, only their behavior.
- Convert the energy that is locked up in our shadow sides into something positive.
- Provide an outlet for the shadow sides that are created by the organization.
- Communicate openly and honestly about all the motives behind your policies or plans, both the lofty and the prosaic.

7.2 How Diversity Can Help Achieve Better Results

In this section I want to approach diversity from the perspective of organizational performance rather than from an equity and social justice point of view. Therefore, I want to use a more general concept of diversity that goes beyond typical categories such as gender, age, nationality, race, sexual orientation, or religion. In this section, diversity is also about differences in vision, working style, values, beliefs, and approaches, often called deep-level diversity. In contrast surface-level diversity, deep-level diversity includes characteristics that are not visibly distinguishable. The key question is this: How can we bring together radically different ways and styles of working to achieve better results?

Usually, the issue of diversity in organizations is focused on the typical discrimination categories above. It's about equality in treatment and opportunities. This kind of diversity is just part of good employment practice and of moral and legal obligations; it should no longer require discussion. Many organizations today fully subscribe to the principles of equality and inclusion and take measures to ensure it in daily practice.

However, the traditional approach to diversity is quite superficial. It's often limited to the introduction and fulfillment of certain diversity quotas, and that's it. Organizations rarely asked afterward if we have achieved true diversity in our team or organization. Do these "diverse" people really have a different and potentially enriching approach or view? Or do we select people who have the external characteristics of the target group (gender, age, skin color, etc.) but who otherwise resemble ourselves in many ways and fit seamlessly into the existing way of thinking? Do we try to assimilate these "diverse" people into the mainstream as quickly as possible to smoothly iron out all the differences? Real diversity should be about valuing and encouraging differences and using their complementary nature to come to better strategies and decisions.

Deep diversity raises some fundamental questions and challenges: Are we really open to what makes others different, and do we really want to use the power of diversity? Is diversity a necessary evil, or could it actually be advantageous? Are differences and diversity actually desirable in a team or organization that needs to work like a well-oiled machine? Isn't it better and easier to employ people who have the same approach?

7.2.1 How Diversity Can Work Positively or Lead to Tension and Conflict

The discussion about diversity in organizations should focus on whether it's useful or not useful to bring together different, and even opposing, views, approaches, and styles. From a paradoxical perspective, a diversity policy should make differences explicit, with the aim of using tensions productively to achieve better results, rather than smoothing out the differences. The productive confrontation of different perspectives will often ensure a more balanced and integrated approach; it will urge people to go beyond the obvious and search for innovative solutions. Done right, this can significantly increase the effectiveness and strength of a team or organization. Done wrong, it could waste the energy of a team or organization on irritations, tensions, and conflicts, causing everything to grind to a halt. Let's look at two examples of how diversity without any accompanying measures can easily go awry.

FINDING BALANCE INSIDE THE PRISON SYSTEM

In a fascinating article entitled "The Paradox of Social Safety,"[7] organizational psychologist and change management expert Heleen Lieffering describes an important polarity in the Dutch prison system and how to deal with it. There are two opposing styles among the prison officers who are in daily contact with prisoners: one

---

7 Published in Dutch as chapter 6 in *Zorg voor zin! Leiderschap en zingeving*, ed. Adriaan Bekman (Assen: Van Gorcum, 2013).

showing understanding and trust, and the other applying general rules and power. In every work team studied, there was a mix of people of both styles. In Lieffering's words:

> The officers with a more lenient style are viewed as very indulgent, showing prisoners lots of empathy and believing that a good relationship helps to create a safe environment. The officers with a more restrictive style are thought to believe that safety can only be guaranteed if everyone follows the rules and protocols in the same way. The fact that a team comprises both types of officers, and thus both approaches, brings about misunderstandings and frustration: A prisoner, who is suddenly not allowed to do something that they were allowed to do the day before, might get angry. Would it not be much clearer for the prisoner if they worked the same way? The current mix also leads to a lot of tension among prison officers and to major safety and security risks. It seems to be a matter of aligning the two approaches, but it's not that simple.

This polarity between showing understanding for the individual and laying down general rules is a fundamental one. It emerges in many roles that work with people, such as teachers, parents, service desk operators, healthcare workers, insurance claims officers, and line managers. But in prisons, this polarity is all the more relevant and a good balance all the more important because of the direct security risks involved. Both a too lenient and a too strict approach can create significant risks.

In her research, Lieffering discovered that there were also large pendulum-like shifts in prison policies: from a high degree of freedom and independence to a strong tendency for power and control. Whenever the undesired negative effects of one policy became too prominent, the pendulum would swing to the other side. Prison management therefore also faces the challenge of finding the right balance between being strict and showing empathy.

A creative combination or a new synthesis (something like "empathetic strictness" or "strict empathy") that would be supported by all prison officers looks very attractive, but this might be asking too much. It would already be a big step forward if the officers were more aware of their own approach, that of their colleagues, and the advantages and disadvantages of both.

"HARDLINERS" AND "SOFTIES": THE CHALLENGE OF GOOD SERVICE

I identified a very similar phenomenon in the social services department of a large municipality I worked with. In the teams that assessed applications for social welfare allowance, there were two different styles. Some colleagues took a more formal and procedural approach and focused on strictly applying the rules and doing thorough background checks; others were more people-oriented, personal, and empathetic, focusing on trust and support. If we had plotted all team members along an axis, we would have seen a wide variation, with quite a few people at both ends of the spectrum. In black-and-white terms, there was a tension between "hardliners" and "softies."

These conflicting approaches not only caused a high degree of inefficiency (lots of corrective action and communication back and forth) but also, and above all, great frustration for individual citizens, who no longer knew what to expect, and therefore felt like they no longer had control of their own lives. For example, an individual who applied for social benefits was allowed to pass through by a "softie" but was then sent back by a "hardliner" in a subsequent step of the application process based on a different assessment of the same case.

The relative influence of "hardliners" and "softies" has shifted from one side to the other along with the political climate. In the past, the political emphasis was more on social responsibility and care, with the "softies" flourishing and setting the tone. Subsequently, the political climate focused more on control and on detecting fraud. As a result, the natural "hardliners" felt even more convinced of their approach. But when the political pendulum starts to swing toward the other side, the "softies" will once again have the wind in their sails.

Due to these differences, customer satisfaction with social services was very low, and complaints were hailing down on the ombudsmen. This reflected negatively on the municipality's credibility and became a priority on the political agenda. The municipality quickly created an integrated plan to increase customer satisfaction, but the majority of the actions and investments described in this plan focused on tangible technicalities, such as longer opening hours and better telephone service. Strangely enough, the crux of the matter ("two different approaches under one roof") was not addressed or discussed. In fact, it was not even on the radar until we took a closer look at the issue and spoke with individual citizens about their specific complaints. This is not surprising because organizations often don't know how to deal with these less tangible aspects, and line managers feel uncomfortable and unsure about how to talk to their staff about more elusive and sensitive behavioral aspects. Different approaches are a source of regular irritation, but they are rarely openly discussed. People accept the situation as an unavoidable fact of life. However, without explicitly addressing the differences in approach, all other investments in better service provision will not pay off.

A CHALLENGE IN NEED OF A NEW APPROACH

So what's the best way to tackle this challenge? Should the organization formulate a uniform and consistent approach, make it applicable to all staff members, and train them in it? Perhaps not ... The idea of asking everyone to be equally strict or empathetic does not take into account the specificity of each situation. There are clearly situations (and clients) where applying control and being strict is much more important than showing empathy and trust, and vice versa. And is it possible or even desirable to completely change people's natural style? It's certainly not very motivating or satisfying to have to try to be someone else.

To make this work, the first and most crucial step is to uncover and explicitly name the different approaches and to recognize their equal importance and strength. Depending on the context, different and even opposing approaches will be required, and you will need both in your organization to be able to easily adapt to different situations and changing circumstances. But it will take more than that to turn diversity into a real advantage.

7.2.2 The Growth Model for Making Diversity Work

The following growth model can help you turn different styles or approaches within a team or organization into something positive that will boost results, process efficiency, customer satisfaction, and staff motivation. It doesn't consist of seven magic steps that will lead straight to paradise, but rather of elements that belong to a gradual and iterative process.

1. SELF-AWARENESS
Make people aware of their own preferred style, of the impact it has on others and on work. Once people know the strengths and limitations of their style, they will have more control over the undesired effects. They will be more able to consciously adapt (soften or intensify) their style to situations that require a different approach and be able to avoid extremes and polarization.

2. A COMMON LANGUAGE
Learn to identify and talk about differences in approach and style, but be careful that people don't start categorizing and labeling others in a binary way as this actually evokes polarization and pushes people with a moderate approach to identify themselves with extreme positions. It can help to constantly think in different shades of gray rather than in

a bipolar world of black and white. It's also important to indicate the situational nature of a particular position. We're not always A or B in all circumstances; our position can change significantly depending on the situation. To physically demonstrate this, you could draw a line on the floor representing the continuum between the two poles and invite people to stand on it and explore together whether certain situations cause them to shift their position (see also the team constellation exercise on p. 254). It's all about creating a common language to enable people to talk about their differences in a nonjudgmental way so that they can refer to them when irritation or friction arises.

3. A COMMON GOAL

Team members can have different views on the "how," but there should be a clear common understanding of the "why" and the "what." It's therefore crucial to regularly keep the underlying purpose of the work alive in team meetings (see also section 6.3.3 about finding a common ground). In the social services case, it might be something like "to give people the responsibility, the confidence, and the means to build their own lives and not be dependent on social welfare." How the organization can best achieve that goal may strongly vary from one client to another: Does a direct and even confrontational approach work best with this person, or is it more appropriate to reduce anxiety and rebuild self-confidence? Or could this situation use an effective mix of both?

4. THE STRENGTH OF OPPOSITE STYLES

Encourage people to recognize the values and strengths of approaches that are opposite to their own. In other words, challenge people to look deeper than well-known stereotypes and caricatures which emphasize the extremes, and beyond familiar negative labels such as "bureaucratic" or "softie." They could, for example, ask themselves: In which situations is this style useful? What are appropriate and comfortable ways to put it into practice?

For example, is it also possible to be strict and critical in an empathetic and friendly way?

5. STEPPING OUTSIDE OUR COMFORT ZONE

Motivate people to experiment and play around with an opposite style, but at all times with respect for their own authenticity and individuality. You could ask questions like these: How can you shift slightly toward being "stricter" or being more "empathetic" without trying to be someone you're not? What happens when you do this? How do others react? Do they really find you a bully or a softie, or not as much as you thought they would? This means encouraging people to stretch themselves a little, but without crossing their own boundaries or denying who they really are.

6. SWITCHING BETWEEN STYLES AND COMBINING THEM

Encourage people to broaden their palette of styles and to switch between being strict and empathetic depending on the situation (Strategy 4 of the Polarity Wheel). This can also lead to the creation of new combinations of styles such as "strict empathy" or "empathetic strictness" (Strategies 6 and 7 of the Polarity Wheel). We can all think of a teacher we had at school who was extremely strict in applying certain rules, but once these rules were established, they could be very gentle and understanding. There was usually more respect for these types of teachers than the ones who were too lenient or too severe (where it was great fun to misbehave as soon as they turned their backs to the class). However, in order to successfully integrate both poles, one first needs to differentiate between the two and experience each one on its own.

7. COMPLEMENTARITY

Make it normal practice for people to ask others for help and to make maximum use of their complementary qualities when their own style might not be the most suitable. Seeking complementarity should not be seen as a sign of weakness but of strength, and the notion of complementarity should be embedded in the company culture. Allocate roles and responsibilities to people based on their strengths. Forget about the idea that everyone should be able to do everything. Instead, assign specific clients, dossiers, or projects to team members who have a natural talent for dealing with the particularities of the case. For example, clients (in the broad sense of the word) who need clarity and guidance will benefit more from a strict style than a more accommodating style.

The polarity of being strict/lenient is just an example. This growth model also applies, of course, to all other polarities that can exist in a team: "hunters" versus "farmers" in a sales team, the content-focused versus the presentation-focused in a team of marketers, or high-volume workers versus meticulously accurate workers in a team that handles insurance claims.

FINDING THE RIGHT TONE

This is undoubtedly a very sensitive process, and finding the right positioning and tone are crucial to make it work. Here are some practical tips:

- **Neutral and nonjudgmental approach**: Talking about different styles is a sensitive subject that can trigger many emotions and make people feel personally attacked. Many of these styles can be traced back to deeply rooted values and beliefs and are part of a person's basic sense of identity. This is why it's important to start this process in a nonjudgmental way and to create a safe environment in which to speak freely and experiment.
- **Acknowledge mutual irritations without sweeping them under the rug or stirring them up**: State things as they are, clearly but tactfully. Being nonjudgmental does not mean that the feelings of resistance, disapproval and even disgust toward the other style

should not be mentioned. Ignoring these negative feelings only reinforces them and feeds an undercurrent of tension.

- **Bring the team to a higher level**: This process shouldn't be used as a means of quickly solving a problem but as an impetus to take your team to a higher level of performance. Team members will learn to recognize and name polarities in this process as well as to talk about their own and each other's styles and behavior. If team members learn to apply this to one specific polarity, they will also be able to apply it to others. The learning process will make people more aware, flexible, and agile as individuals and as a team.

7.2.3 Organize Your Own Opposition

Strong leaders who have a clear vision and are very determined need to be surrounded by equally strong people who can provide the necessary criticism, opposition, and counterbalance. However, this doesn't often happen in practice. Assertive leaders can be quite intimidating and their verbal skills very convincing. People need to be pretty confident to stand up to them, and who wants to risk being knocked down? Standing up to strong leaders also takes a tremendous amount of energy, especially when people consider their (hierarchical, contractual, economic, social, or emotional) position of dependency. "Will the leader see my criticism as a lack of motivation, dedication, and guts, or even as a betrayal?" "Won't this hurt our relationship and my career prospects?" Going along with such leaders is much less of a risk. It is easier to think: "It's *their* decision and responsibility, and if it goes wrong, it's not my fault."

However, this lack of opposition does carry a huge risk for the leader. A leader who only gets gleaming reports of how well everything is going has no idea what is really happening and may not know until much too late when things are going totally wrong.

When they are isolated, protected, and out of touch with reality, many leaders perish because they fail to notice what is really going on. All they see in the reflection of those around them is their own view of the world.

There are certainly leaders who enjoy this, who love feeling like kings and queens surrounded by a court of like-minded people all nodding in support. On the other hand, there are also strong leaders who long for firm opposition and critical feedback but who fail to break through the hesitation and reluctance of those around them. As such a leader, what can you do?

- Surround yourself with people who will **challenge** your ideas, and actively search for people who view things from a completely different perspective. Include people in your team who are your opposite on some key attributes. If you're a hands-on, action-oriented person, make sure you have someone in your team who is reflective and looks at things from all sides. If you're conceptual and visionary, find someone to work with who is practical-minded and will bring you back down to earth.
- Take the **initiative** to ask for advice and feedback from colleagues and staff members. Ask people to say what they really think and be prepared to hear everything – that means literally everything. Listen carefully, try to take on their point of view, and don't become defensive. Stay open-minded and put aside all your prejudices (especially your ego), even if what you are being told feels like personal criticism. After all, it's not about how uncomfortable you might be feeling but about the well-being of the organization. Keep your judgments to yourself, even if you immediately have associations and thoughts. Let yourself be surprised, even if this means that you might have to completely readjust your view of reality. Thank people for their feedback.
- Show people that you **have done something** with their feedback, that you are **willing** to consider it and change your

approach or point of view. If you don't do this, asking for feedback becomes a pointless, politically correct ritual that only feeds cynicism.

- **Create a safe environment.** Never use the feedback you've received from someone against them at a later time or in any other situation because it looks like you've been gathering sticks to hit them with sooner or later. Even an innocent-sounding statement such as "this is what you said to me back then" can completely break down the feeling of trust.
- **Talk to people at all levels of the organization** but first ask their direct line managers so that they don't feel threatened.

Obviously, what applies to leaders applies to everyone else. Asking for critical feedback may seem cumbersome at first, and it takes time (which we often don't have), but it greatly improves the quality of our actions and decisions, provided we do something with it.

KEY POINTS

- Use the strengths of opposite and complementary approaches.
- Make the opposite poles in your team explicit and talk about the qualities of each pole.
- Make people aware of their own personal style and that of others.
- Encourage people to broaden their range of styles.
- Seek both/and solutions together.
- Invite people to make the most of each other's complementary skills.
- Regularly solicit critical feedback and be open to what you hear.

7.3 Creativity and Innovation: A Winding Road

Creativity is primarily a nonlinear process that needs a para-doxical environment in order to flourish. Psychologist Mihaly Csikszentmihalyi, known for introducing the concept of *flow*, discovered with his research that creative people usually have a dialectical personality with apparently contradictory traits.[8] He describes ten paradoxical characteristics of creative people. They

1 have a great deal of physical energy but they're also often quiet and at rest;
2 tend to be smart yet naive at the same time;
3 combine playfulness and discipline;
4 alternate between imagination and fantasy, and a rooted sense of reality;
5 tend to be both extroverted and introverted;
6 are humble and proud at the same time;
7 combine both masculine and feminine characteristics in unique ways;
8 are rebellious as well as conservative;
9 are very passionate about their work, yet they can be extremely objective and critical about it as well; and
10 are sensitive and open, which makes them vulnerable and ex-poses them to pain but which also enables them to experience great joy and fulfillment.

It is this unique tension and dynamic interplay between opposites that sparks true creativity and allows it to thrive. Or in the words of

---

8 Mihaly Csikszentmihalyi, *Creativity: The Work and Lives of 91 Eminent People* (New York: HarperCollins, 1996).

Mr. Csikszentmihalyi: "If I had to express in one word what makes their personalities different from others, it's complexity. They show tendencies of thought and action that in most people are segregated. They contain contradictory extremes; instead of being an 'individual,' each of them is a 'multitude.'"

In order to get the most out of creative people in your team or organization, you have to create an environment that provides and maintains these paradoxical areas of tension. And that is extremely difficult for an organization that tends to stick to a single direction, where traditional organizational values prevail, like: "energetic," "businesslike," "extroverted," "masculine," "structured," "planned," "output-driven," or "measurable," just to name a few. The same applies, however, to an environment where *anything* goes and where there are no limits on creativity; these types of organizations won't reap the full benefits either. A concrete assignment with a well-defined focus is often needed to give creativity an impulse. Defining boundaries, setting limits, and creating scarcity will stimulate creativity because it provides clear focus to the creative process, and it intensifies the creative effort as the boundaries force people to look beyond the obvious.

7.3.1 Allowing People to Play, Experiment, and Fail

In order to tap into real creativity, it is important not to focus too much on output and results. There should be room for experimenting freely without knowing for sure that this will lead to concrete results. People should be allowed time and space to just "mess around" in addition to going about their regular work. This also means accepting the fact that some experiments will fail. Major breakthroughs are often not planned but arise as unexpected by-products of exploring side paths or having a project fail. This is a challenge for organizations that are very target-oriented, especially for those that focus on short-term results.

An effective way to manage and focus creativity is to stimulate and facilitate the exchange of ideas among professionals. Such an exchange provides the opportunity to share creative thoughts and projects and to question, challenge, and enrich each other with new ideas. However, the right timing for sharing is crucial and can be different for each idea or project. Sometimes an idea needs time to ripen, and in a collective process, it would be dismissed too quickly because it is, for example, too new or still difficult to explain. In short, it's important to maintain a good balance between the individual genius and the collective brainpower.

It also helps to allow for recreation time during which people can recharge their batteries and find new inspiration. Brilliant solutions don't come by focusing even harder; they often come out of the blue. Research in neuroscience shows that the brain is most creative in periods when there is nothing specific on the mind. While relaxing, unconscious problem solving goes on in the background until suddenly an unexpected solution pops up. It helps to let your mind run free by going for a walk in the woods, working out, dancing, or meditating. You could provide time and space for this. Since the subconscious works on problems while we sleep, the best ideas often come to us as we're waking up; it might be a good idea to set up some beds in the organization for afternoon naps. Instead of staring blankly at a problem during an after-lunch lull, we could take an invigorating half-hour power nap and return to work feeling energized and recharged with new inspiration. It's then that the pieces of the puzzle often suddenly fit together and in an unexpected way. It could boost productivity enormously, but "sleeping on the job" is still a big taboo: "Who knows, maybe some people will take advantage of it and stay in bed all afternoon … ?" Leave this control thinking behind and just see how this can work.

When I talked about Strategy 6 of the Polarity Wheel, I referred to the example of the tech company that allowed its staff to work on their own projects for one day a week using the company infrastructure, provided that they shared the results with their colleagues. This is an ingenious way to balance individual passion with business goals, and a great example of how individual entrepreneurship and working for an institutionalized company can fit seamlessly together without uninspiring compromises.

7.3.2 Innovation: Organizing Creativity in a Paradoxical Way

To make optimal use of the existing creativity and to strengthen the innovative capacity of an organization, it's important to bring together and find the right balance between different approaches, qualities, domains, and parties. The following paradoxical challenges are linked to innovation.

MARKET-DRIVEN AND VISION-DRIVEN

Many organizations spend quite a bit of time passionately discussing which of these two strategies is best, with strong arguments for both. Some will say, "We can try to come up with what we think is good for our clients, but wouldn't it be better to ask the clients themselves?" or "Innovation is most effective when it results from co-creation with our clients." Others will refer to the famous statement by Henry Ford: "If I had asked people what they wanted, they would have said faster horses," or to the innovative success of Apple, which proudly believes in developing products that Apple's designers themselves are excited about rather than letting the company be swayed by market research.

Rather than investing time and energy in ideological discussions, it's better to make full use of both innovation strategies and achieve a good mix. After all, both strategies can be effective and fit perfectly together. The vision-driven approach entails more risk but the chance of coming up with revolutionary innovations is also much greater, while the market-oriented approach greatly reduces the risk in advance but often builds on what is already known and what already exists. By including both vision-driven and client-driven projects in your innovation portfolio, you can spread the risks and the potential benefits.

You could also try combining both strategies. The question is then in which phase of the innovation process it would be best to engage the market and clients: at the very beginning when determining market demand, or during the development process itself by extensively consulting with clients, or even through co-creating products with clients? Or should you wait until you've developed an initial concept, a minimum viable product, or even a ready-to-use prototype and then test it in the market to be able to refine it further? We already mentioned the iterative approach of Agile development as an efficient way to bridge the gap between conceiving a new product and aligning with customer needs. It's a good example of a Strategy 6 solution in the Polarity Wheel.

USE ALL COMPETENCIES NEEDED FOR INNOVATION

Innovation isn't just about coming up with a brilliant idea; the success of this brilliant idea depends entirely on how it's designed and executed. Innovation requires complementary competencies: creative and conceptual thinking on the one hand and the ability to make something work in practice on the other. Both qualities are necessary and should be regarded as equally important. We may tend to rate creative ingenuity higher than practical execution (because it's scarcer, more elusive, and we feel it has a greater impact on the final result), but without having someone who will fully dedicate themselves to working out an ingenious idea right down to the minutest detail, this idea will be of no value at all.

BRING DIFFERENT WORLDS TOGETHER

Sometimes innovations emerge when very different worlds and disciplines come together, such as entomology and space travel (biomimicry), big data and psychotherapy, or art and technology. Mental models and paradigms that work well in one domain suddenly appear to open up a completely new perspective in another domain. Instead of focusing primarily on the trends in your own sector, it might be worthwhile to stimulate interaction between completely different sectors. Allow people to dive into areas that may seem unrelated to their own field of work and invite them to investigate whether and how they could use paradigms from these other areas. Sometimes surprising results appear just by letting people from different disciplines or different parts of the organization (including clients, partners, suppliers, and stakeholders) work together on an assignment. To make this work, it is important to have the ability and willingness to open up to the language and conceptual framework of another discipline and become, as it were, conceptually multilingual.

ALONE *AND* TOGETHER

To take the previous point one step further, innovation can be greatly stimulated by a fervent exchange of ideas. The places where ideas are freely exchanged are the birth places of renewal, like Alexandria in antiquity or Silicon Valley today.

Traditional innovation consists mainly of investing in an in-house R&D department, with the focus on secrecy and protecting intellectual property. However, organizations are more and more innovating outside of their own "laboratory" by co-creating with others, such as by collaborating with direct partners (suppliers, clients, users, sector peers, nonsector peers, or academic institutions) or even with a broader field, as in the case of open innovation. The clearly defined boundaries of traditional organizations are losing importance; it's the exchange of thoughts and ideas with the environment that leads to the creation of new things.

However, this doesn't mean that development and innovation within organizations are at an end, or that they do not need to be involved in this process. Open innovation processes also require a clear contribution from the organization. The strength and added value of large organizations in particular lie in their ability to scale up and commercialize new products and services. Moreover, large investments in R&D infrastructure remain essential for complex technological developments, and appropriate scaling is indispensable; not everything can be conceived and developed in a garage. Finally, organizations play a vital role in creating and nurturing a platform for co-creation and in steering efforts in a certain direction because without direction, creativity rarely leads to anything concrete.

It boils down to finding the right combination of internal and external sources and the complementary use of "open" and "closed" innovation processes. Many large corporations combine internal and external sources in a very simple way: they bring in external sources by acquiring and incorporating innovative start-up companies. This often works well for a particular product, but is this also an effective way to innovate on a continual basis? A lot depends on the deviation and freedom that the large corporations allow. Can the start-ups still retain their passion for pioneering and experimentation, their unconventional ways of working, and their freedom and space, or will they be swallowed up and paralyzed by the bureaucratic rules and financial logic of the large corporation?

PUSHING *AND* LETTING THINGS HAPPEN ON THEIR OWN

The threshold for innovation is especially high for traditional organizations that have a strong focus on compliance and efficiency. "Innovation" alone, as management's new buzzword, will not spark concrete initiatives to happen on their own. On the contrary, if someone did come up with a wild idea, chances are that it would quickly be thrown out the window under the well-known regulatory and business case scrutiny. In such cases, removing barriers and giving room for innovation is not enough. Nothing will happen until the leadership team provides the necessary counterbalance and actively pushes for innovation. This initially means spending a lot of time and effort on going against the existing logic and turning relationships upside down, for example, by paying attention to those seemingly "wild ideas" and spending time and money on their further development. Only when the leadership team shows by their intense engagement, perseverance, and concrete deeds that the innovation ambition is more than a nice slogan, will it be possible for initiatives to pop up and grow spontaneously.

THE INNOVATION DEPARTMENT AND THE REST

I have already discussed the example of a traditional organization creating a few trendy innovation cells because "we have to do something with innovation." The innovation challenges are then typically assigned to these separate units, relieving those involved in day-to-day business operations of the obligation to be innovative ("that's what these innovation incubators are there for"). Innovation and day-to-day business operations often stay in their own independent worlds. Sometimes such innovation cells lose their motivation because they are unable to connect with the entities responsible for daily operations, which are mainly focused on meeting their short-term production targets. The key challenge is to make the entire organization innovative and connect innovation with day-to-day business. To do this, you first have to strip "innovation" of its bigger-than-real connotation, which makes it daunting and discouraging. Innovation doesn't only have to take place on a large scale, in a disruptive way, or in big projects. Everyone has ideas and can be innovative in their daily activities. It's important to keep these ideas circulating and to include them in the regular team meetings as a standard topic of discussion. Making optimal use of the diversity of approaches and styles within a team will be an important lever of innovation.

Innovation is something that can be expected from every team and staff member. It is not helpful to introduce an overkill of KPIs:

"You're expected to come up with twenty new ideas this year, three of which should be realized and put into practice." Innovation should certainly not become an extra obligation or performance objective but something that people are allowed to spend time on and that is above all fun and energizing – playing rather than working.

Innovation cells should not only focus on the content of innovation but also on enabling the innovation *process*, for example by sharing stimulating ways of collaborating and by connecting the various parties within and outside of the organization. They should be masters at connecting opposite poles.

KEY POINTS

- Create an environment that supports and empowers the paradoxical characteristics of those who are creative.
- Allow people to feel free to experiment and to fail, and at the same time provide direction by stimulating and facilitating an exchange and learning process.
- Ensure balance between creativity, on the one hand, and execution, on the other.
- Innovate with both an inward and outward focus.
- Innovate together with other parties and know your own strengths.
- Try to steer innovation in the direction you want it to go but without stifling or killing it with bureaucracy.
- Sometimes innovation can be stimulated by simply removing restrictions, but sometimes it needs to be actively "pushed."
- Do not keep innovation locked up in a separate department, but make sure it's the responsibility of all parts of the organization.

CONDUCTING THE PARADOXICAL DIALOGUE

This chapter explores how to enable your team to work with polarities and how you can deal with conflicting demands yourself when you are in an intermediary role. Being able to establish a process of ongoing professional dialogue is the critical success factor for both challenges.

8.1 The Inner Compass

The previous chapter highlighted the importance of diversity in making organizations and divisions capable of flexibly adapting to different situations. It is definitely an asset to be able to engage people with different styles and approaches in different situations and to actively use the specific qualities of each individual. However, it would be even better if everyone had a kind of inner diversity on an individual level. Professionals should be able to recalibrate the balance between opposite approaches and values to respond differently to different situations.

It's therefore important to allow professionals to make their own considerations and trade-offs within the overall objectives of the organization. The primary characteristic of a professional is someone who can determine the best course of action themselves, even if they work for a large organization that strives for predictability and control. As complexity and unpredictability increase, this skillset becomes even more important since it becomes impossible to cover all potential cases with clear if-this-then-that rules.

8.1.1 Why It's Appealing to Have Clear Rules

It may not be obvious why one should abandon clear and unambiguous regulations, procedures, decision trees, and instructions. There are actually several good reasons for sticking to them, both from an individual as well as from an organizational perspective. From an individual perspective:

- **Avoid paradoxical confusion**: Some people have difficulty with ambiguity and prefer to follow a clearly defined set of rules, which they can apply systematically. They feel insecure and nervous when confronted with conflicting demands and may get stuck in confusion or paralysis. They may find it difficult to deal with changes of direction: "First management told me to go left, and then I had to go right again. What do they want me to do now, and do they actually know what they want?!"
- **Tiring and risky**: If there are no clear rules, every situation requires assessment, choice, and possibly justification. It can be difficult, tiring, and risky to analyze instead of simply applying a general rule. A patient might ask for a hug – which might be too intimate or might be very comforting for the patient in an intense moment of grief – making a healthcare worker feel unsure and uncomfortable. It would be easier for the healthcare worker to refer to a general rule such as "no intimacies between caregivers and patients" rather than to make a very rapid assessment of every individual case, both for the patient's good and their own.

From an organizational perspective:

- **Predictability and consistency**: An organization wants the outside world to see it as one organization with consistent practices. What if clients feel that they are not treated in the same way? If an organization does not have clear-cut rules, what would then be the explanation to back up differences in treatment? Shouldn't the advantage of bureaucracy be that it ensures uniform, objective, and equal treatment for all and excludes any form of subjectivity and favoritism?
- **Control and accountability**: What if a professional makes the wrong choice? For example: What if a government official makes a decision in an asylum procedure which later turns out to be wrong? If this becomes widely publicized in the news without all the background information, the organization may be put under considerable pressure. Will scapegoats be sought out to take the fall? Or will senior management protect its staff member and publicly reveal the considerations and trade-offs of the case and how difficult it was to make such a decision? How will they make clear that despite the risk of a wrong decision, the opposite approach – blindly applying bureaucratic rules – would have been far worse?

8.1.2 Balancing in Dialogue

The advantage to having professionals who are by themselves able to weigh the options and to choose for each case the best approach is that an organization doesn't need a complicated, confusing, and sometimes contradicting jungle of decision trees, rules, exceptions to the rules, exceptions to the exceptions, and so on. People just navigate decisions with their own professional compass.

However, the challenge is to give people the space and confidence to make contradictory decisions and still maintain a certain degree of consistency at the organizational level. Therefore, it should not be a purely individual process, but a collective one, requiring organizational support and guidance. Important steps include making the tensions that professionals experience explicit, acknowledging the value of both sides, and providing some form of a shared assessment framework. The following interventions may help.

THE PARADOXICAL DASHBOARD

In order to give people guidance in dealing with polarities, you and your team can design a concise dashboard with some key polarities, either for the business in general or for a specific project. Ask all team or project members: Which tensions do we experience in our daily work and what are the underlying conflicting values and goals? A paradoxical dashboard for a project could look like this:

Figure 8.1. The paradoxical dashboard

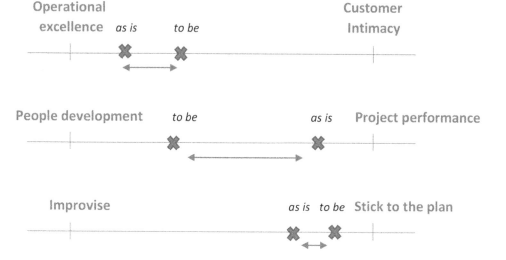

After listing a top three or five team polarities, you can reflect together on each, pointing out where the team's current balance point is on the continuum between the two poles ("as is" on the dashboard). This is of course a rough estimation, but it provides significant insights into the team's culture. Then you can examine if this current balance point still reflects the challenges of today or tomorrow. You may collectively choose to aim for a new balance point on the axis ("to be"). For example: "The focus in our project team is currently on rapid project delivery, sometimes at the expense of people development. We should shift the balance considerably toward individual development by providing more room for people to experiment with new roles and skills."

The team can regularly return to this dashboard and see where they are in comparison with where they want to be and to major changes in context and environment. It is an interesting way to create a platform for your team to share their experiences of daily tensions and deal collectively and consciously with polarities. It gives individual team members an indication of what the desirable direction is for the long term, although everyone in the team should be able to use the full polarity scale to cope with specific situations in the short term. The dashboard also provides a good starting point for conducting the paradoxical dialogue in individual cases (see 8.1.3).

Another tool that can be very helpful is the Polarity Map® developed by Barry Johnson.[1] This highly visual mapping tool enables you to quickly identify the strengths of each pole and the negative effects of over-focus. It will also help to define some early warning indicators to prevent you going too far in either direction.

DUAL VALUES AND CULTURE CHANGE 2.0

It is common practice for organizations to formulate singular corporate values such as "result-focus," "collaboration," "proactiveness," "innovation," "empowerment," or "customer centricity."

---

1 Barry Johnson, *And: Making a Difference by Leveraging Polarity, Paradox or Dilemma* (Amherst, MA: HRD, 2020).

Although they are often quite vague notions with which you cannot disagree, people are encouraged to embrace these values and adopt the required attitude through all sorts of company culture programs, including awareness, motivation, conviction, coercion, and training. If the organization later changes course, people have to be "taught" the new values, usually in a similar way. Change management professionals and training institutes make oodles of money from this.

Alternatively, it's interesting to see some organizations start working with dual values. For example, the Dutch financial market authority has in its value set the polarity "autonomy and collaboration." This represents the dual purpose of taking an independent controlling role toward financial institutions AND working with them in partnership. Professionals within such an organization are expected to be able to manage the tension arising from this polarity, seeking the right balance in every situation, and probably performing both roles simultaneously. For example, they might "provide financial institutions support to self-monitor."

Dual values offer much greater freedom and recognize the professional judgment of every staff member. Introducing these dual values requires a completely different approach than getting people "aligned" through a traditional cultural change program. Culture Change 2.0 requires people to learn how to deal with these polarities in a conscious way: to learn how to adapt their approach to a given situation through interactive experiences, such as simulations and cases, concrete work situations, feedback, peer review, brainstorm sessions, and self-reflection; to learn to explore the limits and the tipping points; and to learn how to find new ways of integrating two opposite poles at a higher level.

Culture change under this dual model could be focused on the specific set of core polarities of the organization, but it's even more important to support people in mastering the art of balancing in general. See also section 9.2 on developing paradoxical skills.

THE ORGANIZATIONAL PURPOSE AS INNER COMPASS

The whole point of balancing between opposite or complementary values is to serve the mission and purpose of the organization in different contexts. Every time professionals have to make decisions, they should ask themselves which approach best serves the overarching mission and purpose of the organization.

For example, the purpose of consultancy firm XYZ is to support its clients in realizing successful and sustainable change and in building a strong sense of ownership across their organizations. This purpose ultimately determines whether in a specific change project the consultants need to take a more driving role or an enabling one, to apply a data-based or a more intuitive approach, to set up a master plan or go step by step. Consultants must continuously check in with this overarching purpose and navigate with their inner professional and moral compass to determine the best approach. The key questions should be if and how the approach chosen contributes to the overall purpose. This is why it's important to instigate an ongoing dialogue about the purpose on all levels of the organization, not hiding it under all sorts of sub-goals and KPIs.

If we imagine that the ultimate organizational purpose points out the direction and the professional's inner compass helps them choose the path to follow, then dialogue can provide the necessary compass calibration. This dialogue should take place systematically, with professional decisions being weighed against the organization's purpose. The dialogue doesn't at all have to be conducted in a top-down way ("ask the boss"); it can easily be conducted among peers.

8.2 How to Shape the Paradoxical Dialogue

Rather than spending a tremendous amount of time, energy, and money trying to achieve compliance, it's much more effective to take advantage of the power of differences. This can be done by setting up a "paradoxical dialogue" process within a team (or among teams). The paradoxical dialogue is about how the team deals with some key polarities in its daily work, and how to balance between these poles on a case-by-case basis.

This is a practical way to achieve more peer-to-peer management and self-organization (as described in section 5.3) and to rely less on top-down control mechanisms, detailed procedures, and hierarchical structures. This approach is especially effective for teams of professionals and knowledge workers, or in more complex and unpredictable environments where flexibility, adaptability, and quick response are crucial for success.

Just like in the paradoxical dashboard of the previous section, the best place to start is a specific polarity that every team member experiences daily and that everyone struggles with to some extent. This polarity is usually related to the core business or customer relationships. In a service team, for example, there might be tension between the delivery of "standardized" and "customized" solutions or between "personal attention" and "efficiency" with respect to customer contact.

The paradoxical dialogue consists of several building blocks that can be arranged into steps for implementation. I will illustrate the implementation of these building blocks with a real-life example: a team of project controllers within a government agency monitors a portfolio of capital-intensive infrastructural projects, for financial soundness, spending within budget, and compliance with procedures, policies, and regulations. The project owners ("The business") are complaining that the project controller team is too controlling, rigidly setting boundaries and restrictions. Furthermore, in their view project controllers don't take enough of an advisory role, helping the business to look for opportunities and find creative solutions. For the business it is clear: the controlling team needs to make a shift from controlling to advising. However, the board recognizes that both controlling and advising are important and wants to avoid pendulum swings too far in either direction. Instead of opting for a traditional turnaround from A to B, the board therefore decides to experiment with a process of paradoxical dialogue, enabling the controller team to find the right balance for each project or situation themselves.

The building blocks of the process are shown in figure 8.2: (1) a core polarity, (2) the diversity in preferred styles and approaches of team members plotted on a gradual spectrum between the two poles, (3) the commonly defined boundaries between functional and dysfunctional behaviors, (4) the gray zones, and (5) the ultimate goal or purpose.

Figure 8.2. The paradoxical dialogue

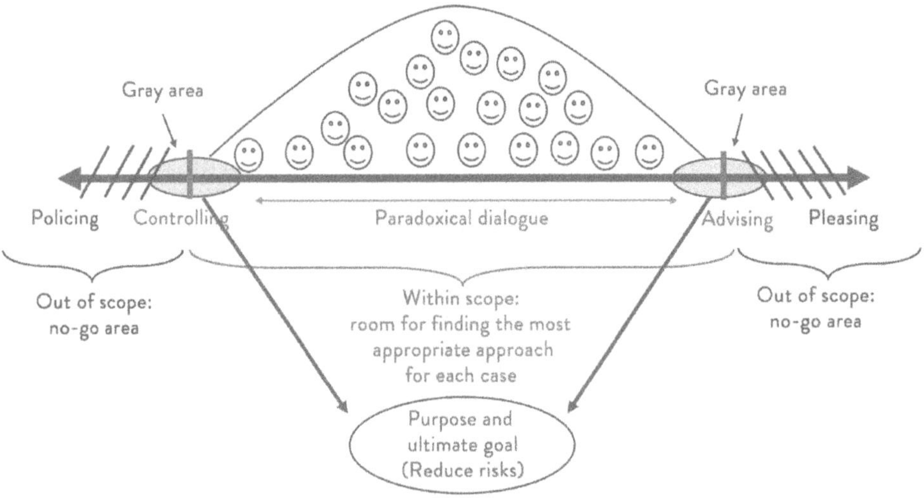

The building blocks can be established in the following steps.

1. Identify the core polarity of the team

The first step is to explore and name the core polarities that have a critical effect on team performance and atmosphere. As a team leader or coach, you can ask the team members which tensions and opposing values they have to navigate every day. You will soon identify common themes. Focus on the polarity that is most strongly felt by everyone. It is important to refer to it in a neutral way, without implicit or explicit preference for either side; not "orderly" and "chaotic" or "bureaucratic" and "client-oriented," but "structured" and "flexible" or "customized" and "standardized." The key role for the team leader or coach is to create a safe environment by highlighting, in word and deed, that both opposite poles are essential for doing a good job as a team.

In the case of the project controllers the most important polarity was obvious: controlling and advising. However, the process uncovered additional polarities, such as the tension between "working on demand" and "developing own initiatives," between the "strategic" and the "operational" roles, and between "loyalty to their business unit" and "loyalty to the municipality as a whole and the interests of the city." Although these other polarities were out of scope for the time, they were also documented and saved for a later moment. All polarities were formulated as both/and paradoxes and not as either/or dilemmas.

2. Mapping differences in style and approach

If you were to plot the natural style of all team members along the axis between the two poles, you might see a normal distribution pattern, or perhaps a curve toward one or both of the extremes, or even a division in two camps around the extremes with only a few people in the middle. The shape of the curve gives an interesting visualization of how like-minded or diverse the team is and where tensions may arise between different parties. It is also a dynamic and systemic process. For example, if a majority of the team positions itself on one side of the spectrum, some will feel the need to position themselves toward the other side, not necessarily because they have a natural predisposition for this pole, but just to keep the team in balance.

A useful tool for mapping is the team constellation exercise described on p. 254, in which you invite team members to physically take a position on a line between the two poles. I should note that taking a position on the line between the two poles is also situational and should not lead to any sort of fixed classification or typecasting. Throughout the process of the paradoxical dialogue it cannot be stressed enough that both poles are equally necessary and valuable.

In the case of the project controllers, there was a clear split in the team between the older generation (more toward the controlling pole) and the younger (more toward the advisory pole), with only a few individuals standing in between.

3. Define the boundaries together

It's fine that people have different styles and approaches, but what are the limits? What is still acceptable and where does it become dysfunctional? In our example: "It's good that we're closely monitoring the business, but if we stick too much to formal procedures, we can lose touch with complex day-to-day reality. Moreover, it will undermine our relationship with the project owners, who will try to avoid us and start experimenting with workarounds beyond our control." And the other way around: "It's great that we're creatively looking for solutions to satisfy the needs of the business, but if we are too lenient, we might end up with solutions that are not only legally and morally disputable, but also entail considerable risks for the municipality as a whole." Therefore, it's important to set boundaries. What are the no-go zones? For example: Returning a project budget proposal covered in red ink and recommending a fresh start – which sometimes happens – might be the right thing to do from a strict controlling point of view, but this won't go well in practice. Likewise, thinking creatively is fine, but stretching the rules to justify a questionable course of action is clearly not. It's interesting to see in the dialogue that people may have different perceptions of what is acceptable and what isn't. What might be "standard controlling practice" for one person could be "plain bureaucracy" through the eyes of someone else.

It will also become clear through dialogue that different people can mean very different things with the same words (like "advice" and "control"). This often leads to confusion and an unfounded sense of consensus or disagreement. It is therefore important to clarify the concepts that everyone uses with many concrete examples.

Examples from daily practice are the best way to build a shared view on what the boundaries are. By making them very concrete, you avoid the typical misunderstandings of vague general concepts that are open to multiple interpretations. You can explore a specific case: "What do we think of this approach in this case? And what if we went even one step further? What would happen then? Would it still be within the range of what we consider to be acceptable, or would it be over-the-top?" Based on real-life and hypothetical examples, the team explores the boundaries of what they consider acceptable and makes these boundaries explicit. Of course, as a leader, you also have an important contribution to make because your role is to ensure that everything is still in line with the overall goals and boundaries of the organization.

As a leader, it's important to be clear on the extent of team members' freedom. How wide or narrow should the authorized bandwidth for different approaches be? Do team members really have a lot of room for intervention options, or is it rather restricted?

4. Make the purpose clear

The differences in approach or style are merely means to achieve an overall goal, which in this example is to reduce the risks to the organization. "Controlling" or "advising" are just two ways of getting there. This ultimate goal often gets buried beneath well-intended derived goals, KPIs, guidelines, frameworks, procedures, and checklists. That's why it is essential to go back to the purpose again and again so that it's at the top of everyone's minds. "That's why we're all here." The purpose should be simple and understandable and touch people emotionally. It shouldn't just be formulated as a list of beautiful-sounding values; if you have to rack your brain to remember them, you can already be sure that the values don't reflect the essence of the organization. Stories are a great way to make an overall goal stick; stories can be told, retold, enriched, and adapted to the changing context, like a living fabric.

5. Allow for mistakes and recognize gray zones

The fact that you are working within a margin inevitably means that judgments will be made that afterwards may prove to be wrong. No matter how clearly you try to define what is and what is not acceptable, there will always be gray zones. You can never anticipate or think up rules for all possible cases. What you can do is set up a process of peer review and consultation where these kinds of borderline cases are systematically discussed. The dialogue must simply start with open minds regarding the issue at hand and with the ultimate goal as a beacon.

Even if there is no consensus reached on what course of action should be followed in a specific case, the exchange process still has value, as it stimulates professionals to better understand the complex trade-offs and to make more conscious decisions. Such discussions don't necessarily have to involve management but can also take place among colleagues. However, people should feel safe and supported by their management when inevitably professional judgments are made that afterward prove to be wrong.

6. Create both/and solutions

The team of controllers came to the following both/and solution: by being involved in the earliest stages of shaping the project, a controller is able to indicate from the outset the financial and regulatory boundaries, but subsequently supports the business in finding workable solutions within these boundaries. By taking an advisory role during the setup of the project, it is less likely that the controller will need to elaborately review the project plan at the end, when it is already in its final decision phase. As a result, the decision process can run smoothly, without annoying surprises, hiccups, or delays. In short, investing in a stronger advisory role early on allows a much lighter controlling role later. However, a both/and solution may not be always possible or even desirable, so people should have the freedom to move across the whole polarity spectrum, within the boundaries the team has set.

7. Ongoing process: Create consistency through peer review

Once this framework of balancing, agreed boundaries, purpose, identified gray zones, and rules of engagement is established, room is created to make professional trade-offs and considerations, enabling approaches that match the specific requirements of each case and situation. Encountered complex and gray zone cases can be discussed within a team along the same lines: Which approach would work best given the context and overall purpose? Which professional or complementary mix of professionals could we best assign to this case or project, given the required approach and skillset to take it further? This process of joint evaluation ensures a certain level of consistency and alignment within a team without imposing one way of working for everyone. It enhances learning from each other, although differences are valued and allowed. From the client's side, it avoids unexplainable and arbitrary decisions, merely depending on the particular point of view of the professional they have in front of them. The key question for complex cases should rather be which approach and professional are best placed to reach the overall purpose in this specific case, instead of which approach or professional happens to be available by chance. This process should not slow down production rate: with less complex cases, a brief check with a colleague may suffice, and for most regular cases people can make their own professionals judgment. Of course, the availability of people and resources is also one of the key elements in any consideration.

This entails a different process of control and accountability. Instead of professionals having to demonstrate that they have handled everything in the same way in accordance with the protocol, it now comes down to being able to provide insight into the considerations made. They must be able to explain the chosen approach in a substantiated manner to the customer, their colleagues, and management.

As a leader, you can help initiate and stimulate this process by working with your team:

- To identify their **core polarities**. What is everyone struggling with?
- To define the **margins**. What is considered acceptable and what clearly isn't? This should be based on concrete examples.
- To keep the **ultimate purpose** at the front of everyone's minds by regularly sharing with each other concrete stories and anecdotes.
- To name the **gray areas** and regularly discuss examples. What are possible approaches? What are their advantages and limitations? Make "dealing with borderline cases" a standard item on the agenda of the team meetings.
- To establish and apply the **rules of engagement**, such as "listen before judging."
- To encourage team members to slightly **broaden** their own behavioral repertoire, to experiment with other styles and approaches, and to become more skilled in using the competencies of colleagues.
- To challenge and help team members to **substantiate and explain** their professional trade-offs.

PRACTICAL TOOL: TEAM CONSTELLATION EXERCISE

This practical team constellation exercise can be a powerful tool to make team members aware of how they all cope with the same polarity and to kick off the process of professional dialogue. It is often an eye-opener to everyone in the team to see how their individual positions regarding a specific polarity may differ or be very similar. This exercise is a variation of the individual constellation exercise on p. 96, instead done with a whole team.

The aim of this exercise is to

- make team members aware of their own position regarding a particular team polarity;
- provide insight into the position and views of their colleagues and achieve mutual understanding; and
- allow team members to learn about and appreciate other positions and points of views.

Proceed as follows:

Step 1: Invite your team to choose a key work-related polarity. This should be a polarity that everyone recognizes as a challenge in their daily work (e.g., the tension between "accuracy" and "speed"). Write each pole on a piece of paper and lay them on the ground, with enough space between them.

Step 2: Invite the team members to take their *natural* positions – based on their personal preferences, not their roles at work – on a line between the two poles. The advantage of a line is that it represents a continuous range and not a division into two categories. You can use a concrete example or a controversial statement to trigger responses. The participants tell each other why they have taken this position and enter into a dialogue with each other. Do the participants end up changing their position as a result of the dialogue?

The way the participants are spread across the spectrum will tell you a lot about how the team works. Maybe they are evenly distributed across the line (wide diversity), or perhaps there's a normal distribution, with most people in the middle. There may also be a cluster at one or both ends, or someone might be standing all on their own at one end while the others are all huddled together at the other end, as in the case where nearly everyone wants to be engaged in new creative developments, while the one person crying out for more structure and focus feels like they're talking to a brick wall.

Step 3: You can then ask what position the participants would take in their current role or job. This can be very different from their own personal preferences. As mentioned before, the systemic context plays an important role here, in two ways. First, there's the specific requirements of the role. You might have a fairly easy-going and accommodating preferred style, but in your role as the one responsible for quality control, you're expected to dot the i's and cross the t's. Second, there's the position of the other players in the team. You might work in a creative environment where there's a lot of freedom, and things are slightly chaotic; as a person, you're fine with this but, due to your sense of responsibility, you take on a more procedural role to offer some counterweight: "I'm standing at this point because everyone is mainly on the other side, and someone has to keep the boat balanced." How is that person going to feel in the long run? If there's a big difference between your personal preference and the position that your role or the system requires of you, how long will you be able to maintain this position, and what do you need in order to compensate for this?

Step 4: The next step is to ask the participants to stand in the position of someone else: a client, a stakeholder, a colleague with a different role, a director, or someone from a different division. It's interesting to see, for example, that a counsellor who typically has a soft and compliant approach with clients might clearly prefer – in the role of client – to have a counselor who is quite direct and decisive. The rebel in the team, when considering the role of director, might want to be very much in control. This exercise encourages people to look at an issue from different sides, to put themselves in someone else's shoes and, in doing so, to put their own position into perspective.

Step 5: Finally, you can invite the participants to return to their personal preference positions. Have they changed their original position? How exactly? And what has brought about this change? Have certain insights made them more flexible with respect to other positions along the line?

INSTILLING CONFIDENCE AND ALLOWING FOR MISTAKES

If people are punished for making mistakes, they will be discouraged from taking any initiative that deviates from bureaucratic rules. In an environment with a strong focus on control and reporting, a lot of energy will be wasted on collecting evidence to cover one's back. A thriving environment for professional initiative is created by giving professionals both freedom *and* confidence, by fully accepting the risk that mistakes will be made and by using them as a collective learning opportunity.

A seemingly open and free culture can change from one moment to the next into a culture of fear and mistrust if a mistake is met with an accusing tone ("We didn't mean that you were allowed to make such *big* mistakes!"). The ultimate test is when a mistake reaches the ears of the general public, particularly if the press pounces on it to produce sensational headlines. Will the organization start looking for a scapegoat? Or will it explain both internally and externally that this mistake, although extremely regrettable, is an unavoidable risk in any complex decision-making process? The organization should of course also take full responsibility for any mistakes and do whatever it can to minimize their negative impact.

Another interesting question is whether the same level of trust can be maintained when mistakes are made after careful contemplation or when they arise from carelessness. There is a big gray zone between these two types of mistakes, so it's best not to make too much of a difference between them, although it's quite challenging to treat the second type just as mildly as the first type. The first type is a normal risk when doing business, whereas the second type probably indicates that the professional dialogue within the organization is not working properly. Both types of mistakes should be used as crucial opportunities to learn and to share the lessons with all levels of the organization. It's important to look at mistakes from a broader perspective and to resist the immediate temptation to make another new rule based on one isolated incident.

When creating an atmosphere of trust, openness, and learning from mistakes, a leader's exemplary role is particularly important. It means a lot when someone at the top admits to having gone wrong somewhere, without trying to justify everything or blame someone else. Rather than trying to appear infallible, it's much stronger to say, "The direction we carefully chose last year has turned out to be the wrong one. We made a mistake. Let's see what we can do differently together this time."

SWITCHING TO RULES AND GUIDELINES WHEN REQUIRED

None of the above alters the fact that clear and unambiguous rules and guidelines can be very useful in certain situations or with certain people. Some people will continue to find it difficult to make their own decisions and choices and will want nothing more than clear instructions. In these cases, strict rules and guidelines can help make people feel safe and give them a sense of direction. Providing more space for deliberation and situational flexibility is not necessarily suitable for every type of work either. Some more predictable processes, where routine, standardization, efficiency, and/

or following strict protocols are important, may benefit more from being straightforwardly managed.

This requires leaders to also be flexible in their management style and adapt to different people and contexts. But that doesn't mean that leaders can't encourage people or divisions who strongly adhere to rules to take small steps toward a more multi-perspective and contextual approach. It will be important to create a general sense of safety, with basic rules in place to fall back on and to actively boost self-confidence.

KEY POINTS

- Make a paradoxical dashboard for your team or project with the key polarities in order to regularly monitor where you are and where you want to be.
- Formulate your organizational values in terms of polarities. Stimulate and teach people to balance between opposite poles according to the given situation instead of "educating" them in one direction.
- Invest time and effort in sharing the underlying organizational purpose as a reference point for the inner compass.
- Establish a process for a paradoxical dialogue on core polarities and how to cope with them at all levels of the organization.
- Instill confidence, especially when things go wrong.
- Accept that there may be people who like to have clear guidelines and adapt your approach accordingly.

8.3 Caught in the Middle: Reconciling Different Worlds

For organizations to function, they need interfaces on all levels. For that purpose, they create a number of intermediary roles, which

counterbalance all kinds of specialized and often self-absorbed silos. The main focus of these intermediary roles is to make connections and to build bridges. You'll find bridgebuilders on all levels:

- between the organization and its customers or the public, such
  as sales and service roles, community workers, care professionals, teachers, or consultants;
- with other organizations, such as relationship managers,
  negotiators, or liaisons with external partners, suppliers, government agencies, or acquired companies;
- between the top of the organization and the shop floor, such as
  middle managers, team leaders, controllers, support services, or
  compliance officers; and
- between different parts of the same organization, such as internal account managers or business partners.

What these roles have in common is a focus on bringing together
worlds with different and sometimes conflicting goals, priorities,
concerns, and interests, and on finding solutions that work for all
parties.

All these roles face the same paradoxical challenge: they are paid
to represent the organization (or a specific part of it) and to safeguard its interests. However, they engage with other parties and
have to accommodate their needs and interests, too. People in these
intermediary roles need to keep both parties happy. They often develop double or divided loyalties.

In an ideal world, this natural tension is hardly noticeable because
both interests are aligned. For example, focusing on the needs of
clients, providing them with adequate solutions, and making them
happy also creates value for the organization in the form of money,
appreciation, customer loyalty, or reputation. At the end of the day,
everyone is satisfied. Or, by investing in people, providing mean-
ingful and satisfying work, and making sure that everyone can fully

develop their talents, an organization improves its own performance, and business success soon follows.

For some organizations, these interests are closely intertwined.
Companies that focus on providing fully customized solutions,
for example, serve clients who can afford to pay the high price for
unique customization: one-on-one teaching, custom-made furniture, unique jewelry, or personal assistance. The more the organization caters to its clients' needs, the higher customer satisfaction will
be and, as a result, the more the organization will profit.

However, in many cases there are areas where interests diverge or
even clash. For example, an organization may want to standardize
as much as possible to be more efficient in operational processes and
costs. Its customers, on the other hand, feel unique and would like
a solution that fully meets their specific needs. This creates tension,
with the professional or manager in the intermediate position feeling trapped between these two worlds, bending over backward to
appease both parties. People who are good at this work need to be
flexible, excellent communicators, capable of connecting and convincing people, and creative in finding out-of-the-box solutions. But
above all, they need to enjoy the often-difficult challenges involved
in being "caught in the middle."

In many sectors pressure increases because all sides continually
set higher expectations. Market pressure plays an important role in
this development because organizations need to become more efficient in order to survive, and that often means less customization
and more standardization for economies of scale. Individualization
and empowerment are important trends in the opposition direction:
everyone feels unique and wants something that suits their specific
needs ("We're paying for it, aren't we?"). Consumers are becoming
increasingly demanding and critical about the products and services they pay for, even when they choose the cheapest options.

Sometimes intermediaries find themselves under extreme or even
unbearable tension. Teachers, for example, are required to teach

larger classes while students and parents are increasingly asking for
more one-on-one attention. The time caregivers can spend on a single care home resident may be very limited, but the residents and
their families each make extra requests and require special accom-
modations. Team leaders want to give team members the opportunity to broaden their knowledge and skills, but they experience a
lot of pressure to achieve short-term production and cost reduction
targets. These intermediaries can try to go the extra mile and connect both worlds, or they might conclude that it's no longer possible
to satisfy both sides. Whatever they do, they can seldom do it right;
they can't sufficiently accommodate the specific needs of their clients, and they also fail to meet their organization's goals.

When intermediaries fail to meet the conflicting expectations of
both sides, their identity and sense of belonging are at stake as both
parties see them as representatives of "the other side." For example,
business analysts are the linking pin between the business units and
IT. They set out to be bridge builders, but business units may see
them as advocates of IT, and IT might consider them "foot soldiers
for the business." Similarly, team leaders can be seen by their team
members as "puppets of top management" while top management
experiences them as "delegates of the workforce."

In this situation, it may feel tempting to choose between the two
poles/parties: either go all in for the organization and don't bother
with the specific needs and aspirations of customers or team members, or fully commit to clients and staff and resist adapting to the
rigidity of the organization. However, soon it will turn out that
they are equally uncomfortable positions to be in, and neither can
be maintained for long. Some people in intermediary positions let
this drag on for so long that they end up suffering from burnout or
depression.

How can we deal with this in an effective way? This question applies not only to those who are sandwiched in the middle, but also
to the organization that is struggling with this area of tension. It's

clearly a shared responsibility. Although the following list is certainly not exhaustive, here are some suggestions to avoid getting caught in the crossfire:

ON A PERSONAL LEVEL

- Stay **connected** to both poles/parties and invest in strengthening the relationship with both sides. If you don't, and you align with only one side, you may find yourself in an uncomfortable and frustrating position.
- It's important, for both you and those around you, to **explicitly name** the area of tension that you're dealing with. Share this tension with both parties and make them aware of it, even if they are not willing or able to change their behavior. Make all expectations clear on both sides and pass the ball back when it's not possible to meet certain expectations. The pitfall is not seeing the underlying polarity in which you're trapped and ending up reacting to the specific content of each friction that arises or blaming yourself ("I'm not good enough because I'm failing to satisfy both sides"). Remember that tensions are inherent to the role and not tied to you personally.
- Connecting two parties in the outside world can only be done if you are able to connect both sides **within yourself**. It all begins with regular reflection and understanding how you relate to both sides. What do both parties stand for and how strongly do their values resonate with yours? Do you really believe in these values or are you just paying lip service? What would be a good balance or synthesis for you and how does that relate to the preferred balance of the organization? Being conscious about this enables you to make better decisions for yourself and the organization.
- Be **creative** with both/and solutions. For example: How can you give your client/patient/student the full attention that they need

in the limited time that you have? You can only come to both/ and solutions that go beyond the level of superficial compromises when you are deeply connected with both sides.

ON AN ORGANIZATIONAL LEVEL

- Be **honest** toward your clients and your staff. For example, if your organization is under cost pressure, be transparent about this and state very clearly what this means for your staff and your clients. This will generate much more understanding than presenting yourself as an organization that wants to deliver customized solutions while in fact you can only supply standard products. Nothing hurts your credibility and image more than when you don't live up to your words.
- **Mention** and acknowledge existing tensions, the difficult position of those in intermediary roles, and the dedication, energy, and creativity that is expected from them. Take your own responsibility as an organization to reduce these tensions and don't just leave it to the intermediary to "solve" them. Make the tensions that everyone experiences part of the daily conversation and work together to find effective ways to cope with them. Talk about how this trend will evolve in the future and the position you want to take as an organization. Do you want to let this tension rise further (because this may be the only way to effectively "re-educate" the somewhat spoiled clients), do you want to maintain it at a constant level (because it is inevitable), or do you actually want to reduce the tension?
- Be **creative** in finding both/and solutions. For example, there may be very simple ways to give proper attention to clients and their needs, and to positively surprise them, even when you're under cost pressure.

KEY POINTS

- In many roles, people are caught between conflicting interests.
- In an intermediary role: share your struggle with the parties involved and keep the dialogue open with both sides.
- As an organization: identify and acknowledge the tensions and the difficult position for those in the intermediate position. Take organizational responsibility to reduce these tensions and don't leave it exclusively to the intermediary professional to "solve" them.
- Help each other to cope with these tensions and work together to find creative solutions.

PARADOXICALLY COMPETENT

In this chapter, I will focus on the competencies required to effectively handle paradoxes. First, I want to answer that question at an individual level: Which underlying qualities and skills are important to develop and stimulate in order to become paradoxically competent? Second, I will conclude by raising a similar question for the organizational level: What makes an organization as a whole competent in effectively dealing with polarities?

9.1 The Paradoxically Competent Professional and Manager

In principle, all tasks for which a set of linear rules can be formulated, no matter how complicated they are, can also be automated. This development is already underway and will continue, not only in operational processes but also in highly qualified, specialized work, such as medical diagnoses, mortgage advice, or stock exchange transactions. People and their talents will continue to make the difference in tasks that require creativity, and in all complex areas where there is no one right answer but where a specific balance needs to be sought in every different situation. It no longer suffices to specialize in just one "trick." Real strength lies in being able to combine different and often seemingly opposing approaches. As I mentioned earlier, creativity arises mainly in people who bring together and combine opposing qualities. In section 3.2, I referred to several studies showing that effective leaders and managers are characterized by an ability to think in terms of both/and solutions and to be flexible in using different styles; the broader the range of roles, approaches, and styles leaders can rely on, either in themselves or with others, the more effective they can be. What does this mean in everyday practice?

9.1.1 Recognize and Value Our Contradictory Nature

We tend to categorize and seek clear profiles of ourselves and of others. Our whole culture is permeated by the myth of some sort of unambiguous "true self" which we feel we must live up to, whereas, if we take a closer look, we're in fact all bubbling pots of contradictions. For every characteristic we have or think we have (extroverted, rational, planned, innovative, etc.), we are also to a greater or lesser degree the opposite (introverted, emotional, improvisational, conservative, etc.). But we like to simplify. For example, the Myers Briggs Type Indicator (MBTI) actually measures a continuum between pairs of opposing qualities, but what we tend to remember about this indicator is the general type: "Ah, are you also an ENTJ?" However, the real strength of the MBTI® lies in the fact that it expresses the need for both sides: introverted and extroverted, concept-driven and fact-based, thinking as well as feeling, convergent and divergent.

We always carry both sides of the coin. It's often the situation that determines which of the two aspects we bring to the front and which we move to the back. In fact, it is often difficult to distinguish which side is actually the front. Exhibiting extreme distance and coolness can be a form of protection, hiding extreme sensitivity and empathy. We may work hard to fight a natural tendency to laziness. We may show off and seek the spotlight to overcompensate for timidity. Aggression could hide an underlying lack of confidence.

Which is our "true self"? Or are we simply always both? As I argued earlier in 4.1.6, maybe trying to define one's "true self" is just one big illusion and a waste of energy.

People who are very good at something may highlight this strong side of themselves in a job interview. Sometimes, however, people emphasize qualities that they have the most trouble with. If an interview candidate keeps mentioning the importance of good communication, is it their strong point or their weak point? After all, we tend to focus on the things we struggle with. When we have a natural talent for something, we might take this for granted and not think about it much. The job interviewer might get the wrong impression that the qualities that people mention the most are their strongest skills, when it's the other way around.

We would therefore be staying much closer to the truth if we were to describe our identities in terms of polarities instead of trying to reduce them to one pole. In job interviews, it would be much more interesting to know how well the candidate can cope with these tension and polarities. Instead of trying to find out whether the person is more introverted or extroverted, ask how well the person can play with both characteristics in different situations. This would provide the job interviewer with much deeper insight, instead of measuring singular qualities and matching these with a linear competency profile.

An organization that is really concerned about its people doesn't try to make them fit a certain profile or reduce them to only those characteristics that are directly useful. Such an organization recognizes the versatility of people and their inner contradictions, creating a culture where people are allowed to develop their different sides. This makes people feel truly valued as human beings (and not just as instrumental "human resources"), which in turn stimulates them to go the extra mile. For example, this means that we shouldn't always tap into the well-known qualities of people (such as action-driven, result-oriented, or assertive) but also provide people with the necessary space at work to practice their opposite sides (such as contemplative, explorative, or compassionate).

Instead of going on about the same thing all the time ("sales, sales, sales" or "production, production, production"), it can be refreshing and stimulating to give people the opportunity every now and then to do something completely different at work. It's important to prevent people from feeling drained and to allow them to recharge their batteries. As employers, we might assume that people will make up for work in their free time, but then we're forgetting that for most people, work takes up the better part of the week. And it's also only fair to compensate for the fact that work is increasingly invading people's private lives and that everyone has to be more or less available 24/7. In any case, this would be an effective way to help people stay energized and motivated, and for the organization to avoid problems such as burnout and long-term absenteeism.

9.1.2 Multiple Careers: From a T Profile to an M Profile

Most jobs don't require every one of a person's sides. Many people practice their "other" sides during their free time, with a hobby or passion. You might work on an assembly line during the day and write a historical novel at night. Or you might spend the work week sitting at a desk or a conference table, and on the weekends use your hands to make your own furniture. There's a growing tendency for people to have two or even several "careers" in order to develop different aspects of themselves. Activities that were formerly only seen as hobby-like pastimes are gaining importance in people's lives and are getting a more equal status to the "official" work. These parallel paths may have a clear connection with each other. For example, an HR manager might also teach at a college for a few hours a week or do some consultancy on the side. But sometimes they belong to very different worlds, such as a farmer-lawyer, working in the field in the morning and receiving clients in the afternoon, or an IT specialist with a massage practice.

A T profile is characterized by a broad set of general skills and one in-depth specialization; one step further is an M profile, with several parallel pillars of specialization. An M profile can be very enriching because it allows us to develop and broaden our knowledge in various areas. It provides different, independent sources of motivation and energy, making us less vulnerable to burnout and bore-out. If one of the pillars is slightly wobbly at a certain moment, we still have the other pillar or pillars to stand on. It also helps us deal more easily with change. Our professional identity doesn't exclusively depend on one role but is spread over two or more roles. If there are major changes in one domain, we still have solid ground to stand on in the other domains, and that gives us greater peace of mind.

These parallel paths can reinforce each other and lead to new ideas and initiatives where they cross. The entrepreneurship, for example, that people demonstrate in their own business, hobby, or voluntary work may also reflect positively on the work they do for an organization. Organizations should facilitate multiple careers, both inside and outside the organization, as they can contribute to more complete, satisfied, and broadly developed people and foster "crossover" innovation. The paradoxical challenge will be to safeguard the boundaries and focus of each role so that work in one area is not at the expense of other areas, while stimulating cross-fertilization. The least organizations can do is remove the barriers to those multiple paths. The bottleneck is usually the lack of time to combine everything, but organizations can allow more flexible ways of working, focusing more on output than on input and physical presence, or by giving employees the freedom and flexibility to go on sabbaticals, temporarily work part-time, or simply adjust their working hours.

It might also be possible to offer parallel careers within one's own organization: someone could work at the help desk in the morning and be a programmer in the afternoon, or be a financial analyst and an HR consultant in one, or work part of the week in sales and the other part in production planning. It will undoubtedly help to connect different organizational silos. In many small companies, this multifunctional way of working is common practice (often from necessity), but many large organizations still work traditionally with "mono positions." Offering parallel careers and "multi-roles" in an organization opens the door to a realm of talent that is currently going unused. A team member who doesn't show much initiative in their work might be totally passionate about promoting and doing fundraising for a nonprofit organization in their spare time. Perhaps they don't feel like doing such promotional activities for the organization and want to keep the two worlds strictly separate, but perhaps they have sought out these opportunities for personal development and fulfillment outside the organization because there was no chance to apply them at work.

9.1.3 Beyond a Prescribed Line of Conduct

We could try to describe paradoxical leadership in terms of a specific line of conduct. For example, we could say that a paradoxical leader is someone who is more focused on looking for connections than emphasizing differences. We could also say that they typically try to unite conflicting interests, such as the aspirations of staff members and the goals of the organization. Or we could try to characterize a paradoxical leader as someone who is always looking for integrated and sustainable solutions: How can we link economic growth to planetary health? How can we ensure short-term profitability and long-term sustainable growth at the same time? How can we combine financial, ecological, social, and spiritual goals?

However, all these characterizations are too restrictive because when the situation requires, a paradoxical leader might also propose the complete opposite approach, actively seeking confrontation or going straight for the short-term goals and nothing else.

Paradoxical leadership thus involves more than just having a number of alternative values, views, and beliefs because these views can also become rigid one-sided dogmas. It's much more about looking at the world in a different way, seeing situations as a continuous balancing act between interdependent opposing forces which should sometimes be brought closer together and at other times moved further apart. Sometimes enlarging the difference and raising the tension may be helpful in overcoming resistance, enabling a breakthrough, or realizing change. However, paradoxical leadership always requires leaders to monitor and safeguard the overall balance in the long term.

9.2 The Paradoxical Skill Set

Paradoxical leadership starts with ourselves. We first need to learn how to recognize and consciously deal with our personal polarities before "tinkering" with those of our teams, colleagues, or organizational structures. The inside and outside worlds are inextricably linked. We explored how to play with opposite poles in chapter 4; it requires a number of skills that many of us possess but have not always fully developed.

9.2.1 Eight Paradoxical Skills

Talent expert and coach Silvia Derom and I have worked to identify the core skills needed to deal effectively with paradoxes. Based on our own professional experience and literature research,[1] we have distinguished eight skills, all on the level of inner leadership and self-awareness:

1 Self-observe and take a metaposition
2 Self-analyze and put the inner world into words

---

1 Including authors such as Susan David, Adam Grant, Carol Dweck, and Brené Brown.

3 Allow discomfort
4 Practice an exploratory attitude
5 Consciously deploy different personal styles
6 Use both/and thinking
7 Engage in dialogue
8 Demonstrate vulnerability and humility

These skills apply to everyone, regardless of role or position, although the contexts in which they are used may strongly differ. Each skill has an internal as well as an external aspect: how to harness the opposing forces within ourselves and how to use tensions in our relations with others in a productive way. We can link these skills to the steps that we need to take to deal effectively with polarities (see section 4.1):

How can I deal effectively with polarities? (8 steps in section 4.1)	What skills do I need? (8 paradoxical skills)
1. **Recognize:** become aware of polarities and how they work	1. Self-observe and take a metaposition
2. **Name and explore:** identify and get to know our own Polarities	2. Self-analyze and put the inner world into words
3. **Allow:** allow for tension as a productive force	3. Allow discomfort
4. **Value:** both sides	4. Practice an exploratory attitude
5. **Play:** switch back and forth between opposite poles	5. Consciously deploy different personal styles
6. **Integrate:** experiment with combining and connecting opposite poles	6. Use both/and thinking
7. **Connect and communicate:** Engage Others and Reach Out	7. Engage in dialogue
8. **Serve:** Contribute to a Higher Purpose	8. Demonstrate vulnerability and humility

The eight paradoxical skills are interconnected and build upon each other. For example, in order to associate with a polarity in an open and exploratory way (Skill 4), we need to have noticed it (Skill 1), explored and named it (Skill 2), and allowed it despite discomfort (Skill 3). To consciously switch between the two sides of a polarity depending on the situation (Skill 5), it helps if we have already been able to explore both sides in an open and appreciative way (Skill 4). I illustrate this interconnection in figure 9.1.

Figure 9.1. Eight interconnected paradoxical skills

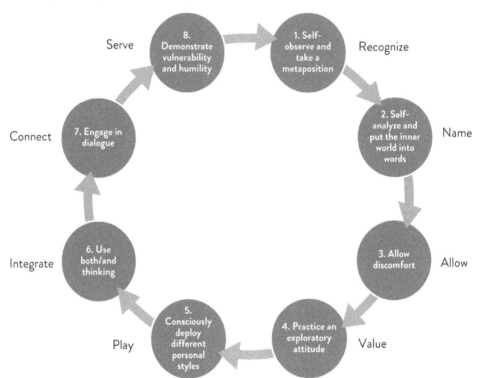

However, you do not need to develop these skills step by step and master the first one before moving on to the second one. Personal development is not linear; it is an iterative process in which all the skills develop together, in a continuous cycle. It's important to start somewhere in this cycle; this will automatically trigger all the other required skills.

Let's illustrate these eight skills with the following case. Sarah is a team leader. Due to the COVID-19 crisis, the interpersonal relations and the mood in her team have changed significantly. Economic uncertainty is causing a lot of unrest and stress. Working from home might remove the stress of the morning commute, but it makes it much more challenging to keep in touch with colleagues. Everyone deals with it differently: some struggle with drawing a strict line between work and private life, others have difficulty coping with the lack of personal contact, while a few unexpectedly blossom. The situation increases the existing tension between "extroverts" and "introverts" even more. And finally, Sarah is used to having her team physically around her and holding all the reins, but that's not possible now. Which skills can help Sarah deal effectively with all this?

SKILL 1: SELF-OBSERVE AND TAKE A METAPOSITION

This skill is the ability to consciously monitor and consider what you are feeling, thinking, or doing in a situation. Essential to this skill is the mental flexibility to fluently switch between focusing on the external world and being aware of what's going on inside yourself. You monitor your moods, tensions, emotions, beliefs, motives, and needs as if you were observing another person. You can temporarily step out of the action and take a moment to self-reflect. However, this process can even take place simultaneously: you are both in the action and taking the position of inner observer.

Taking this metaposition gives you a broader context. You may be trapped in a certain role that does not necessarily help you or the situation. Or your behavior may be based on ingrained trigger-response patterns, which have proven their usefulness in the past but are not functional in the current situation. By observing these patterns within yourself, you are no longer completely coinciding with them. Becoming aware of your inner world enables you to take full responsibility for it and provides the necessary space to make changes.

This requires more than detached intellectual activity. It requires paying attention to subtle and concrete signals (physical, emotional, mental). What do you feel and experience? What does the situation do to you? This sensitivity also allows you to better feel which response a particular situation requires.

But no matter how self-reflective you try to be, you will always have blind spots. That is why it is so important to actively seek feedback. Where self-observation inevitably falls short, feedback from others can tell you what you need to know.

Sarah's situation: Instead of immediately switching to a problem-solving mode, Sarah has learned to zoom out for a moment and to take the time to self-reflect: "What tensions does this situation evoke in me? What do I feel about them? What seemingly conflicting things do I want at the same time?" For example, she finds it especially difficult not to have clarity herself. Therefore, she cannot provide clarity to her team, which makes her feel inadequate as a manager. She also questions her team about the tensions they experience.

SKILL 2: SELF-ANALYZE AND PUT THE INNER WORLD INTO WORDS

This skill is the ability to actively explore and explicitly name the areas of tension that you experience. It is a combination of further investigation and finding the right words for what specifically affects you. The challenge here is to pinpoint the root cause of the tension without getting sidetracked or focusing on superficial forms or manifestations.

The challenge is to dig deeper: what is this tension really about? Which sides of yourself seem to contradict each other? How would you best describe the underlying polarities? Can seemingly different tensions in your life or work emerge from a common core polarity? Is it possible for you to describe these polarities in neutral terms, without a pronounced positive or negative emotional charge, such as the tension between "deciding" and "exploring" as opposed to that between "getting things done" and "indecisiveness"?

This skill also involves being willing and able to raise difficult issues in your relationships with others. Everyone may feel these issues that no one dares to talk about. The challenge here is to make these issues as specific and concrete as possible, while remaining close to your own perception and responsibility, and without accusing or attacking others.

Sarah's situation: Sarah has made it clear to herself what she finds most difficult. She is mainly concerned with the tension between wanting to provide structure on the one hand and going with the flow on the other. Sarah also tries to get a hold of the underlying tensions within the team. She notices that the more extroverted colleagues struggle the most with the lack of stimulating feedback, confirmation, and encouragement, and that the more introverted team members are often relieved that they have less distracting stimuli to deal with.

SKILL 3: ALLOW DISCOMFORT

This skill is the ability to allow tension, resistance, loss of control, not knowing, making mistakes, and negative feedback to exist without trying to brush them aside or fix them. Tension and discomfort may lead to new perspectives and ideas because you are no longer able to rely on familiar routines and existing patterns. Do you dare to critically question yourself and go outside your comfort zone? What will happen if you step outside the boundaries of a familiar and safe position? Will the ground under your feet disappear, or will something new arise and provide you with the means to create a new balance? Can you learn to be comfortable with discomfort?

Discomfort arises from the confusion of contradictory values. It is the fear that your solid and cherished identity and your basic convictions about the world are at risk. One way to make this bearable is to articulate and express your distress and feelings of discomfort.

Another aspect of this skill is the willingness to face parts of yourself that you don't like. You may notice things about yourself that do not please you or match the image you have of yourself. Most people also have a conscious or unconscious tendency to filter out perceptions, convictions, and intentions that are undesirable in order to maintain a bright and shiny version of themselves. But these are aspects of yourself that play a specific role in who you are as a whole. They are necessary for your inner balance. In some cases, they may even be hidden talents that you could use in a constructive way. This also applies to allowing emotions that may be difficult to understand or may seem inappropriate or undesirable; these emotions tell you when something inside of you is out of balance. "Allowing" in this context means allowing these aspects to exist. You don't have to like them, but you shouldn't fight them or push them away.

Finally, this skill is about showing compassion toward yourself and others. No one is perfect and everyone has rough edges; fighting imperfections takes a tremendous amount of energy, without any guarantee of success. You can benefit much more from being kind and compassionate to yourself and by spending this energy in a positive way.

Sarah's situation: Instead of trying to be upbeat and energetically moving forward in a contrived way, Sarah offers herself and the team the space to share their feelings of discomfort. She expresses to her team how uncomfortable she sometimes feels. In turn, the team recognizes these tensions in themselves and the discomfort they all experience becomes more bearable. This openness brings them closer together as a team: everyone seems to be struggling and looking for answers.

SKILL 4: PRACTICE AN EXPLORATORY ATTITUDE

This skill is the ability to be open and curious about views, values, beliefs, or behaviors that are unfamiliar or, at first glance, contradict your long-standing convictions. This skill goes beyond allowing tensions and contradictory aspects of yourself; it's about discovering the value of both sides and diving into each of them. Your first reflex might be to judge and condemn, or perhaps to feel apprehensive or afraid. But after this initial shock, you can try to understand where these views are coming from, what they mean, and what role and function they play. You should maintain the underlying assumption that there's a positive motive and function behind every view or behavior even though the apparent form may be despicable or destructive.

You may recall the "golden triangle" (figure 6.2), where two apparently oppositional poles overlap; this is when you leave behind the level of appearance (which might be negative) and explore the underlying (positive) needs, concerns, values, and goals. The best way to do this is to be curious, ask questions, listen, observe attentively, and withhold judgment. Withholding judgment is difficult because humans are undeniably emotional beings, and emotional judgments help determine which way to go and how to survive. This doesn't mean that you need to agree with every position, but you can make an effort to understand where oppositional impulses come from and how they might be channeled more positively.

Sarah's situation: Once Sarah and her team have opened up to each other, Sarah realizes that there is power behind uncertainty. It can be a breeding ground for innovative ideas that would never arise under normal circumstances. She also notes that her more introverted colleagues enjoy working from home because they have time to work on their own, without distractions. She wonders how she can maintain this strength, even after the COVID-19 crisis. How can she better take into account the different styles and needs of individual team members? How can her more extroverted colleagues also reap the benefits of low-stimulus moments or days?

SKILL 5: CONSCIOUSLY DEPLOY DIFFERENT PERSONAL STYLES

This skill is the ability to consciously activate or deactivate your different sub-selves, identities, roles, or styles, depending on what the situation requires. For example, in one context, you might call upon your action-oriented side, whereas in another you may need your reflective side more. Using the previous skills, you are already aware of both sides and have accepted them as part of your multifaceted identity. But with this skill, you can call upon both poles when necessary. In other words, you control these opposite sides to some degree and are not just controlled by them. This makes you flexible and able to respond quickly and appropriately to different situations. It also provides you with more space and freedom to choose your own course of action. You are no longer trapped in automatic stimulus-response patterns but can consciously decide to take a completely different path.

Sarah's situation: Sarah uses the current situation as an opportunity to develop a side of her that has up to now remained untapped. When team members come to her with their questions and concerns, she learns not to immediately look for the solution herself, but to respond with a question in return and leave the responsibility with them. The team members feel more ownership, and Sarah frees up some time and space. Within the team, Sarah can now alternate between driving for results and reflecting together on team atmosphere and perceptions.

SKILL 6: USE BOTH/AND THINKING

This skill is the ability to come up with new combinations of seemingly opposing elements (Strategies 6 and 7 of the Polarity Wheel). This requires you to look beyond the world of concrete manifestations and to get to the essence of both poles. From there, you can develop new creative combinations. In short, this is the ability to fully grasp the complexity of a given situation, use your imagination, and think outside of the box. Or, as F. Scott Fitzgerald aptly put it: "The test of a first-rate intelligence is the ability to hold two opposing ideas in mind at the same time and still retain the ability to function."

Sarah's situation: Sarah experiments with a new meeting format in which, in addition to all operational matters, there is also room for deeper exchange and personal contact. She abandons the classic agenda structure, leaving operational matters for her team to sort out among themselves. Instead, she starts every team meeting with something unexpected, whether it is a meditation, an inspiring video, or an exciting story. Soon, team members come with their own inspiring suggestions; thus providing inspiration has now become a team effort and responsibility. What Sarah retains is her ability to create a safe environment and to provide guidance when needed.

SKILL 7: ENGAGE IN DIALOGUE

Where the previous skills focused on how to deal with your own polarities, this skill focuses on your relationship with others in a polarity-driven interplay. You are part of many different social systems and thus also part of all kinds of polarizing movements that take place within these systems. For example, in a working relationship, you might be the creative pole and your colleague the procedural pole, or "the system" might be forcing you into the role of caregiver, leader, or rebel.

In addition to an open and exploratory attitude (Skill 4), dialogue requires you to empathize with others who might be very different from you and to try to recognize these points of difference in yourself. The challenge is to acknowledge that what irritates you in others is often a part of yourself that you have not yet accepted.

Dialogue also requires you to consciously switch between different levels of communication: between abstract and concrete, content and process, rational and feeling, explicit and implicit, surface and undercurrent, the expected outcome and the relationship, and between different idioms and paradigms. The challenge is to fully engage in the exchange, but at the same time be able to take a meta-level position and switch to another communication level when required. It requires you to listen and observe carefully, being attentive to unspoken messages, body language, and processes that happen just below the surface (such as mood changes, role switches, or power plays).

Finally, being able to conduct effective dialogue means balancing between many opposing values, like a tightrope walker. For example, it is a challenge to be open to the views of others without losing sight of your own values and interests.

Sarah's situation: Sarah puts "introverts" and "extroverts" together in pairs to work on improvement projects, with the challenge of arriving at a joint approach by listening carefully to each other. If she notices that in a discussion about business content other sensitivities play a role, Sarah stops the conversion to reflect together on what is happening below the waterline. As Sarah shows a strong commitment to put the principles of effective dialogue into practice – which is not always easy to do – she also sets an inspiring example for her team to do the same.

SKILL 8: SHOW VULNERABILITY AND HUMILITY

This skill is the ability to put your own position (perspective, role, contribution, pride, image, status, etc.) into a broader perspective and acknowledge its relative importance. It means you are willing and able to put aside your ego when it gets in the way of a better solution or a higher goal and admit your own failures, mistakes, and shortcomings. However, you should be able to admit to your shortcomings without losing your fundamental sense of self-worth. Adam Grant named this interesting paradoxical concept "confident humility."[2]

When you dare to be open and honest about your needs, drives, fears, and emotions, to share your dilemmas and struggles in a vulnerable way, and to sometimes drop your facade of having everything under control, you create the opportunity for authentic connection with others.

Finally, it is helpful to not always take yourself too seriously. If you can look at yourself with humor, you can also bring a necessary lightness to tense situations.

---

2 Adam Grant, *Think Again: The Power of Knowing What You Don't Know* (London: W.H. Allen, 2021).

Sarah's situation: Sarah originally thought she was indispensable to keep the team afloat, but she now sees that the team can often manage just fine without her. This frees her to pursue new projects and ideas. She can now make jokes about her urge to control situations, which reduces tension, creates an atmosphere of openness and trust, and stimulates others to do the same.

Practicing all these paradoxical skills helps Sarah to be much more confident and resilient in situations of uncertainty and tension, and to give more responsibility to the team. Team morale has been boosted as people feel recognized and know that their different sides and talents are valued. They feel free and safe to share their concerns and struggles and empowered to find creative solutions. As a consequence the team is very engaged and highly productive in a context where one might expect exactly the opposite.

9.2.2 How to Use the Paradoxical Skills

METACOMPETENCIES

How do these paradoxical skills relate to the competencies we have always used, such as result orientation, conscientiousness, sociability, teamwork, or persuasion? Classic competencies usually focus on how proficient we are in single qualities or skills. The eight paradoxical skills are instead metacompetencies. They define how good we are at activating, deploying, combining, and balancing these classic qualities in different contexts. For example, should we take control, let the process run its course, or work out a combination of both?

DEVELOPMENT OF PARADOXICAL SKILLS

The paradoxical skills are all strongly related to self-awareness and the ability to observe your inner world. Some people are more naturally inclined to introspection, while others need to learn it through active and conscious effort. However, this is a muscle you can train with exercise. Introspective methods like mindfulness exercises can be helpful here, along with interactive methods like systematically asking for and giving feedback.

Every development process starts with a good baseline measurement. To give managers and professionals a clear insight into where they stand on the paradoxical skills, Silvia Derom and I have developed the Paradoxical Skills Inventory. You can fill it out freely at https://paradoxical-leadership.com/assess and receive your profile with practical development tips.

A number of contextual factors, both internal and external, influence how easy or difficult it is to develop the paradoxical skills and put them into practice. These include the following:

Internal factors	• **A basic feeling of safety:** feeling safe will help you open up.
	• **Attachment style in relationships:**[3] having a secure attachment style help you to keep balance in relationships.
	• **Personality traits:** for example, "Openness to experience" as one of the Big five personality traits[4] will be helpful in developing these skills, especially Skill 4 (exploratory attitude and learning mindset) and 7 (dialogue).
	• **Self-confidence/self-esteem:** A little self-confidence will help you to cope with negative input in a constructive way.
External factors	• **Stress level:** The higher your stress level, the more difficult it is to step out of fixed behavioral patterns.
	• **Energy level and physical health:** The better you feel and the more energy you have, the easier it is to react in a balanced way.
	• **Fulfillment of basic needs:**[5] If you are focused on survival, you will be less inclined to see the broader picture.
	• **Context:** A safe social environment invites people to openly share their tensions and struggles with polarities.

---

3 Four attachment styles, derived from the Attachment Theory of John Bowlby, are (1) Secure, (2) Dismissive-avoidant, (3) Anxious-preoccupied, (4) Fearful-avoidant.
4 In psychological scientific literature there is a broadly accepted concept of five basic personality traits: (1) Openness to experience (inventive/curious vs. consistent/cautious); (2) Conscientiousness (efficient/organized vs. extravagant/careless); (3) Extraversion (outgoing/energetic vs. solitary/reserved); (4) Agreeableness (friendly/compassionate vs. critical/rational); (5) Neuroticism (sensitive/nervous vs. resilient/confident). "Big Five Personality Traits," Wikipedia, accessed 2 September 2022, https://en.wikipedia.org/wiki/Big_Five_personality_traits.
5 See Maslow's hierarchy of needs.

SKILLS AND COUNTER-SKILLS: LOOKING FOR A BALANCE

Paradoxical thinking assumes that every force evokes its counterforce, and that also applies to the paradoxical skills. You shouldn't try to use these skills at all times and in every situation, as there will also be situations that require you to do the opposite. If you apply these skills to their extreme, dysfunctional effects will start to prevail. You may be too open and too sensitive, overanalyze yourself, or lose your decisiveness, direction, stability, cause, or identity. Therefore, you need to maintain the opposing skills in order to keep the balance. You will recognize in the counter-skills some traditional leadership and professional values:

Paradoxical skills	Risks when overdone	Skills to counterbalance
1. Self-observe and take a metaposition	Dissociation from yourself and loss of spontaneity	• Keep touch with reality and have both feet on the ground • Act spontaneously, following and enjoying the flow of your passions, feelings or activities
2. Self-analyze and put the inner world into words	Analysis paralysis; overly self-centered reflection and rumination	• Look outward • Focus on action, results, and practical solutions
3. Allow discomfort	Focus on the hard and the difficult; constant self-improvement; passivity; inability to relax	• Give yourself a break • Maintain lightness, playfulness, fun, and comfort • Self-protection and action
4. Practice an exploratory attitude	Too much openness; inability to maintain boundaries or to rely on your own judgment; inability to settle on conclusions	• Draw and maintain your boundaries • Make clear judgments • Focus on action and results
5. Consciously deploy different personal styles	Over-adaptation to the environment; loss of self and loss of direction	• Keep a steady course and stick to the plan with determination • Stand for what you believe in with self-confidence
6. Use both/and thinking	Overcomplication by connecting everything with everything else; boundlessness	• Simplify where possible, separating complex issues into manageable pieces • Make unambiguous choices
7. Engage in dialogue	Loss of own interests when too empathic with the other; loss of spontaneity in self-expression; inconclusiveness	• Be convincing and build your case • Be spontaneous • Draw and maintain your boundaries • Focus on action and results
8. Demonstrate humility and vulnerability	Failure to take yourself seriously; loss of self-worth	• Maintain self-confidence • Practice self-respect

AN INCLUSIVE CONCEPT OF SELF

It will help you develop these skills if you stop seeing your identity as a perfectly streamlined and consistent story, but rather as an eclectic and messy hodgepodge of conflicting elements, which is just fine. You will of course have your own preferences, values, and particularities that make you "you," but you will also always have the opposing elements in yourself to some degree. If you can connect the conflicting parts of yourself and experience this "self" as something greater than its parts, it will be easier to switch between these parts without feeling that you no longer have solid ground to stand on. You know that you can choose which selves to put in the foreground and move to the background.

Such an inclusive concept of self is much more robust and resilient to change than a streamlined all-or-nothing identity. If circumstances confront you with unfamiliar or unknown aspects of yourself, your existing identity does not fall apart, because it can easily accommodate and incorporate these newly revealed elements and use them productively.

The principle of a flexible, resilient, and inclusive identity is more a matter of mindset than a skill. There is a positive interaction between the two: developing the paradoxical skills will contribute to your development of a flexible, resilient, and inclusive identity, and a flexible, resilient, and inclusive identity will facilitate your development of the paradoxical skills.

The relationships between the eight paradoxical skills, an inclusive identity, and the contextual factors are shown in figure 9.2.

AUTHENTICITY

You could also use the paradoxical competencies instrumentally to prove yourself right or even to manipulate others. For example, you might pretend to value the other person's point of view, to conduct

Figure 9.2. Paradoxical skills in a broader context

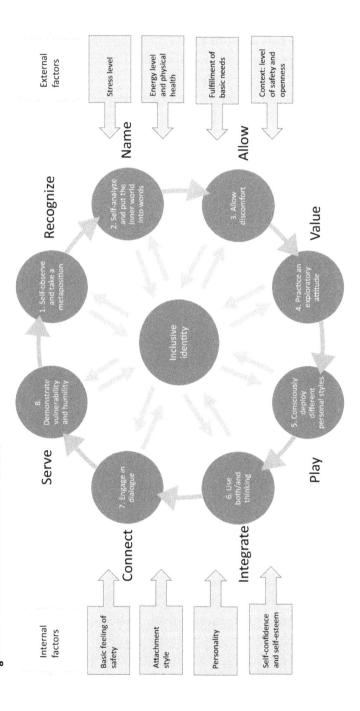

an open dialogue, or to be willing to question your own principles, when in fact you're only going through the motions to get what you want and to push your agenda.

Having the right intention is just as important, if not more important, than mastering the skills. The true aim is to achieve more balance and openness; it should not just be about using some new tricks.

9.3 The Paradoxically Competent Organization

Having started with the individual, I would like to end with the organizational level, raising a similar question: What makes an organization or a team competent in effectively dealing with polarities?

First, as I strongly emphasized throughout the book, it is a matter of awareness, attention, and mindset: the ability to see the continuous dynamic of polarities underlying daily business, to recognize that opposite poles are inseparably linked and both are needed to keep the balance, and to notice in time when drifting towards one of the extremes. Paradoxical awareness, attention, and mindset are ideally broadly shared across different organizational levels and professional disciplines.

Second, it is equally important that paradoxical thinking is deeply embedded in the way of working and in the different processes, practices, and instruments of the organization – that it becomes a kind of automatic reflex or habit, that people do without needing to be consciously alert all the time.

Both sides – mindset and embedding – are needed and reinforce each other. An organization can try to be very alert to polarities and their dynamic, but attention can also shift quickly and be quite ephemeral. Embedding paradoxical thinking in processes, practices, and instruments makes it much more durable and stable. However, embedding these without a lively paradoxical mindset and attention bears the risk of mechanically executed procedures and may install new forms of bureaucracy.

In part 2 of this book we have explored what this embedding of paradoxical thinking in the different core processes, practices, and instruments of an organization could look like. Based on that work and as a kind of practical summary, I have identified thirteen areas where paradoxical thinking can be embedded in the DNA of an organization. They can be clustered around four aspects of organizational practice.

Strategic direction and steering

1 Direction: to what extent are the organizational vision, mission, and strategy well-balanced?
2 Inspiration: to what extent do vision, mission, and strategy offer practical guidance when dealing with daily tensions?
3 Steering: how effective, efficient, and flexible is the organization in adjusting its course according to the changing context?

Leadership and decision-making

4 Leadership: how authentic, vulnerable, open, and transparent are leaders and managers?
5 Decision-making: to what extent do we actively seek dissenting views and include them in decision-making?
6 Dialogue: to what extent do professionals and departments engage in a dialogue about how to deal with tensions?

Change and innovation ability

7 Structures: to what extent are structures and systems flexible and helpful to the overall organizational goal?

8 Change: to what extent do we build stable anchors to guide and support change processes and how do we preserve what is already working well?
9 Innovation: to what extent do we seek creative tension by bringing together different perspectives and parties?

People and culture

10 Culture: to what extent can people speak about their doubts and fears, openly talk about underlying differences and organizational shadow, and be themselves?
11 Development: to what extent can people develop and practice different sides and talents of themselves?
12 Competence: to what extent are people able to reflect on their own polarities and be open to those of others?
13 Appreciation: to what extent does the organization explicitly value people for connecting different poles and providing different perspectives?

All these enablers of a paradoxically competent organization are closely interlinked and reinforce each other. However, in a specific organization or team some enablers will be more present than others. It can be very helpful to "measure" them: to see to what extent they are present and to identify the enablers that require specific attention. For that purpose, I developed the Paradoxical Organization Scan. You'll find the full questionnaire in appendix B. You can fill it out to assess and compare the results or just use it as a checklist for your own organization.

The key point is that the outcomes in all thirteen dimensions of the scan are about perceptions. They will very much depend on the position people have in the organization, the part that they can see, and the specific perspectives they hold. For example, senior management might have a different, maybe more optimistic view on the organization's paradoxical capability than middle management or professionals. People from outside the organization can also be included.

You can use the scan as a 360-degree feedback instrument on an organizational level: it's all about comparing different perceptions. In figure 9.3 you'll find an example of the outcomes, where the average scores of senior managers, middle managers, and professionals are compared.

Figure 9.3. Outcomes of the Paradoxical Organization Scan

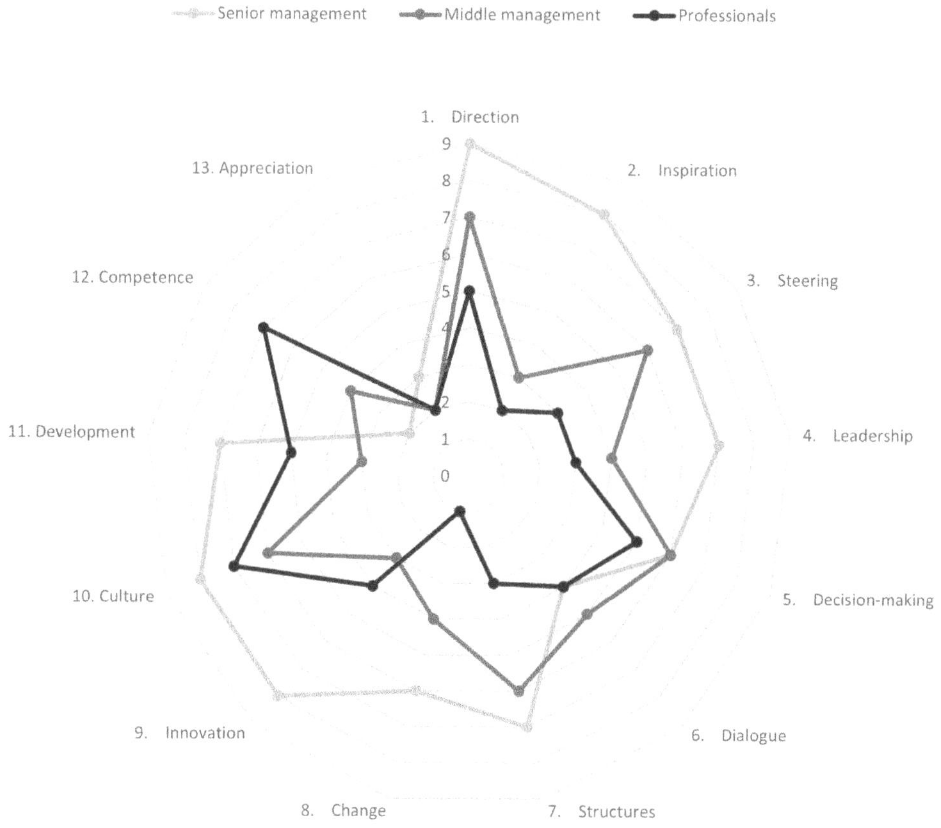

The outcomes of the scan are input for an exploratory but structured conversation about how people experience the organization's paradoxical capability. This conversation could include

several organizational levels, functional areas, or even external stakeholders. Looking together at the outcomes of the scan, one can check for collectively shared strengths and liabilities, but a focus on the differences in perception can be even more revealing. During this collective exploration, it will become clear that the enablers influence each other, and patterns will arise.

This collective exploration may result in action plans and projects. However, even more important than concrete action plans is the quality of the conversation and the awareness-creating effect it has, which will also boost the paradoxical mindset. For suggestions on how you should go about improving specific enablers, you may check the previous chapters.

KEY POINTS

- Describe your professional identity in terms of polarities instead of unambiguous qualities.
- Encourage people to develop their talents on several fronts, in different roles sequentially or even through parallel career paths.
- Learn to embrace and work with your own polarities before starting to "tinker" with the polarities of your team, colleagues, or organization.
- There is no specific approach or prescribed method for paradoxical leadership; the key is to develop a kind of continuous alertness to how polarities work and to maintain a long-term balance.
- The eight paradoxical skills are interconnected and build upon each other. They focus on self-awareness and the ability to observe your inner world.
- These paradoxical skills also need to be counterbalanced as some situations will require the opposite skills.

- An inclusive concept of self will help you develop these skills and make you more resilient to change.
- The intention behind these paradoxical skills is to achieve more balance and openness, not to use tricks to get what you want.
- The paradoxical competence of an organization is a combination of mindset and the embedding of paradoxical principles in the organization's core processes and practices. With the Paradoxical Organization Scan you can check how successful your organization is in doing the latter.

EPILOGUE

WHERE DO WE GO FROM HERE?
BACK TO THE BASICS

You might be feeling overwhelmed by all the lists of tips and tricks in part 2 of this book. How are you going to put these into practice? And above all: Where are you going to start? It's time to return to the essence.

From all the lists, you might also have the impression that applying both/and thinking and paradoxical leadership is a very complicated process. It's completely the other way around! It's a very natural and spontaneous process. The lists can provide guidance and processes to follow, but ultimately all you have to do is remember that every force always evokes its counterforce and that both sides are always needed to achieve a balanced and sustainable solution. It boils down to giving both sides sufficient space. You can contain or suppress the opposite pole for a while, but you won't be able to do this forever. If you don't provide counterbalance, the system will correct itself, often in an uncontrolled and destabilizing way.

Once you are able to view opposite poles as equivalent and can give them the space they require, the next step is to connect, combine, interweave, and integrate them. You will spontaneously feel the need to find new combinations and come up with creative solutions. Creative combinations only arise when you explore the essence of each pole and go beyond the concrete manifestations. It's similar to what happens in the orange parable: There are two people who really want the last orange. After a tug-of-war, they finally decide they are willing to split the orange in half. But it turns out that one person only needed the peel to flavor a cake and the other the juice to make a smoothie. If they had looked beyond the obvious and had questioned exactly what each of them wanted, they would have ended up with what they really needed without the need for conflict.

If this book has one aim, it is to make the reader aware of the paradoxical nature of our actions. Linear processes are more the exception than the rule, even in the seemingly straightforward and rational world of organizational management. It's up to you to be creative in finding new solutions to balance opposite poles. For further inspiration, check out https://paradoxical-leadership.com.

APPENDIX A

LIST OF COMMON POLARITIES

For your inspiration, here is a list of common polarities for individuals, teams, and organizations. I have categorized these under several reference polarities.

Familiar and New

- Preservation – Innovation
- Stability – Change
- Structure – Creativity
- Reality – Imagination
- Comfort – Tension
- Safety – Adventure
- Threats – Opportunities
- Limitations – Possibilities

Hold On and Let Go

- Control – Release
- Actively Manage – Go with the Flow
- Steer – Facilitate/Empower

- Direct – Participate
- Top-Down – Bottom-Up
- Investigate – Trust

Strict and Flexible

- Principled – Pragmatic
- Disciplined – Free
- Hard-Working – Playful
- Serious – Light
- Formal – Informal

Reflection and Action

- Planned – Improvised
- Abstract/Conceptual – Concrete/Practical
- Visionary – Grounded
- Thoughtful – Impulsive
- Thorough – Quick
- Cautious – Risk-Taking
- Wait-and-See – Responsive
- Cerebral – Physical

Broad and Narrow

- Diverge – Converge
- Explore – Conclude/Decide
- Broaden/Associate – Focus
- Long Term – Short Term
- Generalist/Breadth – Specialist/Depth

- Synthesis – Analysis
- Unbounded – Limited
- Comprehensive – Restricted
- Expansion – Back to Core
- Multidisciplinary – Separate Disciplines

Whole and Part

- Central – Decentral
- Corporate – Units
- Cohesion/Unity – Diversity
- Integrate – Differentiate

Ambition and Satisfaction

- Perfection/Excellence – Sufficiency
- Always Better – Satisfied with What Is
- Idealistic – Realistic
- Raise the Bar – Celebrate Achievements
- Work – Rest
- Stretch – Relax

Outcome and Process

- Destination – Journey
- Stick to the Plan – Follow the Process
- Accelerate – Take the Time
- Blueprint Change – Organic Change
- Future Focus – Present Focus
- Useful – Enjoyable

Simple and Complex

- Uniformity – Diversity
- Standard – Customized
- General Rules – Case-by-Case
- Big Picture – Details
- Rough – Refined

Autonomy and Attachment

- Alone – Together
- Freedom – Regulations
- Personal Judgment – Rules and Expectations
- Independent – Connected
- Separate – Merge
- Leave – Join
- Distance – Engagement

Self and the Other

- Self-Interest – Interest of the Other
- Receive – Give
- Self-Care – Care of Others
- Self-Centered – Altruistic
- Loyal to Yourself – Loyal to Others
- Individual – Group

Confrontation and Harmony

- Assertive – Agreeable
- Direct – Diplomatic
- Hard – Soft

External and Internal

- Extroverted – Introverted
- Expressive – Restrained
- Foreground – Background
- External Motivation – Intrinsic Motivation
- Seek Excitement – Reduce Impulses
- Hustle and Bustle – Stillness

Relationship-Oriented and Task-Oriented

- Seek Consensus – Seek Results
- Personal – Professional
- Empathic – Distant
- Compassion – Consistency
- Personal Attention – Efficiency
- Feeling – Rationality
- Subjective – Objective
- Spontaneous – Tactical

Self-Assertion and Self-Inquiry

- Dominant – Compliant
- Hierarchy – Equality
- Confident – Humble
- Strong – Vulnerable
- Judgmental – Open-Minded
- Convince – Listen
- Know – Learn
- Master – Apprentice
- Expert – Beginner

Equality and Distinction

- Collective – Individual
- Collaborate – Compete
- Solidarity – Personal Achievement
- Inclusive – Exclusive
- Equalize – Differentiate
- Democratic – Elitist

APPENDIX B

PARADOXICAL ORGANIZATION SCAN

With this scan we would like to invite you to evaluate how effectively your organization deals with polarities.

We have identified thirteen dimensions of a paradoxically competent organization. These range from more structural enablers (such as structures, systems, processes) to more cultural ones (how we interact with each other).

The scan has a total of thirty-nine statements. For each statement you are asked to indicate to what extent it applies to your organization. It will take you no more than ten minutes to complete the scan. When filling it out, it is important to always interpret "the organization" as the larger whole of which you are an active part. The organization is not an abstract "system" separated from you.

The scan is a tool to facilitate a dialogue. The absolute score is less important than the conversation that follows. People from different parts of the organization – and even people from the outside – are asked to complete the scan from their own experience. The scores are then combined per response group and put next to each other, as input for a dialogue across different levels, roles, and disciplines.

Paradoxical Organization Scan	Scale from 0–3
Note: "We" stands for "the organization."	0 = totally disagree 1 = slightly disagree 2 = somewhat agree 3 = totally agree

1. Balanced mission and goals (Direction)	
1.1 We achieve a good balance in the goals we aim for (e.g., innovation and continuity, standard and customization, profit and sustainability) so that we do not go too far in either direction.	
1.2 If we focus on a certain strategic direction (e.g., more digitization), we also provide sufficient space for the countermovement (e.g., more personal contact).	
1.3 The different professional disciplines or departments have an equal input in shaping the way forward.	
2. A lived-through and practical vision and mission (Inspiration)	
2.1 I feel that the tensions and struggles in my daily work (e.g., personal attention vs. speed) are seen and recognized by the organization.	
2.2 I have the freedom to choose different paths to achieve the overall goal.	
2.3 If there are differences of opinion about the approach or strategy to be followed, the overall goal is always used as a reference point in the discussion (and not positions of power or personal interests).	
3. Versatile steering (Steering)	
3.1 We regularly review the course that has been set and make timely adjustments to either side where necessary.	
3.2 We quickly pick up on early warning signals that we are going too far in either direction and evaluate them carefully.	
3.3 Once we have decided to correct our course, we quickly implement it in daily work practice.	
4. Authentic leadership and transparent communication (Leadership)	
4.1 Managers in our organization dare to show their vulnerability by, for example, speaking openly about failures or admitting that they do not know something.	
4.2 Leaders in our organization share their personal struggles with competing demands and expectations.	
4.3 Leaders in our organization are credible in their communication because they show both sides of the coin with their advantages and disadvantages.	

(Continued)

Paradoxical Organization Scan Note: "We" stands for "the organization."	Scale from 0–3 0 = totally disagree 1 = slightly disagree 2 = somewhat agree 3 = totally agree
5. Thoughtful decision-making through dissent (Decision-making)	
5.1 In decision-making, we actively seek input from other perspectives and visions.	
5.2 We encourage ourselves and each other to examine and question our own beliefs.	
5.3 We include minority views and interests in the final decision.	
6. Professional dialogue (Dialogue)	
6.1 There is room to discuss different visions about the day-to-day business and about the approaches to be chosen.	
6.2 There is an opportunity to have an open dialogue with each other about differences in approach, whereby the outcome is not predetermined, but the best approach is chosen on a case-by-case basis.	
6.3 The lines of communication between the different parts of the organization (e.g., between top and shop floor, between different departments/business functions, between operation and innovation, etc.) are short and effective.	
7. Flexible structures and systems to serve the end goal (Structures)	
7.1 We regularly evaluate the structures (e.g., organizational divisions, procedures, KPIs, roles and responsibilities) to check whether they still serve the overall goal and adjust them where necessary.	
7.2 We deal flexibly with structures. There is room to deviate from established structures if the overall goal is better achieved in this way.	
7.3 We proactively contact other organizational units about matters that may raise tensions due to differences in interest or approach.	
8. Inclusive Change (Change)	
8.1 When changing, we do not only focus on the new, but we also explicitly value the existing. We keep what is good.	
8.2 During change processes, we simultaneously reinforce some beacons of stability so that there is also the feeling of safety and solid ground.	
8.3 After each period of intensive change we insert a period of rest, internalization, reflection, and evaluation.	

(Continued)

Paradoxical Organization Scan	Scale from 0–3
Note: "We" stands for "the organization."	0 = totally disagree 1 = slightly disagree 2 = somewhat agree 3 = totally agree

9. Innovation through creative tension (Innovation)

9.1 We build in creative tension by working together with people from different backgrounds and areas of expertise and with different views and styles.	
9.2 We challenge each other to come up with innovative both/and-solutions by looking at how we can combine the best of different approaches.	
9.3 Our organization provides room for experimentation and pushing the boundaries even if there is a real chance of failure.	

10. Open, safe, and inclusive culture (Culture)

10.1 There is an open culture where differences in interests, perspectives, and beliefs, and the tensions associated with them, can be openly discussed.	
10.2 I can speak safely about my own doubts, concerns, fears, and weaknesses.	
10.3 I feel respected in my individuality and valued for who I am.	

11. Multidimensional professional development (Development)

11.1 I can develop and show different sides of myself at work.	
11.2 People with a one-sided role are given the opportunity and the space to also realize the other side within the work context. E.g., sitting all day → room to move; working according to strict procedures → room for free experimentation.	
11.3 There is the opportunity to combine different roles, functions, or disciplines (e.g., HR and Finance, Sales and Production).	

12. Paradoxically Competent professionals and managers (Competence)

12.1 We reflect on our own behavior and actively seek feedback.	
12.2 We listen carefully to other points of view and are open to enriching, adapting, or radically changing our own perspective.	
12.3 When we face differences in vision, we assess the underlying needs, interests, motivations, and values of one another in order to arrive at a new, connecting perspective.	

13. Appreciation of dealing effectively with tensions (Appreciation)

13.1 Expressing different views and constructive criticism is encouraged.	
13.2 Being able to deal effectively with tensions is explicitly appreciated (e.g., in recruitment and selection, performance assessment or job evaluation).	
13.3 Liaison roles that need to connect different interests or organizational units are valued and receive support from senior management.	

Index

ABOUT THE AUTHOR

Ivo Brughmans (b. 1965) studied philosophy, international politics, and business management. He worked for twenty-five years for a global management consulting firm, supporting organizations in redesigning and transforming their business. Ivo is fascinated by paradoxes and the challenge of bringing together opposite approaches. Connecting opposite poles has been a common thread throughout his own life and work: as a philosopher working with practical business challenges, as a rationalist relying on his intuition, and as a workaholic enjoying doing simply nothing at all.

Ivo has written several books on this theme, developing a "both/and" perspective as a radical alternative to our current way of living, managing, governing, and coaching. He has a deep conviction that this perspective helps create more sustainable solutions to the challenges of the twenty-first century, providing the fundamentals for a fulfilled and balanced life, for better-performing and more innovative organizations, and for a better world.

Ivo lives in Antwerp, Belgium. He gives keynotes, leads workshops and training programs on paradoxical leadership, and works with public and private organizations throughout Europe and around the globe. For more information check https://paradoxical-leadership.com.

Ingram Content Group UK Ltd.
Milton Keynes UK
UKHW011440040423
419630UK00014B/115/J